Toll of the Sea

Stories from the Forgotten Coast

Robert C. Parsons

Also by Robert Parsons:
Lost at Sea, Vol. I
Lost at Sea, Vol. II
Wake of the Schooners

Toll of the Sea

Stories from the Forgotten Coast

Robert C. Parsons

Creative Publishers
St. John's, Newfoundland
1995

Appreciation is expressed to *The Canada Council* for publication assistance.

The publisher acknowledges the financial contribution of the *Department of Tourism and Culture, Government of Newfoundland and Labrador*, which has helped make this publication possible.

Cover: Jim Miles

∝ Printed on acid-free paper

First printing — June 1995
Second printing — May 1996

Published by
CREATIVE BOOK PUBLISHING
a division of 10366 Newfoundland Limited
a Robinson-Blackmore Printing & Publishing associated company
P.O. Box 8660, St. John's, Newfoundland A1B 3T7

Printed in Canada by:
ROBINSON-BLACKMORE PRINTING & PUBLISHING

Canadian Cataloguing in Publication Data

Parsons, Robert Charles, 1944–

Toll of the sea

Includes index.
ISBN 1-895387-51-5

1. Shipwrecks — Newfoundland. I. Title.

FC2170.S5P373 1995 971.8 C95-950174-6
F1123.P 373 1995

To my children
Dale, Nancy and Robert

Table of Contents

Author's Acknowledgements

TO THE INFORMANTS AND INTERVIEWEES who supplied the basic tales, once again I thank you. There are too many to name all, but longer oral stories (slightly edited for clarification), written documentation and/or pictures came from: Captain and Mrs. Harvey Banfield; Winnie Dicks; Reg Pardy; Captain Bernard Whiffen; Walter Dober; William Chapman; Captain George Lace; William May; Waterfield Green; John Douglas; Jack Keeping; Fred Smith; Mary Ellen Moore; Jack Hackett; Ron Grandy; Frank Riggs; Elic Stoodley; Art Ralph; Margaret Mullins; Georgina and Montford Piercey; Les and Lorraine Buffett; Reverend V. Cluett; Margaret Vincent; Annie and Joe Lockyer, Captain Michael Croke; Richard Moulton; George Spencer; Joe Smith; Don Hollett; Harry Bowles; Alex Hardy; Clarence Griffin and Captain Reg Augot. Unfortunately, since the time of this writing, several of these story tellers have passed away.

If any errors occur in dates, information, names or picture credits they are purely accidental or unintentional and I welcome the opportunity in any future editions to correct misinformation.

The Cover Artist

A GRADUATE OF THE VISUAL ARTS PROGRAM at Westviking College in Stephenville, Jim Miles works comfortably on the south coast from his Marystown residence. Miles, whose parental roots come straight out of Fortune Bay, prefers waterbased painting of colourful land and seascapes, wildlife and the occasional portrait. His work has been exhibited at the Greg Seaward Art Gallery in Gander and he has recently instructed adults in drawing and painting at the Burin campus of Eastern Community College.

Preface

Toll of the Sea: Stories from the Forgotten Coast tells some of the sea tales of Newfoundland's South Coast, a rugged and scenic seaboard occasionally referred to in yesteryear's print as the forgotten coast. Tucked away from mainstream Avalon and the more populous northeast corner, the economically stable South Coast was busy around the turn of the century sending schooners to the banks and tern schooners to foreign markets. As a result of rubbing elbows with the old and the new world civilizations, South Coast towns made significant social and cultural contributions to Newfoundland, but their people paid a price in lost ships and men.

Toll of the Sea relates heroic deeds of our forefathers who had no choice but to face the ever hungry and ever relentless ocean — to travel, to socialize, to communicate, and to earn a living. And the vigorous coves, bays, and harbours in which they were born and nurtured struggled on past great odds — changes in technology, resettlement, natural disasters, collapse of the fishery, economic and political setbacks — to become proud, viable, self-sufficient towns today.

The sea stories contained in these pages have been told and retold in song and story. In most cases I cross-referenced or verified verbal retellings with archival records, headstones, church records, old newspapers and museum documentations.

The range of sea misadventures is wide: a description of a trip overseas; survival accounts of men in drifting dories; vessel disappearances where only wreckage tells of disaster; getting home from shipwreck and abandoning schooners in mid-Atlantic.

The community histories tend to be brief; taken mainly from Smallwood's *Encyclopedia of Newfoundland and Labrador Volumes I-V*, gathered from personal interviews and also researched from records in reference libraries and public archives. Several appendices list shipping tragedies and other marine records for various communities. To avoid repetition of my previous works

I have not listed (or sourced) archival newspapers or historical files from which basic information was gathered.

When my first sea-story books were published in 1991 and 1992, I thought most of the major tales of shipwrecks on the South Coast had been recorded. I believe now the surface has only been scratched in terms of uncovering local history and that accounts of many more unique events remain unpublished.

Of the many towns, large and small, along our coast I chose only those that fitted a particular tale of the sea of which I had documentation. Thus some towns are not represented. Also I would liked to have had more stories of the womenfolk who suffered untold mental anguish while waiting for word of loved ones missing in marine mishaps. But I'm sure that could be the subject of another work for someone.

I suppose the basic idea for this collection began at the Marystown, Burin, Grand Bank and Fortune sometime in November and December of 1993 when I met so many people who asked if I knew of this particular schooner or of that special sea story which had happened in their community. In my attempt to verify retellings I discovered that little marine history of the many communities in Fortune and Placentia Bays has been written. Many oral stories which otherwise would not be preserved are, through this medium, now in print.

Toll of the Sea: Stories from the Forgotten Coast gives us a chance to look back and to view the life, times, and communities through the eyes of others: the skipper of the drifting *Mary Wiscombe* or via the retelling of the loss of *Hilda Gertrude* through the personal knowledge of Mary Ellen Moore who remembered the day the little schooner sailed out never to return.

In my own more imaginative moments I look back to see my father, as he told it later on audio tape, struggling for 14 hours to get off the storm-tossed *Mary D. Young* as she lay on her side near St. Pierre harbour a few days after World War One ended. In the summer of 1993 I walked out to Point aux Canon in St. Pierre looking toward the place where he must have been some eighty years before. Never in my wildest imaginings could I envision what he must have gone through in those times.

So it was with all our forefathers who fought the treacherous sea while trying to wrest a living for their families. Shakespeare said in Act V of *All's Well That Ends Well*, "Praising what is lost, Makes the Remembrance dear" and I too praise those heroic pioneers and the home harbours they represent.

The principal towns numbered as they appear in *Toll of the Sea*

2. Bay L'Argent
3. Belleoram
4. Boat Harbour
5. Burgeo
6. Burin
7. English Hr. East
8. English Hr. West
9. Mose Ambrose
10. Flat Island
11. Fortune
12. Garnish
13. Grand Bank
14. Harbour Breton
15. Harbour Mille
16. Jersey Harbour
17. Rencontre East
18. Marystown
19. Little Bay
20. Ramea
21. Red Island
22. Port aux Basques
23. Rose Blanche
24. Rushoon
25. Rencontre West
26. Red Harbour
27. St. Bernard's
28. Brunette Island
29. St. Lawrence

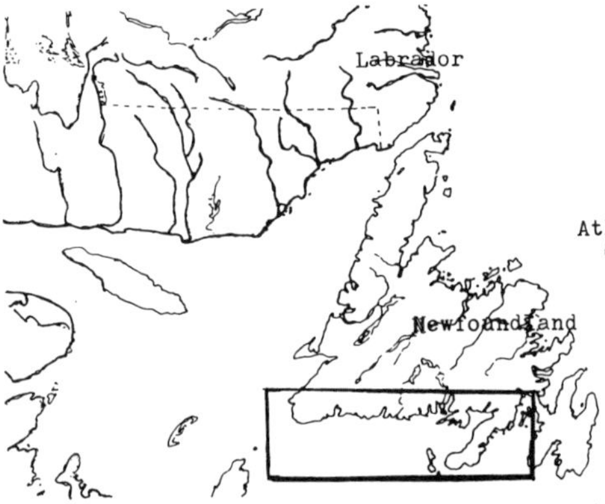

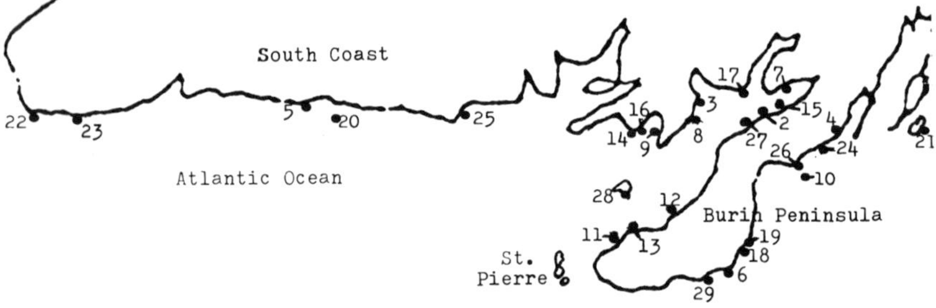

Chapter 1

South Coast Heritage

IN JUNE OF 1497, five hundred years ago, John Cabot claimed that fish were so plentiful off Newfoundland's shores they could be caught in baskets lowered over the side of his vessel. This may possibly be an exaggeration or maybe Cabot lowered his basket into a bank of capelin during scull. No doubt that when the English settled the South Coast from the mid 1700s to 1800s, all species of fish were so plentiful so as to attract permanent settlement. The inshore fishery predominated.

There was, however, a limit to the number of fishermen who could profitably exploit the grounds near the harbour; thus early settlers moved farther and farther west into Placentia Bay, Fortune Bay and along the southwest coast. Populations grew; movement into new harbours near unexploited fishing grounds increased. In time, there were few, if any, grounds located between the Cape Shore Banks near Cape St. Mary's to the Rose Blanche and Burgeo Banks that had not been fished extensively.

By the 1890s pressure on the inshore stocks and the lure of offshore banks lead to the development of the bank fishery. The technology and method was copied from those used in Gloucester and on the eastern seaboard of Nova Scotia. South Coast sailors visited both areas frequently. Some towns emerged as centres of growth — Harbour Buffett, Marystown, Burin in Placentia Bay; Grand Bank, Fortune, Harbour Breton in Fortune Bay; and Ramea, Burgeo and Port aux Basques along the southwest coast. The numbers of schooners, with their attendant dory and hook and line technology, increased until every harbour had a fleet relative to its size. Appendix A enumerates the 1936 fishing fleet in various South Coast towns.

Within the one hundred year period of the wooden sailing ships, Burgeo harboured over eighty schooners; Grand Bank, around three hundred; Burin over three hundred; Harbour Buffett over fifty, and the pattern was repeated for towns of lesser size. The volume of sea traffic around the South Coast was of such proportion that marine mishaps and loss of life were frequent. Despite the heavy loss of lives and ships, the sea was the only way to earn a living.

Although there was little evidence of real cash, the South Coast was a prosperous place in the era of sail. Merchants built themselves fine homes; fishermen were independent and lived adequately. From the 1880s to 1920s and in some instances extending into the 1930s, Britain encouraged its Newfoundland territory to develop the schooner and dory fishing. It was

Courtesy of Marine Archives, Memorial University

Harbour Buffett, one of the busiest harbours along the coast, was the commercial and service centre for Placentia Bay and saw the rise and decline of the schooner fishery between 1920-1960. Here, at Wareham's premises, a Portuguese vessel lands salt and loads salt fish which had been dried on the flakes (centre).

The black-hulled tern in centre is *Stina*, owned by W.W. Wareham. She was abandoned off Portugal in October 1934; her crew — Captain Alex Rodway, Jack Manning, Ralph Dicks, George Gregory, Willis Wareham and Holger Erickson (from Sweden) — was rescued.

The extent to which seamen from the Harbour Buffett area sailed to distant ports can be seen through ships' logs and customs clearance papers of schooners like *Frank Baxter*. She cleared St. John's for Puerto Rico in August 1929 with seven crew: Captain John Murphy, age twenty-nine; Patrick Hayse, thirty-three; Lewis Upshall, twenty-seven; George Marshall, twenty-four; John G. Dicks, twenty-four; Malcolm Masters, twenty-one and Walter Slade, aged twenty. All gave their residence as Harbour Buffett except Slade who hailed from Kingwell.

thought there was too much dependence on the inshore fishery. The government paid a bounty to those who built vessels over 30 tons with incentives to build even larger schooners.

By the 1930s, with a world depression and falling fish prices, men were fortunate to have a job at all. Those who were still employed on banking schooners did not complain of hard work. It was a hazardous occupation taken in stride and something that had to be done to provide a living for families.

Beginning in 1919 and lasting until 1930, the American prohibition of liquor enabled South Coast men and schooners to find a new source of cash — supplying rum and whisky to "Rum Row" off the American coast. High prices for the illegal goods meant risks and South Coast men were killed or disappeared on clandestine rum running missions. Rum running, rather than being considered a criminal activity, was looked upon as part of the economic, social and cultural life of the South Coast.

Despite the lucrative liquor trade, most men were still employed on the large bankers. Work started early. Fishermen baited up in the morning as soon as it was light enough to see the compass, rowed to set their trawls and got back aboard the schooner around four in the evening. All day they would come and go from the trawls to the schooner, bringing fish, lightening the dory, taking up gear and moving to another spot. If, in the 1930s, a schooner fishermen made two to three hundred dollars from February to October he was doing well.

Natural land resources on Newfoundland's coast were, and still are, meagre; especially the soil which was thin and the growing season short. Schooners, employed in the hazardous winter season in the coasting trade, sailed to Nova Scotia and Prince Edward Island for vegetables and livestock and to Nova Scotia for flour and coal.

Often fishermen worked all spring and summer without knowing in the fall how much money they made until they settled up with the merchant. Yet young men hoped and prayed for a berth on a large banker. If a friend or relative volunteered to take a youth in dory with him, only then did the young man assume a feeling of independence. He was helping support his family as a breadwinner.

Two men to a dory with the homebase schooner anchored a mile or two away, bank fishermen unloaded their catch at the schooner. When fishing was done for the day and all dories were nested aboard, the men ate the most substantial meal for the day, supper, for there was still plenty work for all. The day's fish had to be dressed: split, washed, stored and salted in the holds.

Early next morning the routine started again: each man baited two tubs of gear, ten lines to a tub, each line sixty fathoms long with hundreds of hooks on each line.

Within two to three weeks when the schooners were full of

Courtesy George Spencer

Spencer II at the coal pier in Sydney. Built in Placentia in 1924, she once carried the name *Palfrey*. Roy Spencer of Fortune bought her in 1949 and as *Spencer II*, under command of Captain Tom Grandy of Garnish, ferried passengers between Fortune and St. Pierre.

Her chief work was delivering coal to remote lighthouses. From lighthouse to lighthouse from Channel Head to Merasheen Island in Placentia Bay she travelled, bringing coal and vital supplies. On remote island lighthouses sacked coal could be more easily winched up over the rocks and cliffs. Eventually *Spencer II* was sold to English Harbour and was dismantled.

After the deeply-laden vessel and her Fortune crew (above l-r) — Captain Charles "B" Thornhill sitting on rail; Tom Spencer sitting on knee of Eli Thornhill; and Arch Thornhill sitting in front of wheelhouse — left Sydney and arrived in Port aux Basques the coal was bagged, twenty-one bags to a ton.

fish or bait was used up, they set sail for home. Their part was over until the next trip. On shore, fish became the responsibility of the women in large communities and the whole family in smaller settlements; salt bulk cod from the latter was collected by schooners and taken to larger centres.

Teams of women wearing distinctive beach aprons and sun bonnets, spread the fish on flakes or beaches to dry. And these women, who cured the fish on shore, could make or break a ship's catch. They played an important part in the dry fish economy; yet they did not get the recognition, either financially or socially, they deserved. Women as young as thirteen or fourteen and as old as sixty to sixty-five worked long and backbreaking hours. Wages were low. By the beginning of the 1940s, twenty-five to fifty dollars for several months' work curing fish was considered a good season's (April to September) income.

Salted fish would be washed near the harbour and then carried in horse drawn wagons to the flakes or beaches where women laid it out row by row to dry in the sun. Partly dry fish would be stacked in piles and covered overnight. Fish was spread, turned and taken up so that all received equal amount of drying time.

Women worked late. At home, although tired from a day's work on the beaches, they often had to wash clothes, put up bread, bring water, bring in fire wood or make kindling for the next day; usually the man of the house was away on the banking vessels.

It took approximately six weeks to properly dry fish. When cured it was carried to storage sheds to be culled. After fish was culled, or graded for size and quality, it was prepared for shipping to overseas markets in Europe or the Caribbean.

Large bankers or tern schooners carried approximately four thousand quintals of salt dry fish, dependant upon the size of the vessel. The foreign-going voyage to Europe took approximately twenty days. The captain was only responsible for delivery and had no control over the sale which was pre-arranged by the local fish exporting company. Vessels loaded

Newton Lake, a 151-ton tern schooner, was built in Belleoram in 1920 for Lake's interests at Fortune. The advent of the three masted schooners, with their greater spread of sail and increased capacity which owners knew would reduce sailing time and give higher profits, came around 1910. By 1930 shipbuilding costs in Newfoundland and Nova Scotia, where most foreign-going terns were built, and the use of engines doomed the three-master to extinction.

fishery salt for the return journey which often took twice as long as the eastward voyage due to adverse winds.

The schooner fishery declined steadily until 1950 when most towns had only one or two schooners remaining and most of these vessels (now powered by engines) were engaged in the coastal trade. By the late 1940s and early 50s men went to Argentia to work or moved to Boston or Nova Scotian ports. Those fishermen who remained joined steel trawlers which had replaced the wooden schooners.

Still referred to by our forefathers as the most cataclysmic event to ever occur on their rock-girt sea line was Premier Joseph Smallwood's resettlement program. In the 1960s scores of communities were abandoned in favour of life and employment in larger "growth centres". Displaced families left their roots and familiar surroundings where generations had been born and died and where tough seamen had laid down their lives.

By the 1960s schooners, banking dories and a unique way of life had disappeared from all but a few South Coast towns. Thirty years after the demise of the schooner fishery, the once plentiful cod stocks had virtually disappeared. In 1993 a moratorium halted the cod fishery both inshore and on the great offshore banks. The humble but abundant fish that had once given rise to the phrase "Cod is King" became an endangered species.

But the legacy of the days of the schooner fishery still has an influence today. From time to time, in harbour to harbour when communities need a catalyst for some purpose, issue or crisis, they tap the heritage of the sea. The following chapters highlight the towns, men and ships from whence this legacy is drawn.

Chapter 2

Bay L'Argent Seaman: Smoking the Enemies' Cigarettes

LOCATED ON THE NORTHWESTERN COAST OF THE Burin Peninsula, the community of Bay L'Argent is situated in two coves, the Basin and May Cove. The name is of French origin meaning "Bay of Silver" although no known silver mine or other exploitable mineral exists there.

The first English settlers are thought to have been James Banfield (1799-1884) and Robert Thornhill (1817-1899). In the official Newfoundland Census return of 1836, Bay L'Argent is recorded as Bay LeJohn with a population of thirty-two, all Church of England. It first appears as Bay L'Argent in the census of 1857, population twenty-nine. It grew steadily after that, and by the 1880s the Church of England had a mission there, a school, and a teacher named Edwin Snelgrove.

Shipbuilding first appears as an occupation in the census returns of 1884, when a vessel of twenty-five ton was built the previous year. Bay L'Argent people have always been self-sufficient and early records show they raised sheep, cattle, pigs and fowl and grew hay, potatoes and turnip.

By 1921 the population had risen to 266 and, in addition to a productive inshore cod fishery, the town had a salmon cannery and two lobster factories in operation. Vegetable farming was, and still is to a lesser extent, an important part of Bay L'Argent's economy. In 1971, the town became incorporated with a town council and today its population stands at approximately four hundred.

In the era of the bank fishery, from the 1900s to the 1950s, the young men found ready employment on the schooner fleets based in larger towns.

Several well-known schooner captains hailed from Bay L'-Argent: Parmineas Banfield skippered several vessels from Grand Bank and St. Bernard's; Stephen Lawrence who in his lifetime was a teacher, miner, bookkeeper, seaman, captain, soldier and was eventually manager of G.N. Banfield's business in Bay L'Argent. At one time he commanded *R.M. Symonds* and the four-dory banker *Theta*.

Captain Lawrence spent most of his time on Wareham's schooners out of Harbour Buffett and on Parrott's of St. Bernard's. On one occasion he and his crewmates barely escaped with their lives when an ocean liner nearly cut down their schooner. The crosstrees almost brushed the liner's rails when the schooner rolled back in the heavy wake. With white water rolling across deck, Lawrence's crew were ready to abandon ship, but the incensed Bay L'Argent captain would have none of that and instead chased the liner through the fog while trying to determine her name.

On September 11, 1931, Captain Freeman Lawrence, another veteran Bay L'Argent skipper, lost *George and Marion* at Mistaken Point on the Southern Avalon while bound to the Labrador for the fall fishery. He and his crew of twenty-three escaped without injury. In 1936 he was master of *Nina L.O. Davis*, a 68-ton banker owned by W.W. Wareham of Harbour Buffett.

Bay L'Argent Seaman on *Robert Max*

A young seaman from Bay L'Argent, Alex Banfield, sailed on *Robert Max* when she made her fifth voyage across the Atlantic during the war years. As it turned out it was her last voyage, but Banfield and his courageous shipmates, who faced the wrath of the German war machine, lived to tell the story.

With her departure point Bay Bulls, Newfoundland, *Robert Max* set sail for Europe in late July 1941, with six Fortune Bay seamen. Captain Harry Thomasen, born in Denmark in 1898, came to Newfoundland to live when a teenage boy and eventually married and settled in Grand Bank. He rose through the ranks of sailor, navigator and captain in the 1920-30s. Before he assumed command of *Robert Max* he had already been in several shipwrecks: his *Margaret Lake* collided with *Lottie Silver* sending the latter to the bottom; he and his crewmates abandoned *Thomas A. Cromwell* in January 1918 and on March 9, 1928, as captain of *Sunner*, with his wife, two sons and five crew, he abandoned ship in mid-ocean.

Robert Max's crew also included four men of Grand Bank: John Douglas, Gordon Hollett, Sam Pardy and cook Luke Rogers. Douglas, when only a school boy, had made his first trip overseas on the tern schooner *Ria* captained by his father, George Douglas (See chapter 13). Like his father he had been a seaman all his life, sailing mostly on coasting and foreign going vessels.

Rogers, the oldest man aboard, had endured a trying experience on a small schooner *Maggie E* in January, 1926. Her crew of Captain William Evans, William Thorne, Abe Thorne and Rogers left Lawn for Grand Bank, a run of a few hours. They were storm driven for over two weeks before ultimate rescue from the sinking *Maggie E*. Back in Grand Bank they had been given up for lost — grieving relatives wore black and pulled window shades down for the lost men.

Gordon Hollett, son of Neddie Hollett, was a veteran seaman. By the next year he would have been shipwrecked on *James and Stanley*. Sam Pardy lived in Grand Bank. His father, Matthew, had disappeared in 1907 on the ill-fated *Tubal Cain*, a coal and lumber laden schooner which left Halifax for Grand Bank but never reported.

Alex Banfield, of Bay L'Argent, was the son of Parmineas "Min" Banfield, a well-known banking and coasting schooner captain. In later years, Alex, or "Hec" as he was called, was shipmates with John Douglas and George Grant on the iron ore carrier *Louisbourg*, carrying ore from Bell Island to Sydney, Nova Scotia.

These six Fortune Bay seamen on an unarmed merchant

Courtesy of Joanne Wilson

The Shelburne-built *Clara B. Creaser* awaits her cargo of dry fish. Named for Captain Henry Creaser's sister, she fished out of Riverport/La Have, Nova Scotia, for ten years. When Captain John Thornhill bought part shares in this 180-ton vessel in 1929, he renamed her *Robert Max* for his two sons who had died of diphtheria some years before.

According to Nova Scotian tradition, the 13 letters in her name would prove unlucky, but this omen was unfounded; she had a long and productive career.

sailing ship were about to come face to face with German seamen on an enemy sub, in mid Atlantic.

On August 4 *Robert Max* was around 700 miles off the Portuguese coast. A little after midday a German U-boat intercepted the solitary schooner, fired one warning shot across the bow, one over the masts and ordered the boat to stop.

Commander Ernst Bauer of *U-boat 126* ordered Thomasen

and two crewmen, John Douglas and Alex Banfield, to row over while the other three held *Robert Max* into the wind close by. Thomasen went into the conning tower, while Douglas and Banfield kept the dory off from the sub with dory oars otherwise the larger ship's wash would have swamped the dory. Banfield thought they might tie onto the stay running from the sub's stern to the conning tower, but seas were too high.

Recalling the condition of the U-boat and its men, Douglas claimed, "She was full of barnacles — white with barnacles so she must have been at sea a long time. The crew had their pants rolled up to their knees and wore blue sweaters with a large swastika on the front."

While aboard the enemy sub Captain Thomasen gave details of *Robert Max*'s cargo and destination. Although the schooner was not armed, the Germans decided to sink her for in their opinion she carried food for Allied nations. Crew members of *Robert Max* were given ten minutes to gather personal belongings and move away.

From their lifeboat a few hundred feet away, the six seamen watched their schooner go to the bottom. Over two dozen shots ploughed into the hapless schooner, most hitting the fuel drums strapped on near the rear and plowing into the place nearest the engine. Under the onslaught she went down. *Robert Max* became the first Newfoundland schooner sunk by the enemy in World War Two. Appendix B lists other South Coast schooners sunk by enemy action in World War II.

The German crew, especially the sailors, were friendly enough. Several talked in broken English to the Newfoundlanders, offered encouragement and good health, and gave them cigarettes. Bauer offered to tow the lifeboat toward the nearest land which Thomasen refused.

Before he moved away the German commander, Ernst Bauer, said to them in English, "Give my best respects to Winnie Churchill." Captain Thomasen, undaunted by the might and presence of the enemy, had his answer ready. He could speak several languages: his native Danish; English; French, from having spent some time employed in St. Pierre; perhaps a little

Courtesy Robert Stoodley

With her great mainsail taut between the main boom and main gaff, *Robert Max* catches the wind. According to most sources, in this photo she sails out of Grand Bank harbour, bound for the Grand Banks. She measured 136-foot long and netted 180 tons.

Portuguese and a few phrases in German. He replied, "There'll always be an England."

Although the lifeboat was open to the weather and all the unpredictable North Atlantic could throw at her, Captain Thomasen in his foresight had the seaworthy boat well prepared for emergencies. Most likely the good weather and favourable wind would push them to the coast. He organized the six crew members into three two-man shifts for rowing and keeping watch. John Douglas recalled the eerie feeling:

> That evening we were adrift on the ocean by ourselves, the schooner on the bottom and we were two or three hundred

miles from land, out in the Western Ocean. Although Skipper Harry had our little boat well-prepared, no one knew how the weather would turn. It was a lonely feeling.

Home Thoughts from the Ocean

In these solitary hours, when sailors like *Robert Max*'s seamen face the enormity of the ocean and the depth of God's universe touches the individual heart and mind, *The Mariner's Prayer* has more significance:

Oh God, Thy sea is so great,
And my boat is so small. Amen

Undaunted despite the odds against them, the Fortune Bay mariners put their minds and muscles to the thoughts of getting home. Aided by a small sail, a fair wind at night and a good set of oars, *Robert Max*'s lifeboat covered 297 miles in seventy-two hours. Hard bread and corned beef became their daily fare; water, stored in four or five ten-gallon kegs, was issued by Thomasen in empty corned beef cans. He poured it out in the can and passed the precious commodity to each man at regular intervals.

Mainly the men suffered from cramped quarters and hands made sore from rowing and bailing which was necessary because the lifeboat hadn't been in the water for a year.

On August 6, at 1:30 p.m. the weary crew saw the purplish outline of one of the islands of the Azores on the horizon. Twelve hours later they reached and anchored off its lee shores. Alex Banfield, Gord Hollett and the four other Fortune Bay mariners had found the port of Ponto Delgado on the island of Sao Miguel, Azores. They had 120 fathoms of buoy line and an anchor aboard which was put overboard and the crew lay down to rest. They would need their strength to find a landing area and to breach the breakers in daylight hours.

That long night of August 6-7, as they rested on the thwarts and in the bottom of the lifeboat, each man had time to reflect on the ordeal they had gone through. Out of fear of being spotted by the enemy, Captain Thomasen, who was a non-smoker himself, wouldn't allow the crew to smoke or light up at night. By now in the relative safety of the Azores, he relaxed his regulations. Sam Pardy, in a recorded interview made several years after the incident, recalled:

> I started to make a cigarette out of some Jumbo tobacco we had there. I tore a leaf out of the old man's (Captain Thomasen) *Belcher's Almanac*...
>
> I made a smoke out of that. The Germans gave us five packs of cigarettes. But we didn't like to smoke them. We had heard talk that they were given to fellows on those raiders. The Germans gave them cigarettes and it set them frantic. You know, it put them off their heads. We were too scared to smoke them.

Generally, Newfoundland seamen smoked heavily, but for the shipwrecked men waiting off the Azores coast there weren't enough cigarettes to get them through the long hours.

One brave seaman took the chance — Alex Banfield, asked, "Where's the cigarettes they (German sailors) gave us?" But not knowing if the cigarettes were drugged or poisoned added, "If they set me crazy, heave the cigarettes and me overboard!"

The smokers aboard opened a pack to discover they were Turkish cigarettes — unusual in shape, not round but flatter, oval shaped. As Pardy remembered:

> We smoked one apiece and nobody felt the effects; so the Turkish cigarettes didn't last long. I had saved 6 packs of Jumbo from the schooner and after, that's what we used to have a smoke out of.
>
> We were in under this island and we were anchored. By and by, we started to roll back and forth. I was lying down and she rolled. My head went down in the bottom and my legs went up on the oars, sails and that. Someone said, 'Boys, we're drifting; we ain't anchored'. Thomasen asked to try the anchor and it wasn't on the bottom.

The crew hauled up and rowed right in under the land. At daylight fishermen gathered at the beach. The shipwrecked crewmen could see them with a large seine, catching fish at the beach. Pardy recalled:

> They were going to haul sardines with a long net this way and heaving rocks out that way to drive them in. They came up alongside and asked if we were Angle Terres. Skipper said 'Si', that's Yes.
>
> They went ashore and by and by off came a boat. A fellow dressed in military uniform — I don't know what he was, some kind of captain — who could talk good English...
>
> He said he'd take us in charge, but we got in their boat and they took ours.

To the Newfoundland crew, the breakers of Sao Miguel's shores look wild and threatening, but the island people calmly waited for a large wave and brought both small boats over the surf to the beach without damage. *Robert Max*'s lifeboat was pulled 200 feet beyond the shoreline. It was the last the six Fortune Bay seamen saw of the little craft that had been their refuge from the sea for three days and nights. Pardy recalled conditions on the island; the thoughts of the enemy were uppermost in his mind:

> After that they took us in a car and drove us about seventy miles and put us in a hotel. We weren't there long before we got something to eat.
>
> I had a big whisker on and the rest was clean shaven. I was reading sometime before where they (enemy) used to pluck the prisoners'— when they'd get prisoners — pluck their whiskers out, so I thought about it then and got a shave.

In a week or so *Robert Max*'s crew left the Azores by a freighter for Lisbon, Portugal. *Helen Forsey*, another Grand Bank schooner, was in Lisbon to discharge fish. However, this schooner had a three week delay to replace a broken mainmast. Not wanting to wait the extra time, Thomasen, Banfield and

Rogers came back on *James and Stanley*, owned by Grand Bank Fisheries and captained by Hughie Grandy.

At first it looked as if the remaining three, Hollett, Douglas and Pardy, would make the trip with a large Portuguese salt vessel sailing directly to Fortune, only three miles from Grand Bank. But the British Consulate in Portugal reminded them that Portugal was a neutral country in the war and the freighter could not take passengers from another country.

Captain John Ralph and *Helen Forsey*'s crew obtained a mainmast on a country farm with tall stands of trees. Pulled by an ox-team, the mast was brought through the city after midnight due to the heavy daytime traffic on Lisbon's city streets.

To attach the stays and rigging to the stepped mast, the crew nailed junks of wood to the mast which acted as cleats to climb up on.

In due time *Helen Forsey*, her crew of six — Ralph, cook Tom Bolt, mate Joe English, deckhands Bill Keating, Don Baker, Arthur Bond of Frenchman's Cove — and three passengers from the ill-fated *Robert Max* reached Grand Bank without incident.

Bay L'Argent's Alex Banfield and his five shipmates had all survived to sail again; each was ready to face the sea and the enemy again, if necessary, to find employment and to keep the lifeline of food and supplies flowing from Newfoundland communities to war-stricken European countries.

Chapter 3

Belleoram: Home to a Fine Fleet

WHEN *The Gay Gordon* arrived in Belleoram on May 4, 1915, she had made a near record voyage of seventeen days on a westward trip — a voyage not without tragedy. Tern schooner *The Gay Gordon* was one of Belleoram's fleet of foreign going schooners managed by Harvey and Company.

Harvey and Company, with its headquarters in St. John's, began to expand their interests in the fish trade and shipping in the early twentieth century. Several years prior to and during the Great War, Harvey's, as it was known, put branch businesses on the South Coast. In 1915 Harveys built a bait freezer, the first of its kind in Newfoundland, at Rose Blanche and had bought J. Penny and Sons business at Belleoram a few years earlier.

Harvey's recognized the value of Belleoram's sheltered harbour, situated on the west side of Fortune Bay, and its proximity to the rich fishing grounds.

The French had occupied the harbour up to 1713 when they were forced to leave by the Treaty of Utrecht. The French referred to it as Bande de Laurier or Bande de l'Arier and the English fishermen who wintered there soon after called it Belorme's Place after a French settler. By 1800 most of the pioneer families originated from southwest of England and the Channel islands. The first official Newfoundland census in 1836 showed there were 104 people living there. The emerging town, like others in Fortune Bay, depended on the local herring and cod fishery.

Up to the end of the 1930s, Belleoram was the centre of Harvey's South Coast bank fishery and export business. Between 1915-20, Harvey and Company had foreign going tern schooners and smaller banking vessels constructed or purchased especially for their Belleoram fleet. Harvey's also built an artificial fish drier in the early 1920s to cure fish that could not be spread on beaches or flakes. Their business manager in 1920s was Claude Noonan, born in St. John's.

In time, as Harvey's closed out its Belleoram branch in the 1930s, some of these were sold to other South Coast businesses or Belleoram men bought shares in these schooners. The following is a partial list of schooners and terns owned by Harvey and Company, but commanded and crewed by Belleoram seamen.

Schooner	When Built	Eventual Fate
*William Morton	1905	Abandoned at sea, Jan. 1918
The Gay Gordon	1909	Lost in ice, March 1923
*Allen F. Rose	1909	Abandoned at sea, Nov. 1938
*Thomas	?	Sunk by enemy sub, Apr. 1917
Alice M. Pike	1911	Wrecked Lumsden, Oct. 1950
*Stanley and Frank	1911	Lost 1919 or 1920
John Harvey	1911	Wrecked Gabarus, NS, January 1912
Ellen and Mary	1912	Wrecked St. Lawrence R., July 1942
Reading	1914	Wrecked Rose Blanche, March 1938
*Florence	1915	Abandoned on Banks, Sept. 1940
*Sunset Glow	1916	Wrecked at Fogo, October 1949
*Rita M. Cluett	1917	Abandoned at sea April, 1923
Sparkling Glance	1917	Abandoned at sea Feb. 1921
Ruth Adams	1917	Wrecked near Point au Gaul, 1943
Mary Ruth	1918	Beached Southport, NF, 1980s
Antoine C. Santos	1918	Wrecked Miquelon Head April, 1942
Dorothy O	1921	Burned Hermitage Bay June 7, 1950
Lucy Edwina	1922	Wrecked Raleigh, NF, May 1953

* Tern schooner

Bank fishing from a small dory using hook and line, coupled with long hours, dangerous work and economic insecurity, gave rise to an old saying, "Any man who would go fishing for a living, would go to hell for a pastime." Thus there were always seamen in ports like Belleoram who preferred the steady and less demanding work on foreign-going vessels. Although most voyages across to Europe were made in the winter months

Courtesy book American Neptune and Jack Keeping

The 120-ton *Lucy Edwina*, built in Shelburne Shipbuilders Yards, had the same lines as *Dorothy O.* Claude Noonan performed the christening ceremony for *Lucy Edwina.*

when wind and weather threatened ships and lives, it offered more financial security than the banking schooners.

But life was not always easy on the foreign-going schooners, as the following three examples show.

The Gay Gordon

The Gay Gordon, built in Shelburne, Nova Scotia, netted 119 tons and measured 103 feet long, 25 feet wide and 10.5 feet deep. Oddly, she was christened with the word "The" in her name. Joseph Marshall had spent several weeks in Shelburne while *The Gay Gordon* was being built and had been her master until his death.

Laden with dry cod destined for Oporto, *The Gay Gordon* left Belleoram in the spring under the command of Marshall, a resident of Carbonear, but two or three days into the voyage eastward Marshall was washed overboard during a storm. While running before the wind under bare poles, he was at the wheel when a wave rolled over the ship taking Marshall and the wheelhouse over the side into the boiling sea. The ship was put about in hope that Marshall had clung to the wreckage, but the captain was never seen again.

Mate Reginald Keeping, age seventeen, finished the voyage to Oporto, but the insurance company considered him too young to take *The Gay Gordon* back across the Atlantic. Captain George Kearley (Sr.) of Belleoram was sent over to bring the schooner back after loading salt at Cadiz. The westward run, which usually took twice as long, was only seventeen days. That fast voyage brought praise from newspapers in Halifax and Shelburne where the exploits of Nova Scotian-built terns were regularly reported.

Lasting fourteen years — longer than average — *The Gay Gordon* sank on April 21, 1923, crushed by the ice field that practically surrounded Newfoundland in the spring of 1923.

After *The Gay Gordon*, Captain Reg Keeping commanded several of Harvey's tern schooners and was with three when they were wrecked: *Thomas; Sparkling Glance* and *William Morton*. Throughout both World Wars he crossed and recrossed the Atlantic many times; during the second war he sailed on tankers and carriers. Keeping, modest about his seafaring achievements, had service medals for every theatre of war at sea. Between wars he was a sailmaker in Belleoram's sail loft and in later years was mate on Imperial Oil tankers.

Belleoram Crewmen Rescued

"Blown off Course, Liner Saves Seven — Succession of Storms Stripped the Fudge of Canvas, Bulwarks and Rudder." This is how the *New York Times* carried the news of the sinking of a Belleoram vessel. Tern schooner *Gordon C. Fudge* left Grady on the Labrador on September 17, 1922, for Gibraltar. On board were 2350 quintals of cod. Captain Edward Owen Fudge, who also owned the schooner, had as crew: mate Frank Tibbo, Lemuel Gould, Simeon Poole and Patrick Hickey, all of Belleoram. Cook George Bambury was from Pool's Cove.

When the tern was built in Essex, Massachusetts, she was christened *Marne* and had tanks built into her hold aft to hold several tons of fuel oil. Owned by a German company, *Marne* also had a Diesel engine and was designed to supply German submarines in the Atlantic. When the United States entered

With Chapel Island looming in the background, S.S. *Glencoe* backs out of Belleoram harbour in 1910. Two banking schooners are moored just inside the lighthouse on the point of beach. By 1910, the bank fishery reached its highest point in Belleoram with eighteen vessels employing over 250 men. Today Belleoram's population has stabilized at approximately seven hundred fifty.

In this photo many of the residences are one and a half storey wooden houses with a back porch attached. Vegetable or hay gardens are behind the house.

World War One in April 1917, she was seized by the American government, taken to Boston and later sold to Fudge for $28,000. Fudge had the tanks taken out to make more cargo space, had the engine removed and renamed the schooner *Gordon C. Fudge*, after his ten year old son.

Weather was so bad on the eastern journey, the crew had to jettison 250 quintals of fish to lighten the schooner. Heavy seas damaged *Gordon C. Fudge*'s bulwarks, but the crew made Valencia, Spain, and discharged the remaining cargo. At Terre Vaja, Spain, they loaded 230 tons of salt and departed for Belleoram. According to Captain Fudge's story told later:

> After we passed the Azores, it was one gale after another with sails being blown away and bulwarks crashing until a big sea smashed our rudder on December 20th. Our two lifeboats had been crushed in and swept away, and I don't remember the dates for things were happening too fast for me to keep a strict reckoning.

Finally the only sail remaining was a piece of foresail. Water poured in through opened seams despite every effort of the Belleoram men to keep it out. After the rudder was carried away and *Gordon C. Fudge* was out of control, Captain Fudge raised the British ensign as a distress signal. Not long after, that too was blown to tatters and Fudge hoisted the American ensign which was still fluttering when the tern sank on December twenty-first.

Captain Ernest Finch of the Atlantic transport liner *Menominee* reported he sighted the schooner on December 21 at 2:30 p.m. about twelve hundred miles east of the Ambrose Lightship. There was a northwesterly swell on the ocean, but not much wind. Without much difficulty, Chief Officer Miller of *Menominee* lowered No. 2 lifeboat on the port side, which was manned by five sailors, and soon they had the Belleoram men aboard. Officer Miller recalled his part in the rescue:

> At 2:38 p.m. the lifeboat was lowered from the davits and at 2:52 p.m. she was on her way back to our ship with the six men including the Captain. All were in better shape than I expected to see them. It was a hard pull for the men in the lifeboat, as there was a heavy swell running. Captain Fudge suggested that we should try to tow his vessel to St. John's, but she was taking in water too rapidly and there was nothing else to do but abandon her.

To ensure a quick sinking so as the derelict tern would not be a menace to navigation, Fudge set her afire before he left. The six Fortune Bay seamen were landed at New York on December 27, 1922, and from there they had to find their own transportation back to Newfoundland.

Less than ten years later another schooner — some of the crew were Belleoram seamen — went to Davy Jones's Locker, again without loss of life.

J.D. Hazen, a Nova Scotian schooner captained by George Walters of Fortune, left Lunenburg, Nova Scotia, on March 1, 1931. *J.D. Hazen*'s destination was the West Indies, probably for a load of Demerara rum, but adverse weather sent the two masted schooner to the bottom. Her crew list comes straight out of Fortune Bay: Morgan Moulton, Belleoram; George Mullins, Belleoram but originally from Rencontre East (Mullins later moved to Nova Scotia); Reg Hardiman, Point Rosie (Point Enragee); the mate R. Vallis of Coomb's Cove; and two from Fortune, cook Morgan Thornhill and Captain Walters.

Three days out of port or about 332 miles south southwest of Cape Sable, Nova Scotia, the vessel was lashed by a heavy gale. With decks awash and seams strained, *J.D. Hazen* began to leak. Captain Walters ordered his crew to the pumps, but water gained steadily until the forecastle and holds were nearly full of water.

Like bleached driftwood on the shore, the derelict of *Kathleen C. Creaser*, owned in Belleoram by Benjamin Keeping and captained by his son Zina, lies on Dune Sands between Miquelon and Langlade. On September 17, 1943, she carried supplies and coal to Belleoram, but grounded in thick fog. Her six crew — Keeping, Morgan Moulton and Lorne Barnes and three others — escaped; later, insurance agents sold her coal by the doryload to the St. Pierrias.

After that incident, Zina Keeping captained *Betty and Molly* which had been purchased by W.G. Nott from the Northeast Coast. *Betty and Molly* was later skippered by Joe Saunders of Tickle Beach who lost her on the western shore.

Successive days of pumping made no difference to the level of water, but the schooner, now wallowing and labouring in the storm, had her mainmast carried away. With it went the rigging to operate the other sails. Driven back toward Nova Scotia, Walters had no choice but abandon ship, if another vessel came by.

On the night of March 10, the lights of a steamer were sighted in the distance, apparently headed their way. The Fortune Bay crew dipped blankets in oil, hung them in the rigging and set the material afire. Although the steamer passed close enough that her swell rocked *J.D. Hazen,* it did not stop. There was no response.

By the next day, the storm-racked schooner had drifted to within fourteen miles of Cape LaHave, Nova Scotia. This was close to the coastal shipping lanes of Nova Scotia and a passing schooner, *Selma K,* spotted the distress flags. Before Walters and his crew abandoned *J.D. Hazen,* he set fire to the ship to ensure a quick end. *Selma K* landed them in Lunenburg, the same port they left twelve days previously.

Another fine schooner owned in Belleoram was *Effie M. Prior,* built at the Arthur D. Storey Yards in Essex in 1906. *Effie M. Prior* was purchased by Captain Stephen Vatcher Cluett and the Kearley Brothers of Belleoram in 1912. For years while under the command of Captain Stephen Vatcher this schooner was a familiar sight on the Grand Banks. Her end came in 1921 while she was under the command of Captain Brenton when she ran ashore at Savage Cove in the Straits of Belle Isle while returning from the Labrador fishery laden with 1300 quintals of fish. Brenton and his crew made shore safely.

The fishing community of Belleoram has depended on the sea for over two hundred and fifty years, but codfish, once the prime catch, has been replaced by numerous other species. The scores of banking schooners which lay at their mooring in Belleoram harbour or sailed up Belleoram Reach with salt-encrusted canvas are now half-forgotten memories of old.

Chapter 4

Boat Harbour Boatbuilders

With the eastern hills and Rattle Brook looming behind, *Gail* waits in front of Earl and Charlie Lockyer's premises. Dixon's business of Fortune brought their schooner *Gail* to Boat Harbour for repairs. While under the command of Reg Buffett, she struck Fortune's western breakwater and had to be beached for temporary patching until she could be taken to Boat Harbour.

Originally called *Vera B. Humby* when she was built in Summerville, Bonavista Bay in 1935, she netted 68 ton and was 82.7 feet long. At Boat Harbour she had her bowsprit removed, masts cut down and pilot house constructed.

On May 23, 1964, heavy ice at Partridge Point, White Bay, punctured *Gail* and sent her to the bottom.

LOCKYER BROTHERS, shipwrights and carpenters by trade, built the sixty-three-foot *Glimshire* (page 27) in 1944. Named for an island near Flat Island, Placentia Bay, she was used by Alberto Wareham of Harbour Buffett as a six-dory

Tides were not high enough for a launching; schooner *Muriel G. Maxwell* tows the newly constructed *Glimshire* from her slipway at Boat Harbour, Placentia Bay. Charlie and Earl Lockyer of Boat Harbour bought the fifty-three-foot long *Muriel G. Maxwell* from Street Brothers, Epworth where she had been built in 1935. By the late 1940s she was sold to E.J. Green, Winterton, Trinity Bay.

banker with fourteen crew. In 1949 Captain Osborne Hayden and his brother Joseph of Petite Forte, Placentia Bay, bought her. In 1953 *Glimshire*'s work changed to hauling coal after ownership passed to Captain Leslie Cutler of Ramea.

When she collided with S.S. *Perth* and sank on August 20, 1954, off St. Pierre, she was under the registry of William Kendall, Pushthrough.

In the years of wooden vessels, Boat Harbour's economy depended on the sea, not only for the inshore and bank fishing, but also, because of the availability of timber nearby, for logging, saw mill trade, building and repairing small vessels.

Located on the western shores of Placentia Bay near the head of a deep inlet, Boat Harbour is situated on the west shore of the inlet and Brookside, the east shore. It is likely that the first settlers of Boat Harbour came from Brookside/Bay de Lieu; both towns were listed in the 1884 *Census*.

By 1928, families in Boat Harbour North West included: Browne, Denty, King, Keeping, Lockyer, Matterface, Over, Saunders, Senior, Smith, Stacey and Walters. In Boat Harbour

North East, which became Brookside, were Bailey, Brown, King, Pardy and Smith families.

Always dependant on the Placentia Bay fish stocks, the small communities around Boat Harbour were not without vessel tragedies: Denty's vessel of Little Harbour was lost with crew including several Denty men. The derelict drifted in Lear's Cove on the eastern side of Placentia Bay. Patrick Burton's schooner and his seven crew, who probably belonged to Bay de Lieu and Boat Harbour, disappeared in one of the frequent August gales that swept the coast.

In the thirties Boat Harbour's population rose to eighty-three and by this time had gained a reputation for small schooner construction or repairs. *Glimshire; Muriel G. Maxwell; Effie H,* repaired and bought from Petites in English Harbour West, and Thomas Walters' *Alice & Edith* were some vessels rebuilt at Boat Harbour.

Chapter 5

Burgeo: Wreck of Three Vessels

WHEN THE NEWSPAPERS OF THE DAY described the abandonment of the schooner *Elsie L. Corkum,* it didn't mention the names of the hardy South Coast seamen successfully rescued by the S.S. *Heronspool* on December 26, 1920. In contrast, each of the men on the six-man lifeboat rescue crew received a medal for bravery.

Elsie L. Corkum, ninety-seven tons and built in Lunenburg, Nova Scotia, was owned by Burgeo and Lapoile Export Company, commonly referred to as B and L Export, the remnants of a business founded by Robert Moulton in 1890.

Although *Corkum*'s crew was not reported when she was abandoned in the North West Atlantic, it is known (*Evening Telegram,* September 1992) that her crew three years previously were: Stephen Collier, age twenty; William Benoit, twenty-four; cook George King, forty-five; Frank Remmo, twenty-eight; John Swift, twenty-two; John Ingraham, twenty-one. All the crew with the exception of the cook were in their twenties and Collier, who was captain, was the youngest. All belonged to Burgeo.

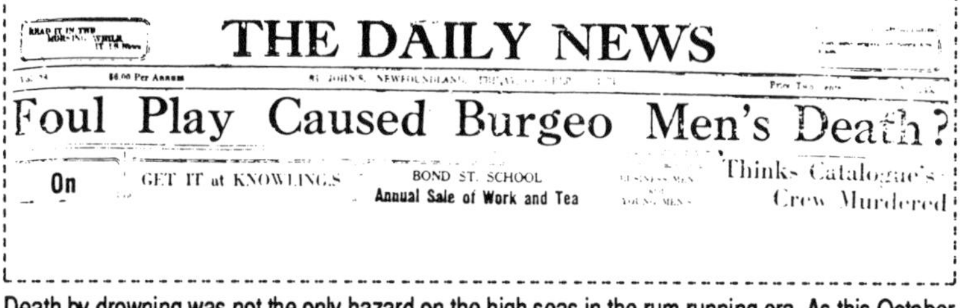
THE DAILY NEWS

Foul Play Caused Burgeo Men's Death?

On

GET IT at KNOWLINGS

BOND ST. SCHOOL
Annual Sale of Work and Tea

Thinks Catalogue's Crew Murdered

Death by drowning was not the only hazard on the high seas in the rum running era. As this October 30, 1931, clipping claims, hi-jackers attacked the schooner *Catalogue* stealing the illegal cargo and killing two Burgeo men — John Spencer and James Carroll.

Catalogue left Port aux Basques bound for New Brunswick, but somewhere off Cheticamp an unusual event mysteriously took the lives of two Burgeo sailors. Two other men — Captain (Teddy) Kirk and Roy Partridge — were missing.

The bodies, which were found in the hold of the schooner, were identified by John Spencer's brother, Simeon Spencer, captain of the Burgeo schooner *Gladiola*. Simeon Spencer's statement to the paper was, "I believe the *Catalogue* was hi-jacked for her cargo of rum and whiskey and that my brother was murdered by boarders."

Catalogue, built in 1910 in LaPoile Bay, was once owned by Abraham Keeping, Burnt Islands, an island settlement located halfway between Port aux Basques and Rose Blanche.

Burgeo, the heart of the South West Coast, is one of Newfoundland's oldest fishing ports. Located about sixty miles east of Port aux Basques, it is situated on an island connected to the mainland by a causeway. There are records of people living in Burgeo as early as the 1700s. Merchants with names like Newman, Clement and Moulton based fleets of schooners in Burgeo's snug harbour and exported fish to ports in Europe and the West Indies.

The origins of Burgeo's name are obscure. Archbishop Howley suggested it may have derived from the French "Bras de Jean." Other historians claimed the Portuguese explorer Joaz Alvarez Fagundez in 1520 named the archipelago. Its name is probably a corruption of Virgeo, a thousand virgins. When English merchants set up business in 1835 there were twenty-three families with surnames Anderson, Matthews, Strickland, Cox, Skeard, Dicks, Cheveilier, Rose, Forward, Read, Harris, Bloomfield, Meade, Major and Collier.

Burgeo's herring fishery peaked by 1887; then the town saw the rise and fall of the banking schooner in its quest for cod. In 1945 Fishery Products built a fresh fish filleting plant which changed ownership and name in 1955, becoming Burgeo Fish Industries.

A significant population influx of over a thousand people from 1961 to 1976 resulted from increased employment oppor-

A major shipping tragedy in the mouth of Burgeo harbour. Debris of *Russell Lake*, built and owned in Fortune, wrecked on Small's Island in Burgeo harbour on March 17, 1929. Her crew was Billy Spencer, Ron Martin, George Witherall, of Fortune; Leo Foote, Lamaline and Frank Stoodley, Grand Bank. Only George Day, born in Harbour Breton and resident of Fortune, survived.

According to veteran Burgeo seamen, the schooner was falling apart with dry rot. The schooner broke up within minutes after hitting a small island almost within Burgeo harbour. Her masts lie in the centre as local men sift through the debris. The section George Day clung to for several hours is barely visible on the right.

tunities from the fish plant and from improved services. In that period people moved to Burgeo from surrounding towns — Rencontre West, Fox Island, Cape La Hune, Parsons Harbour and Francois. Today Burgeo's population stands at a little over 2400.

Up until a few years ago the sea was the only link to the outside world. A road now connects Burgeo to the TransCanada Highway, but its people owe their allegiance to the sea, a friend and foe that provided a livelihood for hundreds of years.

The history of a sea-faring community centres around ships and the men who sailed them. Many of the stately tall sailing ships evoked such feeling of pride that their arrival or presence in a town like Burgeo serves as a reference point when tracing the town's growth.

So it was in the 1920s in Burgeo when the era of the tern schooners came and went; it meant local seamen were in the foreign-trade and made voyages east to Europe or south to Brazil. Many young men had made "a trip across."

Ena A. Moulton, a tern schooner owned by Moulton's business, made a voyage across to Europe in February 1922, one of many in the schooner's career. Most of her six crew for that trip were from Burgeo: Captain Max Vatcher, age thirty-one; Stanley Collier, thirty-seven; William Anderson, thirty-four and John Anderson who at age twenty-one was the youngest aboard. Wallace Smith resided in Flat Island, Placentia Bay and William Peddle in St. John's.

That same year *Gordon E. Moulton* cleared customs at a Newfoundland port for a foreign voyage and had as her crew Burgeo seamen: Captain Stephen Collier, age twenty-four; mate Joseph Ingraham, thirty-four; cook John Caines, twenty-four; Arch Matthews, nineteen and William Clarke. The 195 net ton *Gordon E. Moulton* was built in Dayspring, Nova Scotia in 1919. When this tern was abandoned in late February 1924, off Burgeo, Captain Collier was still in command.

Loss of Moulton's vessels

From the time the first vessel set sail, tales of the treacherous sea filtered back to those waiting on the shore. Ships ran ashore on unseen reefs, were crushed by ice, foundered in Atlantic storms and were cut down by other vessels. Men from Burgeo, like many sailors, paid the supreme sacrifice of ships and lives lost. Island newspapers, written and edited in St. John's, gave little coverage to the loss of a South Coast schooner.

The suffering of men struggling against the elements and the stress of waiting wives and children were often not considered to be particularly newsworthy. William Anderson, John Spencer, Sim Strickland and Jim Buckland, all residents of Burgeo, were reported in good health when they arrived at North Sydney on February 21, 1929. According to the daily newspaper they had been rescued at sea from their tern *Enid E. Legge* by the vessel *St. Dunstan.*

Owned by John T. Moulton, *Enid E. Legge* was en route from Oporto with 200 tons of fishery salt. Battered by storms and heavy seas, the seams opened and eventually salt clogged the pumps. For six days the Burgeo crew battled storms and a sinking schooner until they were plucked off by *St. Dunstan* and carried first to Galveston, Texas, thence to North Sydney.

On September 22, 1931, *Daily News* briefly reported the loss of two vessels owned by Burgeo and Lapoile Export Company: a steamer near home; a tern schooner far from home.

Exhausted from their strenuous labours of four days at the pumps on a rudderless ship that was gradually taking on water faster than it could be pumped out, the crew of the S.S. *Herbert Green* finally abandoned ship.

Steamship *Herbert Green*, owned by Burgeo and Lapoile Export and captained by Stanley Collier of Burgeo, left North Sydney on September 15 with a cargo of coal destined for some port on the South Coast. Well known around the coast as a cargo carrier, the little steamer was a trawler type and had, at one time, been captained by Joe Vatcher.

In the 1930s sailing ships powered solely by the wind continued to be the prime mover of goods along the South Coast of Newfoundland. In other traditional fishing centres, such as St. Pierre and Gloucester, sailing vessels were already becoming obsolete and engine-driven bankers and carriers were increasing more and more. Steam or diesel engines had superiority in speed during calm or adverse weather, thus reducing shipping time. Despite the obvious advantages, the larger towns along the South Coast were slow to adapt to engine-powered vessels. During the salt fish era only a few were listed: S.S. *Illex* owned by Wareham of Harbour Buffett, Captain Alex Rodway and wrecked near Fermeuse on October 27, 1948; S.S. *H.A. Walker* by Patten and Forsey's business, Grand Bank, lost at Pouch Cove, February 18, 1938.

After leaving Burgeo *Herbert Green* ran into heavy gales and high seas. The rudder was stripped and the steamer began to leak. Somehow in the high seas, a jury or makeshift rudder was rigged which kept the vessel under some control. Slowly the ship was navigated toward land.

For four days the nine men pumped to exhaustion — water rose steadily. In the early morning of September 21, the fires providing the steam for power were extinguished by rising seawater. *Herbert Green* now had no power and was being steered in heavy seas by an improvised rudder.

By 4:00 p.m., the vessel was only one mile from land, at the mouth of Chaleur Bay near Francois.

Captain Collier decided to abandon ship. Soon after the nine men rowed off some distance in their two lifeboats, S.S. *Herbert Green* sank.

That same evening another vessel owned in Burgeo succumbed to the elements when the auxiliary schooner *Reginald R. Moulton* stranded at Burnt Point near Seldom on Fogo Island. Her cargo was to be landed at Victoria Cove, Gander Bay, but only part was salvaged.

A tern schooner of 141 tons, *Reginald R. Moulton* was built in 1917 at Dayspring, Nova Scotia and was once under the registry of Robert Moulton. For many years Captain Dan MacDonald skippered her out of Burgeo until 1928 when she was sold to a business in Notre Dame Bay.

Moulton struck a shoal near Grandfather's Reef at 2:00 a.m. during a snow storm and the captain, knowing the ship's bottom was seriously damaged, headed the sinking tern for Seldom.

Seas broke on board and flooded the engine room, the mainboom snapped and *Moulton* became unmanageable. The crew steered for a lee shore and beached the schooner at Burnt Point. The Wreck Commissioner at Seldom reported her as a total loss and took charge of salvage operations.

In the roster of vessels owned in Burgeo there are over eighty schooners listed. Not all their crews were as lucky as those of *Elsie Corkum, Herbert Green* and *Reginald Moulton;* no fewer than eleven schooners were lost with all hands taking over three score Burgeo men with them.

Chapter 6

Burin, Born of the Sea

WITH ITS PRESENT DAY POPULATION OF OVER 3000, Burin's roots go back to the Basque fishermen and whalers, the earliest French colonists and the English settlers with their banking schooners and merchant houses.

"Captivating" is just one word of many to describe the rugged shoreline and traditional lifestyle of this historic and independent community where the encompassing sea is, as it always was, the mainstay of the economy. One of the focal points is the recently restored Burin Heritage House, built around the turn of the century by fish merchant James Reddy; it is filled with authentic furniture and yesterday's tools. The house outlines the area's development through artifacts, an extensive captioned photo display and enthusiastic tour guides.

There is a classic beauty to the physical land and seascapes of Burin and the surrounding communities — although a drive around 'the Scrape' today is not as dangerous as it once was, it is still as breathtaking as it overlooks the islands, bays and homes. Several nearby towns are close enough to take a few hours or a day to enjoy depending on your time frame. Fox Cove, Beaubois, Epworth, Burin Bay Arm, Mortier, Little Salmonier and Bull's Cove all have their own distinctive histories and still are a photographer's delight with their sheltered coves and scenic shorelines.

Here as in generations past, small and larger boats wait at their mooring lines to harvest the ocean, corner stores sell everything from home made bread to local crafts and friendly people are always ready to talk and to help.

Burin's landlocked haven became a frequented centre for

In its efforts to preserve the past, Heritage House (above) now has the old Burin Bank of Nova Scotia restored and filled with artifacts and historic pictures on three levels. The punishment area in back has the ancient whipping post, foot and head stocks.

many early Europeans. Newfoundland historian D.W. Prowse relates that in 1697 the French stopped the Spanish Biscayans and Basque from fishing in Buria Chumea (Little Burin) and Buria Audia (Great Burin). According to tradition the name Burin comes from the French work 'Burine' which means an engraver's knife, for it is said that the shape of the harbour resembles the tool.

The French enjoyed a prosperous stay, but by the time the Treaty of Paris was signed in 1763, ending the Seven Year's War and ceding most of North America to England, French settlers had already left the South Coast. English planters and fishermen settled the land after first populating and later abandoning the offshore islands — Pardy's Island, Shalloway, Titus Island and Burin Island.

Captain Cook's team surveyed the area around 1767 and one of the pleasures on a visit to Ship Cove, Burin, is a hike to panoramic Cook's Lookout named for the famed English cartographer and explorer. Remains of ancient fortifications, cannon and rock walls once found at Cook's Lookout, Man-O-War Hill, Troke's Point, Shalloway and other strategic locations attest to the importance placed on Burin Harbour as the British defended it against foreign warships and privateers. Prowse mentions that an American whaling schooner visited Burin in 1810 but left because there was a warship permanently stationed there.

Although most vestiges of the Basque and French occupation have long since disappeared, the savour of the schooner bank fishery still remains. Documentation at Heritage House shows that around 1718 Spurrier's of Poole, England, established a shipyard at Ship Cove turning out dozens of barques and brigantines until 1830 when it went bankrupt.

The 1857 census indicates sixty-one boats and one vessel had been built during the previous year by other shipbuilding firms. From the turn of the century to the 1960s banking captains and merchants — Vigus, Inkpen, Hollett, LeFeuvre, Bishop — built fish drying premises and sent schooners by the score to reap the riches of the bountiful banks near Burin's doorstep.

But for any town that sends a fleet of ships down to the sea, death by drowning and tragedy go hand in hand and to this end Burin has been no exception. In 1919 *Herbert and Ruby* never reported and in February 1924 Hollett's tern schooner *Roy Bruce* was mysteriously cut down in mid-ocean and all five Burin crew members were lost: Captain Robert Hollett, his son Morgan, Max Adams, Berkley Morris and Max Batten. In 1931 *Wilson T,*

THE DAILY NEWS

ST. JOHN'S, NEWFOUNDLAND, SATURDAY, OCTOBER 31, 1931 Price Two Cents

Burin Vessel Founders With Loss Six Men

Daily News, October 31, 1931, edition, reports the *Wilson T*, lost with all hands in the Gulf. Actually she had left the Gulf of St. Lawrence some hours before and was wrecked on Seal Rocks west of Miquelon.

a small schooner owned in New Brunswick, disappeared and Captain Fred Myles, his son Philip, Charles Keating, Leonard Shave, Charles I. White and Thomas Hartson, all of Burin or towns nearby, were drowned.

Whatever Happened to *Mina Swim*?

To hundreds of fishermen on the South Coast of Newfoundland, the Bank fishery once represented financial security at the end of the year's fishing voyages. So it was with our forefathers; they too went to sea to match their strength and their wooden ships against the forces of nature, to conquer more often than not and to return with the reward — codfish.

Sometimes the sea triumphs and a ship does not return at all. Then, instead of bounty and prosperity, the sea forces wives and children to share a cup of sorrow.

When the previous banking season of 1916 ended in October and *Mina Swim* sailed into Burin, people were delighted that all men had returned home safely and successfully. In terms of fish and money or credit, the voyage had been fair. But there was plenty of work to do during the months between October and February. Houses were repaired; wood was hauled, sawn up and stored; barns improved and kelp was carried to the hay or vegetable gardens.

Women spent their evenings knitting and making clothes: mitts, socks, underwear and other woollen attire for the men. No thought of the coming separation between husband, wife and children was allowed to interfere with busy, happy hours. But schooners like *Mina Swim* — a ten-dory banker built in Essex, Massachusetts, in 1904 — must leave port. Considered in her time a fast and able schooner, *Mina Swim* had withstood several winter storms. She measured 82 feet long and netted sixty tons. She brought her unusual name with her from Essex, but there have been other schooners christened "Mina" built in the Minas Basin in Nova Scotia — *Mina Queen, Mina King, Mina Prince.*

The herring baiting voyage took place in February or early March. Frozen herring, obtained at the heads of the bays, was stored in the holds. The owners, LeFeuvre brothers of Bull's Cove, outfitted their schooners with dories, gear, food and supplies and saw each one off; *Swim* on February 17 at approximately 3:00 p.m. From that point on *Mina Swim* disappeared from human ken.

In *The History of Burin*, a valuable community history researched and written by a committee of Senior Citizens in 1977, there appeared this summary of the tragedy:

> The *Mina Swim* was never heard of after a terrific storm on the first night out. No one can correctly say what happened as at that time it was common knowledge that German submarines lurked around our shores. However, high winds, heavy seas and icing can deal out death and destruction in no uncertain terms. Twenty-three men, including Captain John Jarvis, were sent to watery graves by some still unsolved mystery.

To fish the "herring baitings" schooners headed for the Western Shore, between Port aux Basques and Harbour Le Cou, and this phase of the fishing season was considered the toughest. Along the coast tides ran strong and February/March storms were a constant threat. But despite hardships and dangers, it was a paying trip for the fishermen and vessel owners. *Mina Swim* was due to fish from Rose Blanche for two to three weeks, harbouring in Rose Blanche by night and returning daily to the productive grounds.

On the way to the Western Shore, schooners from Grand Bank, Fortune, Burin and Mortier Bay passed near St. Pierre where fishing supplies like rope, lines, gear were cheap. So were cigarettes and whisky; nearly all schoonermen smoked heavily and most were not averse to having their drink. According to local tradition *Mina Swim*, like many South Coast schooners, was due to stop at the French Islands.

When *Mina Swim* failed to report in due time, inquiries with the French authorities on the island proved negative; the schooner had not docked there. Possibly *Mina Swim* went down off the Western Shore.

By February 1917, the German war machine had resorted to

unlimited submarine warfare. Shipping losses increased dramatically, not only off Europe, but near the North American coast as well. S.S. *Eric,* an old St. John's sealing vessel was torpedoed on August 25, 1918, with no loss of life, a few miles off Gallantry Head, St. Pierre. In August 1918, a sub surfaced in the middle of the American fishing fleet on George's Bank and sank or damaged thirteen vessels. South Coast fishing and foreign-going schooners were not immune to predation. No fewer than a dozen were officially recorded as sunk by German bombs, while another eight South Coast schooners disappeared without a trace during the war.

Mina Swim, while sailing between home port and her destination, passed through an area patrolled by enemy U-boats when the war at sea was at its greatest height. It has been

Courtesy PANL

Hollett and Sons premises and five of the many schooners the business had owned over the years. In 1906 brothers William and Thomas Hollett formed a fish procuring and exporting business. In 1931 the business, like many in the Depression years, went bankrupt and was reformed as Hollett and Sons Limited under the management of Thomas Hollett. The building on the near left was an artificial fish dryer. Built in 1913, it was the first of its kind in Britain's colonies.

The schooners from l-r *Keith V. Colin* abandoned off Nova Scotia, February 1954; *Golden Glow*, sank near Chatham, N.B. in the 1950s; *Trinity North*, renamed *Gladys Wiscombe*, burned in July 1970; *Joan Ella May*, abandoned on St. Pierre Bank in May 1957, 79-ton *Roy M*, built in Essex in 1921, and sold back to U.S. interests.

In the background overlooking historic Burin harbour is the Collin's Cove United Church, built in 1904.

suggested the schooner struck an explosive mine planted by the enemy, but this is unlikely. The route from Burin to Rose Blanche fishing banks was not a frequented sea lane, thus the unlikelihood of mine fields. If mines had been set near St. Pierre, other schooners from South Coast ports would have been destroyed. Possibly *Mina Swim* struck a single, drifting mine.

Captain John Jarvis, an experienced mariner, knew the war-time risks and weather conditions and took all necessary precautions to ensure the safety of his men under his charge. *Mina Swim* was posted "Missing at Sea" and those who disappeared were: Jarvis whose home town was Burin; mate Thomas Riggs and Norman Martin, of Bull's Cove, and James Giles, Path End. Nine men hailed from Salmonier: Robert Lundrigan, Sr. and his three nephews, John Lundrigan, Robert Lundrigan, Jr., and James Hannam; Robert Cook; Thomas Lake; William Butler and two brothers John J. Brushett and William T. Brushett. Two Mitchell brothers — Wesley and Samuel Mitchell of Burin Bay Arm — were crew. Samuel, about 51 years old, was married to Mary (Caines) Mitchell and had four children.

Two men missing on *Mina Swim* are identified by last name only: Thorne, Lewin's Cove and a young man named Moulton, Burin Bay. Robert Goods was aboard, but his place of residence is not known.

The missing schooner's kedgie was Sam Planke of Port au Bras, the oldest seaman on *Mina Swim*. Generally, kedgies were boys between fourteen and eighteen — too young or inexperienced for regular work as a dory fisherman. As kedgie, Planke helped the cook, cleaned the galley, helped catch dory painters when the dories returned from fishing. At times, if a someone was sick or injured, he would dory fish rather than have a man work alone or "crosshanded."

This accounts for nineteen of the twenty-three; the others remain unidentified. There was scarcely a home in the Burin area that was not directly touched by the disappearance of *Mina Swim*, lost in February of 1917 with her entire crew.

It became the duty of part-owner Thomas LeFeuvre, along with the local clergyman, to officially inform families of the loss of *Mina Swim.* He often claimed that it was the hardest job he ever had to do. LeFeuvre remembered visiting one father who had lost an unmarried son. Although the grieving man was devastated, his deepest regrets were for families who were worse off than he; those wives and children who had lost a father and now had no source of income.

Other Burin Vessels Lost

Mina Swim was not the only vessel associated with Burin's trade in the salt fish industry to disappear in the war years. After the war, when German war records were checked in relation to Newfoundland shipping losses, it was learned that *Ada D. Bishop,* a banking schooner owned in Burin but operated out of Twillingate, was sunk by an enemy submarine on January 10, 1918. Built in 1911 in Shelburne, Nova Scotia, the ninety-three-ton schooner had been registered to Charles F. Bishop of Burin.

By 1885 Bishop Brothers Limited (Charles and Robert K.) of Burin was one of the leading outport merchant houses in Newfoundland. Robert K. Bishop associated with Monroes in St. John's to form a general import and fisheries export business — Bishop and Monroe. Bishop and Monroe were early partners, but R.K. Bishop, who was also an active Newfoundland politician, controlled the firm in 1908 until its close out in 1922.

Only one of her crew hailed from Burin: Rufus Burgess, husband of Lillian Burgess of Burin North. Bishop Brothers had branch businesses in other parts of Newfoundland and undoubtedly the schooner operated out of Twillingate. Thus the other crew of *Ada D. Bishop* hailed from New World Island, Notre Dame Bay — Arthur Atkinson, son of Solomon Atkinson; Michael Atkinson, son of Mrs. E. Atkinson, both of Salt Harbour near Herring Neck; Fred Lambert, Mark Button, son of Abel Button of Twillingate and Arthur Howell, husband of Florence Howell of Herring Neck.

On March 1, 1918, *Cecil L. Shave* was sunk off the Azores while en route from St. John's to Gibraltar. None of her crew was ever seen again: Charles Hart, Fogo; William Leonard, British Harbour, Trinity Bay; Robert Hunt, Greenspond; and three men of St. John's, Edgar Kean, 3 Haggerty Street; Scobie McKie, 273 Southside Road; and John Turpin, 2 Lyon's Square.

Cecil L. Shave, a seventy-five-ton two masted schooner, was built in 1914 at Shelburne for Thomas Shave of Burin.

Many sea stories associated with Burin have happier endings: like the rescue of the Burin crew of *Vanessa* off Portugal on November 8, 1918. Captain Harry Brushett, youngest aboard at age nineteen; Alton Brenton; Robert Dear; John Isaacs; Thomas Burfitt and Ernest Kirby were all rescued by the Norwegian steamer *Severne*.

Although the crew was not listed, the January 10, 1912, edition of *Daily News* related how *Portland*, another schooner owned by Charles Bishop of Burin was wrecked at Kemp's Point. She was headed for St. John's from Burin laden with fish. All crew was reported safe.

Built in 1907 in Essex, Massachusetts, the ninety-ton *Richard* was brought to Newfoundland in 1916 upon her purchase by Hollett's business of Burin. On February 5, 1917, while on a voyage from Cadiz, Spain, to Burin laden with salt, *Richard* was abandoned at latitude 40.42 North, longitude 52.21 West. Captain Cecil Lake of Fortune and his crew of six were rescued by a passing steamer.

Wrecks and strandings abound on the many shoals, islets and headlands around Burin. One of the most memorable happened on June 25, 1925, when the steamer *Argos* went ashore at Cat Island, Burin. Although there was no loss of life in the wreck, four Burin men — Fred Abbott, Bert Thorne, Richard Moulton and James Dicks — drowned while attempting to salvage items from the steamer. Eleven years later a Lunenburg banker was lost at Corbin, near Burin.

A Wreck at Corbin

On June 8, 1936, the rocky shores around Burin claimed another victim when *Bruce and Winona* left Burin to go to Garnish for bait. *Bruce and Winona*, a ninety-ton banking schooner built in Lunenburg in 1930, was registered to a Lunenburg business; Arnold Parks of Lunenburg was her skipper. When she came around Corbin Island in the dense fog, Parks must have changed his course slightly and kept her inside too far to clear the minefield of rocks and sunkers in Corbin Bight.

At the time of her loss, the Lunenburg banker was towing a trap boat filled with capelin seines to Garnish. Since it was illegal for Canadian vessels to catch baitfish in Newfoundland waters, it was the practise of Nova Scotian captains to hire local men who owned capelin seines and a skiff. These fishermen would gather the capelin in various locations in Placentia Bay or Fortune Bay, put the bait aboard the schooner and get a tow back to Burin. The foreign captain then paid the fishermen for the bait and this legal loophole kept everyone happy.

As *Bruce and Winona* steamed toward Garnish to obtain bait she had to clear Corbin Head, on that day enshrouded with fog. The town of Corbin, Placentia Bay, is located six miles southwest of Burin near Corbin Head, a conspicuous headland around 180 feet high. Corbin Island is just off the coast and Corbin Bight is a mass of sunkers and hidden reefs. Inshore fishermen of Corbin knew the area well, but for a foreign skipper it was an area to be avoided.

Corbin appears in the first *Census* in 1836 with a population of 57. By 1871 it was connected by road to Little St. Lawrence and during the lobster canning boom of 1900–20 Corbin's population rose to its highest peak of a little over one hundred.

Misnamed Corban in the first census, its name may be derived from the French word corbeau (Crow Head) or corbeil (from the lay of the land). By the 1930s when the wreck of *Bruce and Winona* appeared on their doorstep, prominent family names included: Coady, Dunphy, Lundrigan, Nolan, O'Brien, O'Rielly, Power, Ryan, Slaney, Upshall and Grant.

It was William and Ben Grant, inshore fishermen of Corbin, who first saw the stranded *Bruce and Winona*. Captain Parks, being unfamiliar with the area, had kept well inside the proper course to clear the rocks. As the schooner steamed along she went in over Grant's cod trap leader, then ground to a halt on a reef.

Bruce and Winona tore up a hundred and seventy fathom of

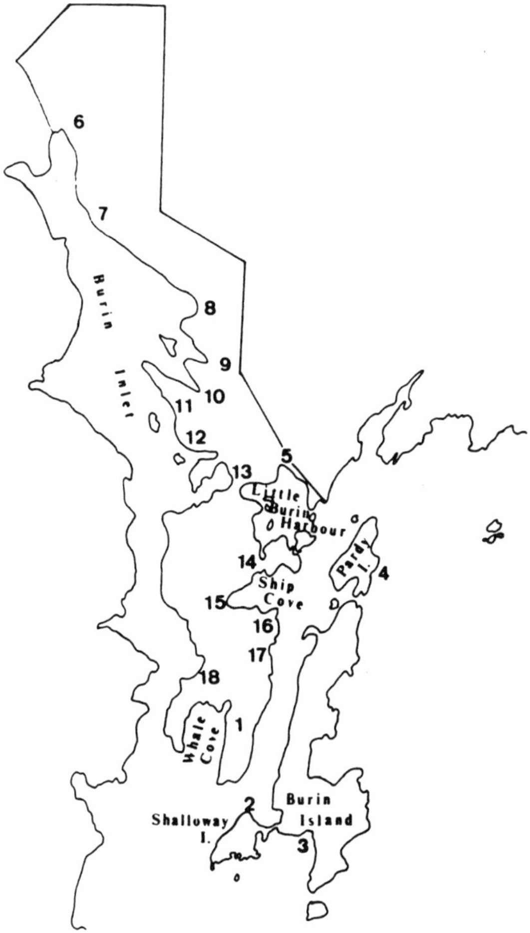

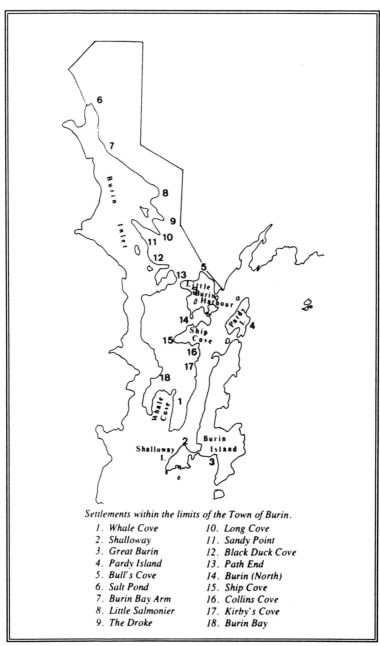

Settlements within the limits of the Town of Burin.

1. *Whale Cove*
2. *Shalloway*
3. *Great Burin*
4. *Pardy Island*
5. *Bull's Cove*
6. *Salt Pond*
7. *Burin Bay Arm*
8. *Little Salmonier*
9. *The Droke*
10. *Long Cove*
11. *Sandy Point*
12. *Black Duck Cove*
13. *Path End*
14. *Burin (North)*
15. *Ship Cove*
16. *Collins Cove*
17. *Kirby's Cove*
18. *Burin Bay*

The many harbours, coves and communities that once made up the community of Burin.

Courtesy of Seamen's Museum

Donald Hollett, built in Shelburne, Nova Scotia in 1911. In December 1918, William and Thomas Hollett's business of Burin lost the 136-ton schooner *Donald Hollett* when she was abandoned at sea.

leader running out to the Grant's trap and ran over the cod trap. When the Grants went out in the morning to tend their gear they saw, not only a damaged cod trap, but twelve or fourteen banking dories in Corbin Bight.

In the early morning haze and fog the twenty-five crew had abandoned the wreck. Dories were keeping off the land a little distance trying to avoid rocks and reefs until the fog lifted. When Ben Grant rowed up to the nearest dory he saw *Bruce and Winona*'s cook sitting up in the dory with his white cap and apron on.

This was an unusual sight for the inshore fishermen of Corbin which prompted Grant to ask what was happening. "Oh," the cook said, "Skipper wanted to take a short cut to Garnish but he couldn't get up over the land."

Bruce and Winona remained stranded on the reef for several days and eventually broke up, but not before the engine, sails, masts and all gear were salvaged by Hollett's business at Burin.

Like most Newfoundland communities modernization has

helped Burin evolve from the yesterday's hardships and tragedy into a stronger and more unified town today. Despite the world depression of the "Dirty Thirties" and the weak market in the 1940s for the salt dry fish, a plant for fresh fish was built in Burin in 1942 by Fishery Products, the first of its kind in Newfoundland. Draggers bringing fresh cod, cutters filleting fish and quick freezing techniques were readily adopted by the Burin workforce.

The traditional game of soccer still attracts large crowds, but softball diamonds, swimming, hockey and movie theatres see hundreds of people participating, young and old. The annual Burin Folk Festival held every July spotlights the Penny Folk Dancers as well as step dancers and folk singers accompanied by the button accordion.

Courtesy of Ron Grandy

Swivel. Built in 1943, the 520-net ton *Swivel* had an iron frame with wooden planks. She was built by the American Car and Foundry Company at Wilmington, Delaware and was later owned by Fisheries Products Ltd. at Burin. From there she carried fillets to Rhode Island and other American ports.

Later after her registry changed to Lake and Lake of St. John's she carried frozen fish from Ramea, Gaultois and Burgeo to Gloucester. In 1962 her crew was: Capt. James Moffatt, Scotland; first mate Bill Grant, chief engineer Hobey Hann, second engineer Jim Parsons, third engineer Eric Parsons, deckhand George Skinner, all of Burgeo; oiler Thomas Young, Grey River; second mate Alfred Carberry, Carmanville; supercargo Hubert Tibbo, cook Louis Kendall, steward Edward Simms, deckhands Harry Bowles, Frank Bowles and Wilfred Bowles of Ramea.

Chapter 7

English Harbour East Connections

BAY OF ISLANDS ON NEWFOUNDLAND'S WEST COAST has a cosmopolitan population. In the 1850s the herring fishery developed there in response to the increased demands of the American fishing fleet. A little later lumbering developed in the area and settlers began to arrive in large numbers. The majority came from the Avalon Peninsula. During the 1860s the failure of the cod fishery on the Labrador coast induced Labradorians to move to the Bay of Islands.

At peak years up until World War One, a thousand and sometimes as many as two thousand fishermen from the Bay of Islands area were involved in catching, exporting, canning or barrelling of herring. As the herring fishery became a large and prosperous industry, some settlers moved in from Nova Scotia and Fortune Bay.

One Fortune Bay town from which the settlers came was English Harbour East, located in northeastern section of the bay north of Bay L'Argent. The harbour had been noted on Captain Cook's 1764 map of the South Coast, and in Newfoundland's first Census report of 1836 English Harbour East had a population of nineteen. Lovell's *Newfoundland Directory* (1871) reported several planters named Dodge and other planters of Hackett, Hines, Kirby, Voter and Saunders, as well as fishermen Phillips, Voter and Hackett.

The cod fishery had always been important to the town. In the 1890s the lobster fishery, including lobster canning factories, increased in prominence; salmon was also tinned at English Harbour East for a brief period. In similarity to the Bay of Islands' herring fishery, vast schools of herring once stocked the head of Fortune Bay. English Harbour East fishermen were well-experienced in the herring trade.

In 1879, when the fisheries patrol boats went to Fortune Bay to monitor the local bounty for herring and to record amounts supplied American schooners, the warden reported that at English Harbour East he "got a fair share of slang (hard language) here from sea-lawyer Hackett who owned two herring seines and five crafts."

So it was that, as the sea and the herring fishery provided a living for men of English Harbour East, the sea also exacted its wages. On the third of January 1924, a terrific gale swept the West Coast of Newfoundland and former English Harbour East seamen fell prey.

Two days after the storm the first news of tragedy reached the Deputy Minister of Customs in St. John's, H.W. LeMessurier, from the Sub-collector of Customs at Robinsons on the West Coast. He reported wreckage had drifted ashore in St. George's Bay and the body of an unknown man had been found. The message read:

> Wreckage and part cargo of herring drifted ashore at Fischell's in St. George's Bay. Schooner unknown. One body picked up.

Meagre information indeed, for a herring laden schooner, either American or Newfoundland, had at least five to seven men. From the location of wreckage and the knowledge that winter sea traffic to and from the herring production plants at Bay of Islands was heavy, it was assumed the vessel had left Bay of Islands for Gloucester. By January sixth more confirmation of the disaster came in a message via the manager of the Newfoundland railway.

Additional bodies had washed ashore at Fischell's. Authorities examining the wreckage found the nameboard *Donald L. Silver* which was known to have left Wood's Island less than a week previously. Built in Lunenburg in 1911, she carried 1010 barrels of loose bulk herring in the holds, 150 barrels of pickled herring and 282 barrels of Scotch-cured herring.

On the sixth, H.J. Russell, manager of the railway received a final official notification of the disaster. The telegraph message read:

> James McIsaac, of Heatherton, reports picking up the body of one man at Berry Head; also reports one more body picked up at Fischell's. Vessel's name was *Donald L. Silver*, with a load of herring. Schooner broken to pieces. Can't identify bodies picked up. Please notify authorities.

Apparently *Donald Silver* left port deeply laden, encountered a severe winter storm and in the attempt to seek shelter in St. George's Bay was wrecked on some offshore bar or rock. Newspapers became silent at this point and further reports ceased. Within a day or so the bodies that had washed ashore were identified: John, Joseph and James Hackett, William Ruth, Alonzo Wheeler, brothers Frank and Harold Swyer, the latter four men from the Bay of Islands area.

In English Harbour East it was another tragedy of the sea striking home. Three of those drowned were Hacketts; namesakes of a family that had left English Harbour East around 1900 to settle in Bay of Islands where work in the herring fishery was readily available.

Nor was this the first time English Harbour East had experienced bad news from the sea. Between April 6–8 in 1907, local papers reported storm damage between St. John's and Conception Bay. Barns, chimneys and a church spire were damaged. Accounts from Belleoram claimed the conditions were the worst in twenty-five years: five craft were driven ashore and eight others received damages.

Grace D. Day, a thirty-nine-ton schooner built in Sable River, Nova Scotia, was bound to Belleoram from Halifax. A four dory banking schooner launched in 1902 and owned by Captain J.S. Hackett of English Harbour East, she was too small to bear the pounding that ships and seamen experienced in the treacherous Gulf of St. Lawrence. On a Sunday night, April 7, while sailing into the teeth of the tempest, Hackett was washed overboard and disappeared. Philip Dicks, a crewman from Belleoram, brought the schooner, with its flag at half mast, into Belleoram.

Hackett, married with a family, had been well-known along the South Coast. *Grace D. Day* was later sold to a business in Belleoram.

Wreck of the *Leopard*

The twenty-ton schooner *Leopard*, owned and commanded by Llewellyn Coombs of English Harbour East, freighted supplies around Fortune Bay in the early 1930s. Coombs had purchased her in 1930 from Henri Moraze, a St. Pierre businessman.

In November 1932, Coombs and three other crewmen — one of whom was eighteen-year-old Michael Hackett of English Harbour East — took *Leopard* to St. Pierre. On the afternoon of November 30, after Captain Coombs had taken his cargo of shop goods, supplies and Christmas cheer aboard, he set sail for English Harbour East approximately eighty miles away.

The weather was threatening — overcast and windy. Before dark the winds, accompanied by thick snow, increased forcing Coombs to make a run into Connaigre Bay, on the north side of Fortune Bay from St. Pierre. While entering Landing Cove, near Harbour Breton, *Leopard*'s mast broke off in the gale. The schooner began to leak and Coomb's decided to abandon ship.

Young seaman Mike Hackett recalled what happened after they launched *Leopard*'s dory over the side:

> All four crew members had to get into one small old dory. We got on board and tried to get ashore. We were nearly frozen with the wind and the cold. Luckily the wind changed direction and six hours later, we reached Landing Cove and saw some friendly house lights. Three of us stayed with the Edwin Rose family (of Great Harbour) for nearly a week. The fourth man was close to his own community and stayed there. This was during the rough Depression years but everyone was kind on the coast of Newfoundland. A seaman was given the best of care whenever hardship befell him and he made it to shore.

Today English Harbour East is a viable incorporated town with a population of over 290. It lost a few households in the resettlement program, but today it has most amenities of small Newfoundland communities. Although its dependence on the sea is less now than in former years, older residents recall the era of sailing craft and the toll of human lives that accompanied the schooner fishery.

Chapter 8

English Harbour West: A Dependence on the Sea

THE TALE OF THE SEA TOLD BY CAPTAIN HORWOOD of the schooner *John W. Miller* when he arrived in St. John's on May 20, 1924, from Barbados contained bad news for two South Coast communities. Howard, while in latitude 41.19 North, longitude 56.09 West, a few hundred miles off the Nova Scotian coast, reported seeing wreckage of a derelict wooden vessel.

Wreckage floating upright included the portside quarter of a large schooner painted white, a large section of the stern, the after bulwarks, rudder, sternpost and after rail were intact. Part of the schooner's name — *EV* —was visible under the broken bulwarks, along with enough wording of her port of registry to show Bridgetown, Barbados. Captain Howard sent a small boat over to investigate, but its crew reported no trace of the forward section nor of the crew.

It was known Monroe Export Company's schooner *Evelyn* left St. John's on February 25 bound for Pernambuco, Brazil, and for over eighty days nothing had been heard from her.

Built in 1907 at Granville, Nova Scotia, for Job Brothers of St. John's, *Evelyn* had a gross tonnage of 324 and was 142 feet long. She carried a crew of seven: Captain Nilsson, a native of Denmark whose wife also sailed with him; another sailor from Denmark; and five sailors from Newfoundland — Ernest Pilgrim, residence unknown; Peter Mullett, Wesleyville; Ronald Burton, Central Street, St. John's. Two others hailed from the South Coast, Frederick Hollett, Spencer's Cove, Placentia Bay and John Yarn of Coomb's Cove, near English Harbour West.

The forward section of *Evelyn* was never located, but it was assumed that the schooner, being in the North American shipping lanes, had been cut down by a large transatlantic steamer. Nor was the crew ever found; they became victims of the sea while carrying on the trade of Newfoundland.

English Harbour West has had a long seafaring tradition and, like most South Coast towns, was not immune from tragedy. Perhaps the most memorable was that of the disappearance of the small schooner *Mary Carmel* in 1939. Only her wreckage was found near Ramea — the bodies of Captain Philip Yarn of Mose Ambrose, Steven Dolimount and George Bishop of English Harbour West were not found.

Located on the west side of Fortune Bay, English Harbour West first appears in Newfoundland's *Census* of 1836. It then

Courtesy Maritime Museum of the Atlantic

Isabel F. Spindler tied on at a mainland port. Built in Lunenburg in 1929, she netted 80 ton and was 122 feet long. Jerry Petite sold *Isabel Spindler* to Victor Fiander of English Harbour West.

On August 24, 1965, Captain Vic Fiander with his crew — Arthur Cox of Wreck Cove, Fortune Bay; mate Stan Savoury, Belleoram; Tom Baker, St. Jacques; John Rose, Mose Ambrose; cook Arthur Evans and engineer Henry Phillips, both of English Harbour West — were headed for Halifax from English Harbour West, but *Isabel Spindler* never completed her voyage.

About forty miles off Channel Head, Port aux Basques, fire broke out. Fiander and crew were unable to control the blaze and were forced to abandon *Spindlor.* Thoy woro picked up by a Fisheries patrol vessel.

had a population of seventeen; numbers grew steadily until 1971 when it reached a peak of 393. According to local tradition, some of the early settlers came directly from England and others moved there from Blue Pinion — a wide, sheltered cove between English Harbour West and St. Jacques.

By 1921 English Harbour West's population had increased to two hundred and thirty, and it was around these years the town was involved in the bank fishery. Prominent among the firms which supplied the fishermen and bought their catch over the years have been Job Brothers and Jeremiah Petite. The latter moved from Mose Ambrose to English Harbour West and bought the business previously owned by Marshalls. Job Brothers of St. John's once ran a branch store including a blacksmith shop and a bakery in the town.

After the turn of the century around 1914, another business was established by Clifford Shirley (first called Clifford Shirley, General Dealer, then Clifford Shirley and Sons) which not only sent schooners to the banks but also ran a herring factory.

The first settlers were of the Anglican and Roman Catholic faith, and both built a church and school, but the Roman Catholic structures no longer exist. Conrad Fitzgerald High School, which serves the eight towns, is in English Harbour West.

English Harbour West is one of a group of interrelated communities on the Connaigre Peninsula: Boxey, Belleoram, St. Jacques, Mose Ambrose, Pool's Cove, Coomb's Cove and Wreck Cove. The extent to which men of these communities were employed on banking schooners can be seen from the crew list of *Ethel M. Petite* — twenty-two of her complement of twenty-eight came from those towns.

On February 5, 1948, the banker *Ethel M. Petite* struck the Three Blind Sisters Ledge off Halifax and sank carrying one hundred thousand pounds of haddock down with her. Owned by Captain Jerry Petite, who lived in Halifax, the 140-foot long schooner was built in Lunenburg in 1935. All the crew escaped in dories. They were:

English Harbour W
Capt. Arch Evans
Wilson Evans, mate
Thomas Evans
Leonard Ashford
Philip Fizzard
Alexander Evans
Stanley Fiander

Harbour Breton
Leo "Paddy" Martin, cook
Thomas Chapman
Edward Reid
George Tom Skinner
Charles Sheppard
Ralph Mullins
Stanley Skinner
Philip Tibbo

Miller's Passage
Thomas Smith
George Lawrence
Aloysius Quann
Charles Abbott

Wreck Cove
James Cox

Jersey Harbour
Claude Stoodley
Harold Mayo

Coomb's Cove
Reg Vallis
Angus Vallis
Thomas Phil Vallis
Albert Drake

Belleoram
William Williams
Simeon Poole

The schooner grounded at 3:00 a.m. and in less than twenty minutes she was abandoned. In the tradition of the sea, Captain Evans was the last to leave the doomed vessel taking Mick, the mascot dog, with him. By the time Evans stepped off, water

Courtesy of Alex Hardy

Crew of the *Ethel M. Petite*

Courtesy of Jack Feltham

Effie May Petite. Shown here moored at Flat Island, Bonavista Bay, the 112-ton schooner was built at Shelburne, Nova Scotia, in 1913 for Jeremiah Petite of English Harbour West and was eventually sold to Captain Job Kean of Brookfield, Bonavista Bay. She was 89 feet long, 25 feet wide and 9 feet deep.

Kean sold *Effie May Petite* to Jesse Howell of Pound Cove, but she ended her days on the South Coast, beached and left to rot near Burin.

lapped around his knees. Captain Evans was also the first man to step on *Ethel M. Petite*'s deck at her launching some thirteen years previously. At that time he was engineer with Jerry Petite, the captain and owner.

In an interview later, eighteen-year-old Charles Abbott, the youngest of the crew who had been asleep when he heard someone shouting, said, "I forgot my suitcase but it wasn't so bad. I'm not through with the sea yet."

It was not the first time the cook Leo "Paddy" Martin of *Ethel M. Petite* had a misadventure at sea. He was torpedoed three times, twice in one hour, during the First World War and was a prisoner for a time on a German submarine.

When *Ethel M.* struck he managed to grab a couple of personal items before leaping into a dory. In his lifetime he had been shipwrecked six or seven times. On August 21, 1954, he disappeared, presumably drowned, from Capt. Earl Winsor's M.V. *Linda Mae* near Battle Harbour as his vessel cruised along the Labrador coast.

Stranded near Louisbourg Harbour

Another well-known and productive captain born in English Harbour West was Captain Arch Evans. He had spent a lifetime on schooners and draggers out of Halifax and Grand Bank. By the late 1940s as the era of the hook and line salt cod fishery was phasing out, employment on banking schooners was becoming hard to find. A few years after the loss of *Ethel M. Petite,* Evans had his own vessel built in Grand Bank — the forty-eight-ton *Joyce and Doreen,* powered by a 150 horsepower Caterpillar engine and equipped for halibut fishing.

On August 13, 1957, Evans and his crew — cook John Fizzard, Montford Piercey, Philip Fizzard, Abe George Hillier, all of Grand Bank; Allen Keeping, English Harbour West and Amos Poole, Belleoram — fished on Sable Island Bank. On the horizon they could see the low land of the island, but kept their distance from the treacherous sand bars off its shores.

They had done well with fishing that summer. *Joyce and Doreen* was almost loaded with around 15,000 pounds of halibut. Although Evans and his crew sought mostly halibut, swordfish was a valuable species bringing good prices in Nova Scotian ports. They had harpooned twelve swordfish, each averaging about a thousand pounds and these were iced away in the holds. *Joyce and Doreen* made for Louisbourg, Nova Scotia, to discharge a good catch.

When the twelve o'clock soundings were made that night, *Joyce and Doreen* was on course. She was not equipped with a radar; thus the helmsman could not see land or danger ahead. Three hours later, the vessel struck land about one and a half miles from Louisbourg harbour.

The noise and jolt awakened the five crewmen sleeping below, but they lost no time jumping into their clothes and boots. By the time they and Captain Evans, who had been asleep in the wheelhouse cabin, reached the deck the small dory was already in the water with one man aboard. *Joyce and Doreen* struck side on, a little offshore, on an underwater ledge and listed out on her starboard side.

Courtesy of Marine Archives, Memorial University

Coastal boat *Glencoe* rounding the Point near Gaultois. The road winds through the main section of the settlement leading to The Bottom. Obscured by the vessel is Whale Island where Newman and Company set up a whale factory in mid-1800s.

Located on the western shore of Hermitage Bay, Gaultois was included in Captain Cook's 1764 survey — Cook claimed both Piccaire and Gaultois would be ideal locations from which to fish the nearby grounds off Hermitage Cove.

Gaultois' name indicates its French origins and probably comes from an old Norman word meaning "like a pinnacle". Some of the established family names according to Lovell's *Newfoundland Directory* (1871) were: Bradshaw, Cox, Grant, Foot, Holman, McDonald, Matchem, Norcott, Organ, Peters, Reynolds, Simms, Snook and Taylor.

Within a few minutes the second and larger dory was hove off on the port side and the remaining crew clambered aboard. To distribute the numbers, two men transferred to the smaller dory. Although some men managed to grab their suitcases, most lost clothes bags, oil skins and personal belongings. Since the crew was in no immediate danger, they waited near the wreck until daylight when they could better see where they were and could make their way to Louisbourg harbour.

About an hour later the lights of the stranded vessel attracted a Louisbourg fisherman who was out tending his gear. In the mutual agreement of help on the sea, the man used his skiff to tow the dories into Louisbourg.

Later that day Captain Evans engaged two longliners to attach towlines to *Joyce and Doreen*, but she refused to budge — the vessel and cargo became a total loss and the crew had to find a ride to North Sydney. There, two Grand Bank schooners were in port: *Freda M*, Captain George Follett and Captain Ben Snook in *Nina W. Corkum*. The crew stayed aboard *Freda M* for a night or two, then took the gulf ferry to Port aux Basques and returned home by train to Goobies where transportation to Grand Bank waited for them.

For Philip Fizzard, it was his second shipwreck: he was crewman on *Ethel M. Petite*, wrecked in 1948; now *Joyce and Doreen*. In 1959 when the side trawler *Blue Wave* went down, he was one of the crew.

On July 19, 1963, the small fleet of fishing vessels owned in English Harbour was further decimated. *Mercedes*, a thirty-four-ton craft built in Grand Bank in 1959, was destroyed by fire. A Matthew II class vessel under the command of Wilson Evans, a brother of Arch Evans, she delivered her catch to Gaultois Fisheries.

Chapter 9

Mose Ambrose Skipper: Wrecked at the Farmyards

FOR A PERIOD IN THE MID-1930s Fortune Bay schooners sailed to Greenland to fish. In Newfoundland the pioneer of the Greenland cod fishery was Captain William Yarn of Mose Ambrose who had heard from the Danes and Portuguese while fishing on the Grand Banks that cod was plentiful in the Greenland waters during July, August and September. Yarn persuaded the owners of the schooners he captained — *Gladys Mosher, Nina M. Conrad* and later *Francis L. Spindler* — to let him venture to Greenland to try those waters.

Greenland grounds extend approximately from Holstienborg north to within one hundred miles of Disko. That area is around 1500 miles from Fortune Bay, Newfoundland. Such a distance meant a seven- or eight-day journey for a sailing vessel with favourable winds.

Francis L. Spindler, a 174-ton knockabout built in Lunenburg in 1920, was owned by Clifford Shirley & Sons business of English Harbour West. From 1935 to 1938 Captain Yarn, a brother-in-law of Clifford Shirley, had taken *Spindler* to Greenland. Each year Greenland waters were bountiful, the crew did well and the schooner proved to be a good fish carrier. In 1937 she brought home a large catch of twenty-seven hundred quintals, but the next year's voyage was to be her last.

Located on the Connaigre Peninsula in western Fortune Bay, Captain Yarn's hometown, Mose Ambrose, first appeared in the 1836 *Census* with nine residents, but there were seventy-three people by 1857. Principal family names were Petite, Evans,

Thornhill and Yarn. Mose Ambrose's name appears on early French maps as Mon Jambe.

Usually Fortune Bay schooners fishing off Greenland had their load by late August or early September. In 1938, fishing had not been good. To make matters worse *Francis L. Spindler* was leaking and four men, or two dory crews, had to stay aboard to pump. Around the second or third of September, Captain Yarn had a less than a full load, but decided to head for home.

A long voyage and a heavy load spelled disaster for Yarn and his schooner. Badly strained from the weight of fish, *Spindler* began to leak severely. The crew altered the intended southwesterly route for Fortune Bay steaming directly across to Labrador. If the schooner made the Labrador coast, Yarn could

Courtesy Shipsearch Marine

Ada A. Petite (right) at a Nova Scotian port. The Petite family established a business at Mose Ambrose; first operated by Jeremiah Petite who moved to English Harbour West around 1902. His brother, Henry (Harry), started a firm in Mose Ambrose around the same time. When Henry Petite, his son Arthur and employee Fred Cramer were drowned on October 13, 1925 bringing a load of freight from English Harbour West to Mose Ambrose, Henry's wife, Ada (Annie) carried on the business until 1965.

Gordon Petite, son of Henry and Ada, had the 97-ton *General Burstall* rebuilt in Marystown (renamed *Ada A. Petite)* to be used as a freighter between Mose Ambrose and mainland ports. She was later sold to Levis Davis' business on the northeast coast and was lost at Snug Harbour, Labrador.

The Yarn family also started a business in Mose Ambrose in the 1880s and is still active today. Of the older established family names only Yarn and Bungay remain today.

work his way southward and perhaps save his voyage of fish and *Francis L. Spindler.*

By September eighth, only continuous pumping kept the vessel afloat. On the early morning of September tenth Farmyards, off the Labrador coast, was thirty-five miles away. *Francis L. Spindler,* well down in the head with water in the forecastle, could not be steered properly. The top part of her rudder was out of water; the Kelvin engine, installed the previous year, had filled with water and stopped.

The crew took to the dories and rowed to Farmyards, today called Kikkertarjote Islands — a mass of small islands and large rocks located north of Nain, south of Okak. Weather was beautiful and sunny with a flat sea; twenty-four Fortune Bay seamen arrived in Farmyards at 10 am. Captain Yarn with three of his men remained behind for a few hours waiting for *Spindler* to sink. She went down taking the potential income of her fishing voyage to the bottom.

Captain Joshua Winsor in M.V. *Winnifred Lee,* a schooner once owned in Grand Bank but at this time a passenger/supply ship for the northern Labrador coast, picked up the crew and carried them to Hopedale. There the twenty-eight shipwrecked crew were billeted in homes to await the arrival of the Newfoundland railway steamer *Kyle* which came four days later.

Kyle was on a return trip to Newfoundland and picked up scores of fishermen with their families travelling to Newfoundland's north east coast. They were going home after another fishing voyage on the Labrador. With such a large number of people aboard, *Kyle*'s cook was hard pressed to provide sufficient meals. But Samuel Vallis of Coomb's Cove, the experienced cook from *Francis L. Spindler,* cheerfully gave his services. All went well in the crowded holds of *Kyle* and she reached St. John's several days later. The South Coast fishermen made their way to Argentia where they boarded the coastal boat *Glencoe,* bound for Fortune Bay.

Captain Yarn's crew (twenty of whom are recorded) came from various Fortune Bay communities: the captain and his son George hailed from Mose Ambrose; engineer Cecil Fiander, cook Samuel Vallis, Garland Vallis, Samuel Blagdon, Coomb's Cove; John Stone, brothers Simeon and Joseph Evans, Reginald Baker, Femme; mate James Fiander, St. John's Bay; Louis Baker, James Wells (Sr.) and his son James, Bay de L'Eau; Harvey Keeping, Lally Cove; Arthur Dolimount, Miller's Passage; James Wells, Grand Jarvis; William and Thomas May resided in Point Rosie but both later moved to Grand Bank.

George Lace who, along with William May, provided the story of *Francis L. Spindler*'s final voyage, was born in Point Rosie, moved to Boxey, then to English Harbour West. Lace, who now resides in Harbour Breton, became a crewman on many schooners and later captained such vessels as *Olga Nita, Philip Wayne, Delawanna II* and *Cape Ballard,* a government vessel.

During the century from 1850 to 1950, scores of schooners visited the smaller communities like Mose Ambrose hidden deep in Fortune Bay obtaining bait, picking up and dropping off the fishermen that manned their dories. These viable towns depended upon the sea and the schooner fishery for their existence. Seven of the towns which provided crewmen for *Francis L. Spindler* — Femme, St. John's Bay, Bay de L'Eau, Lally Cove, Grand Jarvis, Miller's Passage and Point Rosie — are today abandoned. Like several other settlements along the South Coast they became victims of the resettlement programs of the 1960s.

Chapter 10

Flat Island: That Terrible August Day

AUGUST (OR SEPTEMBER) GALES, once the scourge of sailing craft, were very localized and intense windstorms. Throughout the era of sail the wild gales unpredictably ravaged the coast and such was the destruction that stories surrounding them were told and retold, often passing into the realm of legend.

On August 22, 1892, three schooners went down, overpowered by the gale of that season. Two were from Grand Bank and owned by the Foote brothers: *Maggie Foote,* with five crew — Captain Morgan Riggs, brothers George and Clarence Foote of Grand Bank; George Buffett of Jersey Harbour and Sylvester Shea of English Harbour East — capsized off Cape Race while returning home. *George Foote,* a fishing schooner, disappeared on the fishing grounds off Placentia Bay. Only two of her crew of seventeen have been recorded, Captain Sam Patten and Leonard Hartling, both of Grand Bank.

The third schooner lost with crew was from Flat Island, Placentia Bay. The little community of Flat Island, located within a group of islands off the eastern shore of the Burin Peninsula near Red Harbour, was first recorded in the Newfoundland Census of 1836. Flat Island (Lower Island) and Davis Island, later renamed Port Elizabeth, were the most populated. The western end of Flat Island is marked by Little Tolt, about 203 feet high and, on the southeastern part, a flat summit about 236 feet high which gives the island its name.

According to family traditions, a Charles Smith from England was one of Flat Island's first settlers, but later families included: Butler, Chollett, Crann, Dicks, Foote, Frampton, Gosling, Hollett, Joyce, Loughlin, Senior and Whittle. The population depended on a small boat cod fishery until the 1890s when a shift to the larger bankers and sailing vessels occurred.

A Royal Navy captain's report on fishing in 1850 stated: "The best fishing ground for cod in Placentia Bay is at St. Mary's and the Flat Islands. The fish taken in Flat Island is sent to Mr. Falle at Burin." A large number of fish canning factories operated on the islands from 1891 to 1911.

It was during the era of the banking schooners when the little community was hit by a sea disaster which practically wiped out its male population. Jessie Hale, in a *Decks Awash* article, wrote her impressions on the loss of the schooner *Reason*. In August 1892, *Reason*, owned and captained by Isaac Crann, age thirty-three, of Flat Island, carried ten island men to their death: the captain's brother Abraham Crann, twenty-two; John Senior, twenty-four; William Senior, thirty; Henry Senior, twenty-six; Charles Senior, twenty-two; Ephriam Collins, twenty-two; Nathaniel Collins, thirty-three and Charles Clarke, age twenty-six. Hale, whose nineteen-year-old brother Albert Joyce was the youngest aboard, called her story:

That Terrible Day

> I shall never forget that day. The house shook, and its shaking woke me. Things were cracking outside. We were have a terrible storm. I felt it was all wrong. When I was thoroughly awake, I realized why.
>
> This was the day my brother was expected home. He was with Captain Crann in the ship *Reason* and they had been gone to the fishing banks five weeks.
>
> I thought of the morning they had left home. It had been a bright, clear day. The wind was north, offshore, the sailors said.
>
> In the early morning the boys had gone by with their bags. Quite a number of young girls had gone by, too, in freshly laundered dresses and sunbonnets. I had seen my brother stop for a few minutes and talk with Cilia. They had met at the garden gate on his way down to the ship.
>
> Captain Crann loved to sing. He had a singing crew. The boys always sang as they weighed anchor. This morning they

had sung "The Ocean Voyage" and "The Sailor's Farewell." Their voices had been rich and vibrant.

Now I looked out the window. Roofs were blown from some of the buildings. Fences were down. Pails, barrels, and numerous other things were blowing about.

From the front window I could see the harbour. Several boats had drifted from their moorings and the storm was increasing.

Downstairs the table was set as usual, but the place was deserted.

I saw my stepfather going up the road and I followed him. He was a serious man. That day he had cause to be serious. He had two brothers, three nephews, and a stepson on board that vessel. I followed him up the short road by the garden, and when we came to the road under Schoolhouse Hill I walked in the trench by the roadside and held onto the fence rail.

When I reached the road that lead to the hill, or lookout, I think he saw me for the first time and held out his hand to help me.

I assured him I was all right. The wind was strong, and it was hard to walk on the high land. Once I felt my feet leave the ground, but I was holding on to the bushes near the path.

A path had been worn up the hill side. The brushwood and roots had been worn away down to the soft soil. The bushes on both sides were quite high, so the path was sheltered from the storm.

I went up so that I could see over the top and yet hold onto the brushwood. It was breathtaking. Out to sea everything was white as far as the eye could reach. Once in a while you could see two black ledges known as the Western Rocks.

The ocean was mad. It surged, boiled, foamed. Even in the little creeks that were usually so placid, it had gone rampant.

Looking over the island, we could see that a number of buildings had blown down. Boats in the harbour were darting about as if they were creatures that had suddenly gone mad. Some had their crews on board; others were unmanned. Boatloads of men in oilskins were going out from the piers.

There were men on the hill standing near the great boulder called the Pulpit, where they leaned while they looked though their spyglasses. My stepfather spoke for the first time.

Addressing one of the men, he said, "What do you think, Captain Drake?"

"No boat could bide afloat today," the captain answered.

During the day people came, mostly those with relatives on the *Reason*. They spoke in low tones of the Sunken Keys, treacherous rocks that had to be passed on the way home.

In the late afternoon I went up to the lookout again. The storm had abated somewhat, but the ocean was white and angry looking, and where the waves struck against the cliffs, the crest of the waves seemed to break and for a second to be left suspended in the air.

The family gathered together when night came. It was the custom to have family prayer. We sat in our usual places.

My stepfather opened the Bible, waited a minute, then closed it and knelt down. We did the same. Not a word was spoken.

We rose when he did.

It was a blow in both human and economic terms from which the tiny community never completely recovered. The terrible day became a landmark event in terms of weather; veteran fishermen would say "Sure, it's blowing harder today than when the Crann's went down." Although over a hundred years have passed, the saying is still often repeated.

At its greatest peak Flat Island population reached 150; by 1945 it dropped to ninety-one. By the early nineteen seventies under Premier Smallwood's resettlement program, the few remaining residents moved mainly to Burin, Grand Bank, Creston South and St. John's.

Today when one stands atop the high flat summit where Jessie Hale once stood to look across Placentia Bay to the treacherous Western Rocks, Washing Tub, Saddleback and the Black Rock, it is not hard to imagine that schooners like *Reason* once anchored in the sheltered cove of Flat Island. The town is deserted, the people gone, but remnants of island stories live on.

Chapter 11

Fortune's Early Misadventures at Sea

"GATEWAY TO THE FRENCH ISLANDS" is how Fortune, situated at the toe of the Burin Peninsula, is billed in tourist brochures. A thriving, bustling Newfoundland outport with a difference, Fortune handles over 20,000 tourists a year, as they pour through its bottleneck harbour drawn by the French islands, St. Pierre and Miquelon, an hour or two away (twenty-two miles) by sea.

Fortune's busy harbour, with its present-day population of over 2100, has seen the ebb and flow of Europeans for centuries. According to tradition, the name Fortune originated from its first visitors, the Portuguese; their word 'fortuna' literally means good fortune. Later, Spanish fishermen frequented the area often and is listed on their maps dating 1527 and 1529. Newfoundland historian D.W. Prowse claims that the Basque, searching for fish and whales, used Fortune as a base as early as 1650. In the later era of French settlement, a 1693 census lists seventy-two residents including families of Millou, LeManquet and Chartier.

Fortune's English ancestry begins around 1763 with the signing of the Treaty of Paris when several English families left St. Pierre to settle in Fortune Bay. According to local tradition a Lake family chose Fortune. English explorer and cartographer Captain James Cook stopped here in 1765 and in his survey he described Fortune as a place with a '...sand bar allowing boats a passage at quarter-flood tide... a small fishing village with good anchorage.'

Courtesy Fred Smith

Tern schooner *John E. Lake*, named for the founder of Lake's business in Fortune. John E. was an enterprising young man who established several businesses in the town: a boot and shoe factory, furniture factory and a can factory. To export his cured fish he owned several schooners.

Netting 202 tons, *John E. Lake* was built by master shipwright Joseph Miles in Fortune in 1919 for the foreign trade. While under the command of Edward "Ned" Hillier, she was lost in the West Indies a few years later.

In these early years the town's good fortune hinged on the fishery — a sheltered and ice free harbour, an ideal climate for curing salted cod, access to bait, and an abundance of inshore and offshore fish. In 1884 Fortune had ten vessels, owned main-

Courtesy Fred Smith

George Ewart, another tern schooner constructed in Fortune; this one in 1913. She measured 99 feet long, 26 feet wide and 11 feet deep. *George Ewart* lasted only four years. While lying to off the coast of Gibraltar on September 19, 1917, she was rammed by an unidentified ship and sank. Captain Ned Hillier and his crew rowed to safety.

ly by the Lakes and by the Spencer business, engaged in the fishery. Productive salmon and lobster fishing and marketing were conducted in Fortune in the 1880s. To distribute those products to local and foreign markets, John E. Lake built a can manufacturing plant near the waterfront.

The town continued to grow and prosper through the rise

Courtesy Fred Smith

Two masted schooner *Hubert Mack*, built in 1908 at Fortune. In 1911 Harry Thornhill of Fortune took command. Some years later her lines parted in a severe storm and she drifted into First Gulch, east of her home port. Although *Hubert Mack* stranded to total loss, her crew — Johnny Paul, William Keeping and Fred Mario, a Portuguese seaman, escaped.

and eventual decline of the salt fish industry and into the advent of the deep sea trawler fishery. A fresh fish processing plant opened in 1952 which later, under Booth Fisheries modernization, became the second largest frozen fish producer in Atlantic Canada.

Fortune warrants more than a simple pass through. Those who wait near the waterfront ferry terminal for the 'French Connection' — St. Pierre ferry *Anahitra* — should look around and savour the history. On the west side of the harbour under the sheltering lee of Fortune Head once stood John E. Lake's three-storey furniture factory. Opened in 1907, it produced windows, sashes and furniture for shipment all over Newfoundland. Notably, it manufactured 1,000 chairs for the St. John's Nickel Theatre, the first movie house in Newfoundland. Another establishment, Lake's boot and shoe factory, was destroyed by fire in 1908.

If tourists look north across the small, busy harbour to where the fish plant now stands, they could imagine the spit of land where a productive shipbuilding industry once thrived — the 1874 report indicates eight vessels were constructed in Fortune that year. In other years larger ships slid down the ways including the tern schooners *Eileen Lake, George Ewart* and *John E. Lake*, the latter built in 1919.

Today a common sight in Fortune harbour is the St. Pierre ferry slipping in and out of harbour. Generations ago, schooners of all sizes sailed from the port headed for Canadian and European fish markets and the offshore fishing grounds.

One of Fortune's earliest recorded shipping mishaps was documented in the *Evening Telegram*, September 8, 1886 edition: *George A. Tulk*, a seventy-five-ton schooner launched in Fortune earlier that year, was rammed by the steamer *City of Chicago* south southwest of Cape Ballard, about twenty-two miles from land. The steamer carried away the bowsprit, foremast, bulwarks and smashed the dories on deck. Fortunately the weather was settled and Captain John Tulk of Fortune made temporary repairs and reached St. John's without further mishap.

Not all vessels survived the perils of the sea; many failed to return and Fortune was left with the legacy that haunts many fishing communities, tragedy at sea: John Lake's schooner *Sailor's Home* lost Captain Thomas Bennett and cook Ben Miles, both of Fortune, when they were swept overboard in a storm. She struck a reef on Miquelon Head on December 31, 1890. Three remaining crew — mate George Tom Hynes, Phil Elford and Sam Major — although weak and wet climbed the cliffs, walked to Miquelon and survived.

In the fall of 1918 another Fortune schooner met her end near St. Pierre. Built in Essex in 1889, *Joseph P. Johnson*, while under the command of John Sydney Bennett, had been en route from PEI with produce, mainly potatoes. According to local sources the schooner ran into difficulty in Miquelon Bight. None of her crew survived: the captain and his eighteen-year-old son, George; Samuel Coaks; George Morgan and Isaac Kenway.

Kenway, age forty-one, was cook. He hailed from Flat Island but came to Fortune to work for the principal merchant, John Lake. Prior to *Joseph P. Johnson*'s departure the regular cook became ill; Isaac Kenway agreed to go for one trip as replacement. He was married to the former Jane Green of Little Bay East and had three children: John, Randell and Hazel. By November 30, 1918, Kenway and his mates were officially entered in the Fortune United Church records as "Lost at Sea." Appendix C lists Fortune's shipping disasters.

Trying Time on *Rigel*

One sea story with a happier ending is that of *Rigel*. A *Daily News* report of January 9, 1913, carried the headline "Schooner Rigel Still Missing." It went on to say the last report of the schooner — owned in Fortune by Philip Lake — was having left St. Pierre on Christmas Eve for Harbour Grace, laden with coal.

Courtesy of Jack Keeping

Oil painting of Fortune schooner *Gladys S.* On November 14, 1918, this 99-net ton schooner was officially posted "Missing at Sea." Captain Fred Bennett, Gerald Ayres of Fortune and three other crew disappeared.

Her nameboard was later picked by another vessel en route to Sydney.

Lake had contacted Newfoundland's Deputy of Marine Affairs, Goodridge, expressing his concern for the missing schooner. The minister sent inquires of her whereabouts to all telegraph stations between Harbour Grace and Fortune. All reports came back negative. When *Rigel* left St. Pierre she was well-fitted and had plenty of food aboard.

Built in 1889 at Essex, Massachusetts, the eighty-three-ton *Rigel,* under the command of Captain Samuel Mayo, had all Fortune crewmen aboard: mate Berkley Breon; cook Weston Mosher; William Blagdon, Ben Brady and George Lee.

Five days later the barquentine *Gaspe* arrived in Bay Bulls from Maceio, Brazil, with the five Fortune men aboard. The operator of the Anglo-American Telegraph company at Bay Bulls, knowing of the concern for the missing ship, immediately wired this message to St. John's authorities:

> *Gaspe,* Connors master, arrived Bay Bulls at 4 pm Sunday. Brought in crew of *Rigel* taken from vessel. She was leaking and had her sails all gone. Picked them up Saturday just in time to save them. *Gaspe* still at Bay Bulls with wrecked crew still on her. Crew all well.

Not long after, the full story of *Rigel*'s voyage from North Sydney to the place of her foundering became known. According to a subsequent newspaper report, she left North Sydney on the 20th for Harbour Grace with 156 tons of coal. *Rigel* had a fair wind out, but soon after passing Low Point off Sydney, the wind shifted. Captain Mayo had the schooner "close hauled" and still made fairly good progress.

By noon the next day the wind increased to a South easterly gale and *Rigel* struggled for the next two days. By that time Mayo was near St. Pierre and anchored in the roads on December 23.

Weather conditions moderated and the morning of the 24th, Christmas Eve, 1912, *Rigel* ran across to Burin. From there Mayo and his crew decided to make the run to Harbour Grace despite the winter winds. By 10:00 p.m. on December 27, seven days after leaving North Sydney, the vessel was a half mile off Cape

Spear and an attempt was made to enter St. John's. Had she sailed into that harbour safely, the story would have ended there. But a sudden squall forced Captain Mayo to keep her to the land and the wind carried away the jib and jumbo.

At daylight, Saturday December 28, Mayo ordered his crew to take in the foresail as the wind increased to a west southwest hurricane. Suddenly the wind chopped around. *Rigel,* still trying to keep near the land, was swept by a heavy wave. The schooner only carried one life boat and this was washed over the side. Bulwarks on the lee side were smashed, the water cask was torn from its harness, the forecastle and cabin were damaged and fifteen ton of coal carried on deck disappeared in an instant over the side.

The pounding *Rigel* took, while broadside to the wind, opened the deck seams. First soundings at the pumps indicated the vessel was leaking severely. Seas continued to pound over the vessel making it impossible for the crew to navigate.

"It's pump or sink, which?" shouted Captain Mayo. Every man knew the answer and in his turn was lashed to the pumps to try and keep the water from rising. Lashed to the pumps — a heavy rope around the waist, encircling the shoulders with the end double wound around the base of the pump kept the labourers from being washed overboard in the swirl of white water.

The following morning there was a slight drop in the storm. The crew tried to raise the foresail and converted a trysail into a jib. Mayo tried to force the labouring schooner toward land and by midnight saw the Ferryland Light.

With the hope of getting into St. John's, Mayo ran *Rigel* down the shore toward Bay Bulls and eventually as he hoped, St. John's. But it was not to be.

New Year's Day, 1913, another gale blew up — one of a several successive storms — this time from north west with blinding snow squalls and intense frost which forced the crew to take down the sails. Mayo allowed the vessel to drift with the wind. To push her hard against heavy seas would open weakened vessel's seams a little more.

For two days the schooner drifted away from land, all the time with seas washing over her decks. The labouring crew, now for days at the pumps, was exhausted. Water began to gain rapidly in the hold; still each man in his turn, including the cook Wes Mosher, was lashed to the pumps.

To save *Rigel* from sinking, the crew jettisoned cargo. This could only be done by the shovelful from the holds with a hatch cover off. Another problem faced the beleaguered crew: the lower the level of coal, the more likely chance of the coal shifting and moving to one side on the rolling ship. This could cause *Rigel* to roll on her beam ends.

That was the chance the five Fortune men took. Ice on her rigging, bowsprit and headgear weighed her down. Cargo had to be shovelled over the side to keep her above water. According to Mayo's estimate, fifty ton of ice coated the schooner.

George Lee was washed overboard by a heavy wave, but the same wave washed him back on the deck where his shipmates grabbed him.

By now *Rigel* had been storm-tossed for two weeks. Food which had been stored for a short voyage was practically gone. The water supply was depleted except for a few gallons. Mayo gave orders to cook Mosher to bake whatever flour was left into bread and cakes. Tea was rationed to a gallon every twenty-four hours which was not much for five thirsty and labouring men. Plenty of other food — beans, peas, oatmeal and molasses — was in store, but without water could not be cooked.

Mayo, wisely, hid one gallon of water which was to be used as a last resort. By now the crew realized that the end could come by dying of thirst as well as by drowning. When the ship was finally abandoned this gallon of water was the only water aboard.

On Saturday, January 4, *Rigel*'s crew, storm tossed and sinking, sighted another vessel. The schooner *Waterwitch* passed close enough that Mayo tried to hail her. His attempts were in vain. Even if he had gotten a message to *Waterwitch*, it would have been impossible for the latter to launch a small rescue boat. *Rigel* had no life boat — it had been washed away days before.

About daylight on January 11, as the men were beating ice from the headgear, one spotted a sail in the distance. This was reported to Mayo. It could be clearly seen the vessel in sight was coming at a good clip with square yards; most likely a bark or brig. It was bearing north and would have missed *Rigel*, but the wind veered and she bore down toward the sinking ship.

Mayo was well-versed in the lore of the sea. To show his distress he had the Union Jack turned upside down and hoisted as a signal. Within a half hour the vessel, which proved to be *Gaspe* and Captain Connors, was close by.

Connors called to ask if they wanted to be taken off the sinking schooner. When he received an affirmative answer, he asked for volunteers from *Gaspe* to man the lifeboat. Every man of the crew offered, but two were chosen — mate Edward Snooks and seaman William Puddister.

They rowed along to the weather side; then, to the lee side, and successfully managed to take the whole crew from the sinking ship. The five Fortune men brought with them only the clothes on their backs and a few other articles.

Rigel was abandoned, waterlogged and wallowing, 43 miles South South East of Cape Race. Fearing she would get in the track of shipping, the hatches were removed. The cabin stove with the fire still burning was tipped upside down to set her afire.

When *Gaspe* left her a few miles astern, *Rigel* was settling in the water. The men estimated she sank an hour later.

Gaspe brought the weary crew to Bay Bulls. Mayo spoke of the rescue and the treatment Connors and his crew offered. He was also clear in his praise for the hospitable way they were treated on the ship. "Nothing was too great," Mayo claimed.

Upon their arrival in St. John's Mayo, mate Berkley Breon, cook Weston Mosher, William Blagdon, Ben Brady and George Lee were described in the daily newspaper as:

> ...of a class of fishermen-seamen that Fortune Bay has much pride in and while they consider their experience somewhat out of the usual, they look upon their rescue as a cheque and receipt in full for what they underwent, and are prepared to deposit it with "Old Neptune."

Captain Connors was no stranger to wreck and rescue. He was giving back what he and his crew had received the previous March. They had been taken from their brig *Maggie,* just as death on the high seas seemed imminent. He had been bound from Oporto to St. John's, ran into a series of storms which opened her seams and caused *Maggie* to leak. Fortunately they were rescued by a passing ship.

At least one of *Rigel*'s crew came to a tragic end: Breon, who lived in Grand Bank after he married, was a dory fishermen on several schooners throughout the years. On J.B. Patten's *Coral Spray* he was second hand, or mate, and helped inexperienced dory men. On May 6, 1937, he and John Francis of Grand Bank, a younger fisherman, were hauling trawl lines in heavy weather and fog. Both men were having difficulty handling the gear in rough weather and Breon agreed to change places to help him when a swell struck the dory and knocked Breon overboard.

Breon disappeared, never to be seen again. Later when the fog lifted, men in another dory from *Coral Spray* saw Francis waving an oar and signalling for help. Charles Francis of Grand Bank and Allen Rose, Fortune, helped Francis leave the dory. A few minutes later heavy seas overturned the small craft and she drifted away.

Spencer Lake and Other Fortune Ships

Throughout its era of sail the roster of Fortune sailing craft, which numbered well over a hundred, is dotted with words like wrecked, abandoned and lost at sea. In December 1919, the schooner *Aguadilla,* owned and captained by Charles "Chat" Bennett of Fortune, left Sydney laden with 200 ton of coal destined for Lamaline. During a typical winter storm, *Aguadilla* took shelter at St. Pierre before proceeding on to Lamaline on December 20.

Due to the low water in Lamaline harbour and the deep draft of the vessel, the Lamaline pilot insisted he navigate the vessel through the shoals. However the schooner grounded and became a total loss.

Captain Thomas Poole of Fortune, Charles Bennett's father-in-law, met with tragedy while sailing *Dorothy Lake* down through Langlade Channel, or "Langly Reach" as local seamen termed it, on August 30, 1924. She had been returning from Sydney, coal laden.

Usually most tern schooners carried six or seven crew, but *Dorothy Lake* was crewed by only three. According to Parker's book *Sails of the Maritimes*, this vessel was the smallest tern built in the Maritimes. Constructed in Fortune in 1911, she netted a mere 23.8 tons at 63 feet overall length.

When *Dorothy Lake* sank, Poole was washed overboard and drowned in the mishap. Charles Lake of Fortune, and Jim Crant of Swanger's Cove, a town near Head of Baie d'Espoir, lowered the small lifeboat and rowed into Lamaline.

When the crew of the Lake's schooner *Spencer Lake* arrived in St. John's on February 13, 1926, on S.S. *Sachem*, they had a story of shipwreck and mistreatment to tell. *Spencer Lake* left Oporto bound for Fortune laden with fishery salt on December 15, 1925.

Captain Lawson Fox, a resident of Grand Bank, had five crewmen with him: Philip Elias "Li" Strong, George Forsey, Thomas Lake and Amos Cluett, all of Fortune. Cluett was originally from Belleoram, but had married a Fortune girl, Frances Snook, and lived in Fortune. A sixth crewman was Samuel Rideout, most likely from another community.

Twenty-five days out of Oporto fierce winds and mountainous waves battered *Spencer Lake*. The crew pumped for five days until a steamer, S.S. *Ofantz*, saw the distressed schooner and bore down toward them. On January 15, the Fortune schooner slipped into the deep at latitude 25.57, longitude 41. *Ofantz*, Captain Sicle, was bound eastward for Spain.

On board *Ofantz*, Captain Fox and his five crew were well received. Apparently they had saved only the clothes they wore

Courtesy Trevor Bebb, Lockeport, NS

Spencer Lake on her launching in Allendale, Nova Scotia, in 1920. She measured 106 feet long, 26 feet wide with a net tonnage of 148.

Central Fortune in the 1880s

and no doubt the steamer's crew gave them food, a clean bed and extra clothes. Captain Sicle offered every hospitality which was more than the Fortune men could say for the reception they received in Barcelona, Spain, where they were landed. According to Fox, "...treatment at Barcelona was anything but pleasant. We were there for a considerable time without food for want of money to make any purchases."

Several days later they gladly boarded a ship for London, England, thence to Liverpool and finally connected with the Newfoundland steamship *Sachem*, bound for St. John's.

Although visitors won't see schooners in Fortune harbour today, an interesting diversion is to identify the various types of seacraft in port: ferries, deep sea draggers, longliners, dories, skiffs, pleasure craft of all shapes and sizes.

In a walking tour around town visitors can view various architectural styles that have developed from the town's heritage: the older stately homes with unique ornamentation and heavy brackets; the more common salt box house (a one or two storey house with a steep pitched roof and an upper storey bedroom or attic); the main street business establishments that have evolved from the schooner fishing era; the Royal Canadian Legion Hall listing in picture and word Fortune's war heroes;

Marine Archives, Memorial University

Fortune Harbour

and the Masonic Hall, built in 1884, one of the oldest meeting halls on the island although the building has undergone considerable renovations.

Not a town to rest on past laurels, Fortune has its modern facilities too. The Fortune Arena acts as a social centre and sport's complex with figure skating, minor hockey and curling. Soccer is still in vogue, and the softball field attracts young and old. With over sixty trailer sites, Horsebrook Trailer Park is well equipped and has fishing holes and hiking trails nearby. It's not unusual for tourists to find the perfect souvenir in local craft shops or home cooked fish chowder in out of the way restaurants.

For rock hunters and fossil collectors, the slate cliffs of Fortune Head, a few minutes drive by car, have Precambrian-Cambrian trace fossils — one of the world's richest sites. Proposals are now underway to have the area, dubbed by international geologists as the 'Golden Spike,' designated an ecological reserve.

Chapter 12

Garnish Ships and Seamen

WHEN *L.A. Dunton* cruised out into Fortune Bay around noon on October 8, 1963, it was a group of Garnish seamen that helped bring the final chapter of an old fishing schooner to a close. Under command of Captain Harvey Banfield, she left Grand Bank on that date headed for her final resting place, Mystic, Connecticut.

When *L.A. Dunton* passed the sentinel lighthouse guarding Grand Bank harbour, only one schooner remained in Grand Bank which in former years numbered its fleet in the hundreds.

Actually *L.A. Dunton* was leaving one home and heading for her birthplace — Essex, Massachusetts, where she had been launched forty-two years before. In 1934 she was sold from Essex to G & A Buffett firm of Grand Bank. Buffetts commissioned Captain Clarence Williams to bring their banker down. Williams had a Grand Bank crew: Lawson Fox, cook (who had survived the wreck of *Spencer Lake* nine years previously); Alfred Martin, engineer; George Sam Walsh and Len Dunford, deckhands. George Dauphin, of French descent and a relative of the Buffett family, resided in New York and came down on *L.A. Dunton* to visit St. Pierre and Grand Bank.

Captain Williams, born in Pool's Cove but a resident of Grand Bank, commanded *L.A. Dunton* for several years bringing home many bumper catches of cod. In the 1940-50s while softwood Canadian and Newfoundland-built schooners were disappearing, the sturdy *Dunton*, timbered and planked with the best white oak, survived the rigours of bank fishing and the heavy loads of the coasting trade.

Her ten dories stacked on deck, *L.A. Dunton* heads to the banks. In this photo her spiked mainmast is higher than the foremast. When *Dunton* was outfitted for the coasting trade, her rotten mainmast was repaired.

Rather than step an expensive new mast, ten or twelve feet were cut off giving the schooner a distinctive look with a short mainmast and a higher foremast. For that reason, her American buyers were wont to call her a ketch, not a schooner.

Like most South Coast schooners plying the hazardous dory and trawl line industry, *L.A. Dunton* was not immune to tragedy — lost or overturned dories. On April 10, 1947, while under the command of Captain Robert Smith, she sailed into Grand Bank with her flag flying at half mast. The vessel had lost one of her fishermen, Charles Francis.

Francis and his dorymate, Caleb Penwell, both of Grand Bank, were hauling gear when the dory capsized, throwing both men into the water. They managed to climb onto the overturned dory, but the small craft was anchored with her fishing gear out and waves swept over the dory constantly. In April the storm-swept Atlantic is barely above freezing temperatures and both men weakened quickly. Francis was dislodged from the bottom of the dory and swept away to his death.

Penwell remained for quite some time in his dangerous position until he was rescued by *L.A. Dunton's* men who went to his assistance as soon as Captain Smith saw the situation.

L.A. Dunton, pictured above, was fishing for halibut off Nova Scotia and rescued the crew of the burning *Jean and Mona*, a schooner built in Garnish. On September 13, 1951, *Jean and Mona* caught fire and sank on the Grand Banks.

Two years later in July 1953, *Dunton* rescued the crew of the burning *Bessemer* when the latter's engine room caught fire forty miles off Chebucto Head, Nova Scotia. *Dunton*'s crew that year: Captain Arch Evans, mate Caleb Bungay, chief engineer Art Ralph, second engineer Montford Piercey and Wilson Dodge of Grand Bank; cook Sandy Evans, Philip Fizzard, Jimmy Fizzard, Stan Fiander, Aaron Vallis and Maurice Kearley of English Harbour West; Tom Chapman, Harbour Breton; Stephen Drake, Coomb's Cove; John B. Strowbridge and Walter Stoodley of Jersey Harbour; James Cox, Garfield Cox and Philip Cox of Wreck Cove, Fortune Bay; Frank and Theodore Hardiman of Point Rosie; Albert Hillier, Alex Hillier and Simeon Miller of Brunette Island.

Francis' body was recovered and brought to port. He was age 37, married with four children.

In time G & A Buffett sold *L.A. Dunton* to Samuel Piercy's business and then her registry passed to J.B. Foote and Sons of Grand Bank. Over the years *Dunton*'s appearance changed: a gasoline engine installed in the 1920s had been replaced with a larger Fairbanks Morse diesel engine of 160 horsepower; topmasts and main boom shortened; the bowsprit removed and a pilot house built over the wheel box. When *L.A. Dunton* exclusively carried cargoes in the coasting trade, her bunks and sleeping quarters for the dory men were taken out to make additional cargo space.

In 1963, the Marine Historical Association of Mystic purchased the old workhorse from J.B. Foote's with the intention of restoring and preserving the schooner as a floating showpiece. Captain James Kleinshmidt, the assistant curator at Mystic, came to Grand Bank to oversee *Dunton*'s trip back to the land of her birth.

Many of *L.A. Dunton*'s most recent crew were hired to make that last voyage, a 900-mile journey to Connecticut. Captain Harvey Banfield, an employee of Foote's, who was born in Garnish but a resident of Grand Bank, was retained for the voyage as well as his crew of experienced Garnish seamen:

Willy Elias Anstey, mate
Randell Grandy, cook
Guy Moulton, engineer
Herbert Day, sailor
Don Lockyer, sailor

L.A. Dunton was favoured with good weather on her final voyage and in four days, which included a four-hour stop at Halifax for bunkers, the old schooner passed Cape Cod. At 6:00 p.m. she was securely moored at the New London Thames Shipyard where, within a few days, major and minor repairs and restoration were begun.

According to Kleinshmidt, who wrote of *Dunton*'s voyage in the January 1964 edition of the *National Fisherman* magazine, the Garnish crew were fine seamen and made the trip seem easy. He fondly recalled the cook, saying:

> Galley fare on the *Dunton*'s last voyage was plain and generous, fishermen style. Cook Randell Grandy, veteran of a half century in schooners, commanded the ship stores and produced fresh bread, pies and such focs'le delicacies as peas puddin', salt cod, salt beef and pork with boiled potatoes, cabbage, turnips and "Newfie" tea that would tan a polar bear hide.

Their work over, the crew flew by charter plane to St. John's; from there Don Tibbo's taxi brought them to Grand Bank and Garnish.

Located on the west side of the Burin Peninsula, Garnish is built on the western side of Little Garnish Barrasway. The barrasway enters into a shallow channel which, in the era of

L.A. Dunton today at Mystic, Connecticut. She has her bowsprit, her seventy-five-foot main boom, canvas and topmasts restored and the cabin house removed from the after quarter. Ten dories are nested on her deck.

Below deck, the engine was taken out, and some of her fishermen's sleeping berths were rebuilt. Tourists could now see the cramped and confined quarters fishermen slept in — two to a narrow and short bunk.

small schooners, allowed entrance to craft drawing less than six feet of water. Today (1994) its population approaches 750; the first official appearance of Garnish was in the Census of 1836 with a population of seventy-six.

The meaning of the word Garnish is obscure and the years when the first settlers moved there is uncertain. According to family and town tradition, the Grandys moved to Garnish from St. Pierre when the English were forced to leave the French Islands in 1763.

Cartographer and explorer Captain James Cook surveyed the area in 1775 and mapped it as Little Garnish (with Frenchman's Cove as Great Garnish). In the 1836 *Census* all residents were Church of England. At that time, there were eleven dwellings and twelve boats engaged in the fishery. Subsequent census showed steady growth until 1935, after which date the population steadily dropped until recent years.

A livelihood from the sea has always been the economic mainstay of Garnish and various species have been fished over the years: salmon, herring, lobster and codfish. For a brief period some residents hunted seals. Early prosperity from the salmon fishery came because of the productivity of the Garnish River. To protect the stocks, a river warden was appointed in the 1860s. Warden Snelgrove's report of 1872 said four men were engaged in the salmon fishery: Thomas Grandy, Joseph Grandy, John Parsons and Wilson Lovell who sold their fish to Newman's Company of Harbour Breton.

For several decades shipbuilding, chiefly schooners, employed many carpenters and craftsmen. Garnish woods was renowned for its reserves of heavy timber. Not only were many schooners built in Garnish, but the skill of her men who were master boat builders was used in places like Grand Bank.

During Newfoundland's commission government (1934-1949) ship builders were paid a subsidy per ton for vessels built. Although the ship building incentive was short-lived, it was an attempt to stimulate local economy. In one year no less than four schooners were built in Garnish, which then had a population of less than five hundred.

Building *D.J. Thornhill*

In Grand Bank one enterprising and ambitious captain and schooner owner, John Thornhill, took advantage of the government's bounty and made plans to construct a ten-dory banker, the last schooner built in Grand Bank. An *Evening Telegram* article dated March 16, 1935, announced the news with this lead:

> **Banking Captains See Bright Future**
> Building Vessels for 1936 Fishery
>
> Captain John Thornhill, famous fish killer of Grand Bank, has a crew of men in the woods getting timber for a banker of 120 tons to be built this summer at Grand Bank for the 1936 fishery.
>
> Captain Thomas Grandy of Garnish is having a 50-ton schooner (*Jean and Mona*) built at Garnish this summer for next year's fishery. A crew went in the woods last week to cut the timbers for the vessel.

> Capt. Thornhill for years has been a high liner amongst Newfoundland fish killers. He is now on the Banks in command of the schooner *Helen Forsey*.

Thornhill knew many skilled shipbuilders in Garnish and employed one of the best master builders, Bill Henry Grandy, from there to help construct his schooner. Grandy also headed up the team of Grand Bank men sent to the Garnish River to cut timber.

Under his direction, Bill Henry took several Grand Bank men up river: Bob Riggs; brothers Elic and Robert Stoodley; Philip Riggs, Philip Stoodley, Thomas Forsey; Henry (Harry) Hickman, cook Tom Keating and Chas Stone who liked to use a double-bladed axe. Bill Henry's son, Fred, worked there, as well as a young man, Jacob Grandy of Garnish, who helped the cook and brought water to the men in the woods. Bob Stoodley kept an informal set of books tallying wages, amount and cost of food.

Logging lasted for one month beginning the first week of March, ending early April. After supplies were hauled by horse and sleigh to a site five miles up the Garnish River, the men built a camp bunkhouse. The crude bunkhouse had a small barrel stove for heat at night. A cook shack was already on site, but was so small Keating prepared most food outdoors, baking his bread every day in large covered pots. Crusty on the outside, the bread was not baked in the middle. One of the woodsmen would pull apart the stringy dough in the middle of the loaf and say, "Cook, what a sacrifice of good food!"

Large fir, spruce, witchhazel and birch — some measuring twenty-one or twenty-two inches in the top and twice as big around or more on the butt or bottom — were termed "dory sticks" by the Garnish woodsmen. Sticks like these close to Grand Bank had long since disappeared; most had been cut in the shipbuilding era prior to the 1880s. Large timber had been further depleted when five tern schooners were built in Grand Bank harbour: *Roberta Ray*, 1917, 164 net tons; *General Currie*, 1918, 162 tons; *Carl R. Tibbo* 1918, 173 tons; *General Allenby*, 1919, 145 tons and *General Ironsides*, 1920; 157 tons.

Bill Henry Grandy knew what timber he wanted and would go out in the morning to select certain trees, mark them and assign men to get to work with the bucksaw. Two men could cut, trim and pile two or three logs a day. On Sunday, a day of rest, and in the late evening when the day's work was over, the Grand Bank loggers enjoyed Bill Henry's yarns for he was known to be quite a storyteller.

After the spring thaw two to three hundred logs were floated down Garnish River. Heavy birch and witchhazel tended to sink, but a "rampike" of fir or spruce nailed to them kept these afloat until they reached Garnish Gut. From there *Winnie*, a little schooner owned by John Tom Cluett, brought the sticks for *D.J. Thornhill*'s timbers and planking to Point of Beach in Grand Bank harbour.

Overseeing construction was master builder Hughie McKay. Thornhill had asked McKay's Shipyards at Shelburne, Nova Scotia, to send someone to build his schooner. When McKay, who was in his early twenties and had boyish good looks, arrived on the coastal boat someone in Grand Bank remarked, "John Thornhill sent to Shelburne for a man to build his schooner, but look what he got — a boy." But despite his

Courtesy Otto Kelland and Hughie McKay, master builder

D.J. Thornhill on the stocks at Point of Beach in Grand Bank harbour about September/October 1935, a month before her launching. She has a good coat of black paint; masts, soon lying on the ground to the left, are stepped after she is launched. To the right is a pile of dry fish covered in canvas.

youthful appearance McKay proved to be a master shipwright. He, his wife and infant daughter lived in the Thorndyke, John Thornhill's home and boarding house.

Under McKay's direction, Bill Henry Grandy was the head shipwright on the schooner. Grandy's son, Fred, worked with him as a "dubber." Both men were experts with the adze — an axe which had its blade at right angles to the handle and was used primarily for dressing timber. The dubber with an adze trimmed or bevelled edges of the frame or timbers before the planks were nailed in place.

While the raw material was making its way to Grand Bank, Hughie McKay and Bill Henry Grandy were at Grand Bank preparing the site at Point of Beach, in Grand Bank harbour. Not all those employed cutting timber built the schooner, but Chas Stone, Jake Matthews, Harry Hickman, Bob Riggs, Stephen Leonard Grandy and his son, Max, were six Grand Bank men who did. Later in the summer when more casual labour was needed William (Bill) Baker and Ambrose Thornhill were hired.

Stephen Leonard operated the band saw which McKay had shipped down from Shelburne especially for sawing the planks. In the first stages, most of these men were engaged in chopping timbers with a broad axe to make a flat side to fit on the band saw. Bill Henry Grandy, well-experienced in preparing and hewing timber to be sawn into plank, was in charge of this operation and gave directions to his men:

> "Now boys, whatever you do, don't under hew the timber. In other words don't cut it in under, cut it straight. If you do you will spoil it."
>
> Chas Stone asked, "What will happen if a piece was spoiled or under hewn."
>
> "Well," said Bill Henry, "if you spoil a piece, look around to make sure nobody is looking at you. Carry it over and heave it in the scrap heap. Pick out another piece and start chopping that. If you can do that, without anybody seeing you, you'll do alright."

Although he was not employed building the schooner, Elic Stoodley remembered that sometime during the summer he and Bill Henry Grandy went back to Garnish woods for a couple of days. Apparently there was a certain piece of wood, perhaps for the stempost, which Grandy needed. By now it was mid-summer and they travelled by dory which could be rowed or sailed upriver with fair wind. They went deep into Garnish River watershed, crossed overland to Black River where the appropriate stick was cut and hauled out.

The carpenters employed on *D.J. Thornhill* were paid at a rate of "a dollar a day." Local carpenters in their search for work would offer to build a barn or stage under the terms "a dollar a day and dinner." By the 1940s, pay became a little better, rising to $1.10 per day.

All through the summer of 1935 while the schooner was under construction, Captain Thornhill lost no fishing time. He had command of *Helen Forsey*, a banker owned by William Forsey, Ltd. To give his newly-built schooner every advantage, Thornhill ordered a 44-Kelvin engine installed making *D.J. Thornhill* an auxiliary/sail schooner.

He had already decided to use D & J in the schooner's name: his wife Dinah's and his own initial. Highest tides that fall occurred on a Tuesday morning, November 26, 1935, and *D.J. Thornhill* was launched with great acclaim — a school and civic holiday was called. The same evening after the launch McKay and his family left for Nova Scotia via Port aux Basques on the coastal boat *Portia*.

When the schooner slid down the ways, Bill Henry said that all their hard work had just gone out into the water and their employment was over.

By the spring of 1936 *D.J. Thornhill* was outfitted for the fishery, the herring baiting off the Western Shore on Quero, Burgeo or Rose Blanche Banks. Because Thornhill knew where the cod were and usually brought in above average catches, he had no trouble finding a crew — most had sailed with him before. In her crew list for 1937, *D.J. Thornhill*'s twenty-three fishermen hailed from various Fortune Bay communities:

Grand Bank	Frenchman's Cove	English Harbour E.
Capt. Thornhill	Matt Cluett	George Hickey
Charles Parsons, cook	Steven Cluett	Pat Hynes
Am Thornhill	Frank Hoben	George Saunders
Alex Price	Frank Bond	Joseph Hackett
Albert Elms		John Cluett
Alex Bond		
George Barnes		
Bay L'Argent	**Garnish**	**Belleoram**
Reuben Pardy	Albert Grandy	William Fudge
John Pike	George Cluett	
Lally Cove	**Fortune**	
Wilson Dodge	Reg Buffett, engineer	

Despite all her acclaim *D.J. Thornhill*, built of softer, unseasoned local timber and badly strained from heavy cargoes and winter storms, did not last long. Less than eight years later, on January 23, 1943, she succumbed to a severe storm and sank in the Gulf. Her crew — Captain Gordon "Johnny" Williams and Berkley Nurse of Pool's Cove; mate Hughie Grandy; engineer Wilson Price, Grand Bank; James Brown, born in Baine Harbour but a resident of Grand Bank; cook Winston Taylor — abandoned the sinking auxiliary schooner and was rescued almost two days later by a passing Canadian corvette.

Throughout the Burin Peninsula, Garnish was renowned for men with shipbuilding skills and, as well, the area around the town had adequate resources of timber suitable for the trade. A partial list of schooners built in Garnish includes:

Schooner	Year Built	Net Tons (Approx)	Owner and/or Builder
Garnishee	1907	25	unknown
Carrie and Evelyn	1911	?	Foote's, Grand Bank
Millie Francis	1917	42	Phil Walsh, Mortier B.
Andavaka	1934-35	57	James Anstey/F.& Tibbo
Eva King	1934-35	28	Cephas Grandy/F.King

Jean and Mona	1934-35	92	Capt. Tom Grandy
Joan Madeleine	1934-35	28	Albert "Ab" Grandy
Beatrice and Grace	1935	61	G.T. Dixon, Fortune
Harold Guy	1939	104	Sam Piercy, Grand Bank
Garnish Queen	1943	107	Cephas Grandy, builder
Fortune Breeze	1954	48	Eli R. Grandy, owner
Daphne and Phyllis	1956	148	Cephas Grandy, builder

Many Garnish-built schooners were bankers ranging from four-dory to ten-dory, but *Garnish Queen* was a coasting vessel operated by Burchell's of Sydney, Nova Scotia. Her chief work was in the produce and coal trade from Nova Scotia to Newfoundland, although she is known to have once carried a load of Christmas trees cut in the Garnish area to Boston. Her crew for one season was: Captain Chesley Walters, Robert Jensen, Willis Grandy all of Garnish, and Elroy Kelly of Burin.

Garnish Queen was abandoned on November 8, 1952, twelve miles off Cape St. Lawrence, Nova Scotia.

Adrift and Astray

Although Garnish breadwinners were master shipbuilders, fishing was the predominant occupation. By 1891 the number of Garnish vessels involved in the inshore cod fishery dropped to six, due in part to a decline in the Fortune Bay herring stocks. In the same year there were three lobster factories employing thirty-eight men and seventeen women.

In the era of the banking schooner fishery, 1890s-1950s many Garnish men were employed on vessels from Lunenburg, Nova Scotia, and Grand Bank. Many of the traditional family names of Anstey, Banfield, Cluett, Grandy, Legge, Marsh, May, Moulton and Walters began to appear in rosters of schooners lost, ships wrecked and dories missing with their two-man crews.

Dories led a perilous existence on the stormy Atlantic: many were lost in the ever-present fog; overloaded dories were sometimes swamped in heavy seas and run down by their own or another vessel. Two young men from Frenchman's cove, near Garnish had a combination of luck, experience and skill to bring

Garnish had a combination of luck, experience and skill to bring them through a trying ordeal on the sea.

Max Myles and Archibald Rideout, two dory fishermen, rowed 175 miles after they were separated from their schooner. On July 13, 1941, *Beatrice and Grace* had been fishing on the banks about 115 miles off the coast of Newfoundland. Bank fishermen would normally rise at daylight, 4 or 5 o'clock in the morning, bait up the trawl hooks and coil the hundreds of fathoms of trawl line in trawl tubs. Tubs are loaded in the dories and around 6 am, the men set their gear. Myles and Rideout had the trawl lines out and rowed back to *Beatrice and Grace* to have breakfast. At 8 am they rowed back to take in the gear and load their dories with cod.

In the fog they were unable to find their trawl buoys. In their circling and meandering looking for the buoy that would identify the whereabouts of their gear, they lost sight of the schooner. Six hours of rowing, looking and sounding the small horn in the dory was of no use.

They lay back for a while, listening and hoping *Beatrice and Grace* would find them. By then the men had already worked and rowed ten hours and weariness was setting in. Both men agreed their best chance was to row to the coast of Newfoundland. After checking their dory compass for the general direction of St. John's, they began the long pull toward land. Taking stock of what was aboard, they found the usual dory rations: about four pounds of hard bread and a little water, certainly not enough to last several days.

To make matters worse, the weather changed. The wind came up very strong and the dory began to leak. They had to bail constantly. The wind was against their intended direction and they had no choice but drift with it. Myles and Rideout estimated they were driven back about fifty to sixty miles. Then as if to "pile on the agony" as Newfoundlanders often say, one oar broke off.

Nevertheless, they kept their spirits up and pushed for land for another three days. One hundred and seventy-five miles later, they reached Newfoundland off Cape Spear at 11:30 in the night. In the three days of rowing, they had about four hours' sleep when the wind was fair and a small sail could be hoisted. Near the mouth of St. John's harbour, a schooner saw the castaways and towed the dory into port.

Both men, drained and weary, were rushed to the Grace Hospital, but they had no physical damage other than badly galled hands. Both men resided in Frenchman's Cove and were married; Rideout had one child. Myles intended to return home as soon as possible, while Rideout intended to look for work in St. John's.

According to an interview with the *Evening Telegram*, Arch Rideout claimed the worst hardship he had to endure was the lack of tobacco. Both men were concerned that their shipmates on *Beatrice and Grace* would not know if they had been found or had reached safety.

Nor was this the first time Garnish dorymen had been astray from *Beatrice and Grace*. In early October 1935, Samuel Newport and Gilbert Grandy lost their bearings in dense fog while fishing from *Beatrice and Grace* on Misaine Bank. After sixty hours of rowing to reach St. Pierre, Newport, age fifty-five and married

Author's collection

Daphne and Phyllis, a few days prior to her launching. Master builder Cephas Grandy oversaw the building and had with him: John Wilson Grandy; George Wilson Grandy; Albert Legge; Richard Grandy, who did finished carpentry work and liked to work with fine birch; Thomas Grandy; Ernest Grandy; Ron Grandy and Clyde Grandy, both of whom later lived in Grand Bank.

Built across the Garnish Gut, *Daphne and Phyllis* was launched side on and at highest tide due to low water in the Barrisway.

and Grandy, twenty-one and unmarried, were picked up by *Ronald George* and carried to North Sydney. An excerpt from the *Daily News* — brief and lacking details of the mental and physical stress both men had undergone — summarized their trying experience:

> Newport and Grandy told a story of desperate struggling against a hurricane accompanied by thunder and lightning, the waves sweeping over the tiny dory on the Mizzen (Misaine) Banks. Members of the crew of the *Beatrice and Grace* set out in seven dories to fish from the schooner on the Banks last Thursday.
>
> Dense fog caught the men in the dories unexpectedly and a search for the larger vessel proved fruitless. Visibility was very bad and Grandy and Newport became separated from their twelve companions, giving up hope of finding the schooner and turned toward St. Pierre, two hundred miles away.

After an examination by a doctor, Grandy and Newport were deemed none the worse for their experience; however, they voiced concern for their twelve shipmates on *Beatrice and Grace,* which had been caught in a violent windstorm. Their

Courtesy of Y. Andrieux, St. Pierre

A schooner lies stranded on the Dune Sands connecting Langlade to Miquelon Islands, St. Pierre. Here a calm peaceful scene, but often the shoreline has been littered with shipwrecks — over a two hundred in a 100 year period.

In May 1925, four Garnish men fought for their lives when they abandoned *Gladys E. Bullen*, stranded off the Dune Sands in a similar situation as the schooner above.

Bullen was a small coasting vessel owned by Grand Bank's Forward and Tibbo, who operated her out of Garnish. Captain Jim Anstey, Willy Elias Anstey and Ern Anstey of Garnish and William Baker of Grand Bank jumped from the bowsprit into the rollers and scrambled onto Dune Sands beach.

fears were unfounded for she had immediately returned to port, Fortune, to report both men missing. The Garnish seamen returned to Newfoundland via Captain John King's freighter *Administratrix*.

Beatrice and Grace lasted twenty years in the strenuous fishing and coastal trade — above the usual term for locally built schooners — before she sank, coal laden, in the Gulf of St. Lawrence. Five Fortune Bay seamen were rescued by another freighter: Captain Austin Myles, Joseph Myles and Harold Whittle of St. Bernard's; Michael McCarthy, Terrenceville and Steve Drake, Bay L'Argent. Shipwreck was not a new experience for Drake. He was one of the crew of the coaster *Velvet Lady*, wrecked in Newfoundland waters in mid July, 1935 — six weeks previously.

Chapter 13

Grand Bank Seascapes

SOON AFTER THE FIRST FRENCH SETTLERS arrived at the toe of the Burin Peninsula in 1687, the town of Grand Bank became a prime location for the French fishery of the seventeenth century. Vestiges of the community's salty past that once earned the title of "Bank Fishing Capital of Newfoundland" abound throughout the town, and merchant houses, stores, fishing premises and various historical monuments from a by-gone era are remarkably well-preserved.

The name Grand Bank came from the French "Grand Banc" which was likely named after the natural embankment on the west side of the harbour (what is now Water Street) and extending westward beyond Point Bouilli.

For the year of 1687, French census records show a population of forty-five. By 1693 there were only eleven adults living in Grand Bank with the names of Bourny, Comier, Chevallier and Grandin, and the population decline continued until 1714, when the French left the coast altogether, some moving to Cape Breton. When the Seven Years' War ended, the Treaty of Paris (1763) awarded France the nearby islands of St. Pierre and Miquelon, and a few of St. Pierre's English resettled at Grand Bank.

From the outset the livelihood of the people revolved around the sea: the selling of bait to the French, until the Bait Act of 1888 stopped the trade, and an inshore fishery until around 1881 when the era of the Bank Fishery began. The latter marked the beginning of sixty years of relative prosperity for the community with scores of schooners heading for Newfoundland's bountiful Grand Banks.

Incorporated in 1943, Grand Bank was the first town on the island to have its own cottage hospital, and today (1994) this town of 3500 still draws much of its sustenance from the provident but demanding ocean. Located on the Burin Peninsula's north shore a few miles from the French islands of St. Pierre and Miquelon, which attract more than 15,000 tourists annually, Grand Bank is a charming community, steeped in history.

Grand Bank has been listed in the Newfoundland Historic Trust's book *Ten Historic Towns* as a community full of unique architecture. It claims: "Architecturally, Grand Bank is interesting since many of its earlier homes are built in variations of the Queen Ann style, popular in Lunenburg, Shelburne and New England from 1870 to 1890." The Thorndyke Bed and Breakfast Home, designated in 1989 as a provincial historic site, is a unique building. Built in 1917 by banking schooner captain John Thornhill, this is a structure similar to the Queen Anne style architecture with a 'widow's walk' or belvedere on the roof. Traditionally, wives and relatives stood there to watch for incoming banking schooners.

The Grand Bank lighthouse, built in 1921-22, invokes memories of shipwreck and calamity. On January 10, 1923, the tern schooner *Frank R. Forsey*, returning from Oporto deeply laden with fishery salt, attempted to enter the harbour during a storm. Her bowsprit struck the lighthouse and shattered, putting the vessel aground and damaging the lighthouse. The scar on the B in the word BANK is still visible today in the vertical lettering.

Prior to 1900, most schooners used along the South Coast were built in locally, several in Grand Bank. Just after the turn of the century as their business began to expand, South Coast merchants needed larger, more durable vessels, and bought them from Gloucester, Lunenburg, Lockeport or Shelburne.

One of the first round-bowed (unlike the cutwater bows) schooners brought to Grand Bank was seventy-eight-ton *Edith Pardy*, owned by Patten and Forsey. Built in Shelburne and named for the daughter of one of Patten and Forsey's clerks, this 8 dory banker came to Grand Bank in March, 1910. The owners

Courtesy Shipsearch Marine

A Grand Bank vessel built in Little Bay Islands in 1965, *Sybil Eloise* was owned by G & A Buffett and was employed in the coasting trade until 1974. She was 111 foot long, netted 156 tons and was one of the last wooden vessels owned in Grand Bank.

Freights were varied: salt, soft drink, flour and coal, taken from Nova Scotia to Newfoundland ports from Burgeo to Port Elizabeth. Her Grand Bank crew during her last year out of that port was: Captain Randell Prior; engineer George Green; cook Will Handrigan; deckhands Les Buffett and Sylvester Hynes of St. Bernard's.

On March 27, 1974, *Sybil Eloise* sprang a leak in the Gulf between Halifax and Port aux Basques and sank. "We were very lucky," said Wallace Elliott, the new owner, after he and his three man crew — son Arthur, Randy Hollett of Halifax and Reg Galloway, Harbour Grace — were taken aboard Gulf Ferry *Ambrose Shea*. "It all happened within 15 minutes. I guess she sprang a leak because all of a sudden we began taking on water at a rapid rate. We just had enough time to get in the lifeboat and get off her."

gave command of her to Captain John Hickman Matthews. For five years, up to 1915, the nucleus of Matthews' crew remained basically the same: George and Charlie Clements, cook Henry Griffin, kedgie and nephew to the captain, Len Matthews, all of Grand Bank; Richard Banfield, George Myles, George and Richard Legge, Garnish; John Snook and Harry Mavin of Fortune.

Sea disasters are nothing new to most Newfoundland communities, and Grand Bank has had more than its share of missing ships. Reminders of local tragedies can be seen along the town's walking tour route. In Frazer Park, a municipal heritage site steeped in local history, stands the monument to

Grand Bank Heritage Walk

Grand Bank, the Historical and Cultural Center of the Burin Peninsula, is rich in heritage - an important part of all our lives.

Architecturally, Grand Bank is interesting, since many of its earlier homes are built in variations of the Queen Anne style, popular in England and America from 1870 to 1890.

"Lost With Crew - 1936"

First produced in 1987 by the Grand Bank Town Council to help celebrate the town's 300th anniversary, the Heritage Walk brochure guides walkers past historical and cultural points in the town. The vessel shown here is the *Partanna*, lost with her crew of twenty-five in April 1936.

the schooner *Tubal Cain* which disappeared in January 1907 while returning from Halifax to Grand Bank. *Tubal Cain* represents one ship out of twenty-five which has been lost with all crew over the years.

Harold Guy— A Typical Banker

Fascination for sailing ships and schooners affects nearly all who live by the sea. Most of us, like the photographer who went to waterfront sometime prior to 1951 (when the last of the banking schooners sailed out of Grand Bank and out of most other South Coast ports) to take the photo below, would rush to watch a vessel come into port.

It would be easy to dismiss our fascination as a romantic longing for an older and simpler way of life. There is a natural grace of form and rhythm of the vessel and sea that attracts the watcher. Poet Henry Wadsworth Longfellow, who saw sailing ships in their heyday, was as entranced with them as we are and wrote these lines:

Author's collection

Harold Guy, entering Grand Bank harbour with Lewis (Louse) Hill in the background, returns from a fishing voyage with dories and gear on deck.

The ninety-six-foot long *Harold Guy* netted 104 ton and had an eighty-eight horsepower engine installed in 1949. She was named for the son of owner Samuel Piercy, Grand Bank.

I remember the black wharves and the slips.
And the sea-tides tossing free...
And the beauty and the mystery of the ships,
And the magic of the sea.

Several features of South Coast fishing vessels are evident in this photo of *Harold Guy,* a typical auxiliary engine/sail schooner of the period between 1940 and 1950:

1. *Harold Guy* carried twenty-three men for her fishing crew: twenty dory men (two for each of ten dories); a captain, cook and kedgie. The kedgie was the cook's helper.

The only man who was positively identified in this photo is Wallace Pope, Grand Bank, standing nearest the bow with his left hand on the heaving line. Several men are standing in front of the wheelhouse.

2. Prominent in this photo is the bowsprit — a schooner attribute that fell to disuse when vessels like *Harold Guy* relied more on her engines than sail. When the J.B. Foote business bought *Harold Guy,* they removed the bowsprit for it was in the way for freighting, especially when manoeuvring in small harbours and ports.

3. The bobstay, a steel cable or wire, extends from the top of the bowsprit to the stem. Near the top of the bobstay is a turnbuckle used to tighten or loosen the stay. It could be tightened on voyage by getting out on the bowsprit and reaching down with an iron spike to turn the buckle. Attached to the bobstay was a pennant which in turn was attached to a shackle on the stem.

4. The cable coiled on the bow is a nine-inch cable; three three-inch cables braided into one, about 300 fathoms long and used for anchoring while bank fishing.

The pile of cable on the bow often provided some privacy when a man had to use the bathroom. He threw a draw bucket over the side for a makeshift toilet of salt water, answered the call of nature and cleaned himself. There was usually no paper; a piece of old rope was braided out and this replaced today's toilet paper.

5. The anchor on the starboard bow is the cable anchor, weighing about 900 pounds and attached to the cable with a chain extending through the hawse-hole. Anchors could be bought in St. John's at Nail and Foundry Company or at Halifax/Sydney ship suppliers. The wooden stalk through the anchor was slipped in and wedged tight. It could be removed if necessary. Anchor stalks could be cut locally, often in the Garnish woods, but were, for durability, a hardwood such as witchhazel or birch.

6. The chain anchor on the port bow, its fluke barely visible above the railing, had an iron stalk. Weighing about 600 pounds, it was used when a vessel was in the coasting trade and had to anchor while in port.

7. The sail tied down in a jacket in the foreground is the jumbo.

8. The riding sail tied in its jacket extends from the mainmast to the stern. While fishing, the riding sail was used and this helped keep the schooner's head to the wind. While going to and from the banks both the jumbo and riding sail were lashed up out of the way.

9. Although *Harold Guy* had an engine, she carried a foresail used if the wind was right or if the engine was not considered necessary. Thus she would be termed an auxiliary sailing vessel. The foresail (between the foremast and mainmast) is lashed securely between the foreboom and the gaff.

10. *Harold Guy*, as required by marine law, carried four lights: two side lights (two box-like features on the port and starboard rigging); behind the wheelhouse a white light; and a mast head light located on the top of the foremast.

11. Barely visible on the top of the mainmast is the receiver for the Marconi set. *Harold Guy*'s call letters were VOVK and *Nina W. Corkum*'s, VOGR.

12. This schooner was a ten dory banker; five dories nested together on each side. Behind the dories (right, near the rear starboard rigging) are the four crates, four tables and four large tubs — all used when splitting fish on the banks. Not visible is a water hose to wash fish, tables and decks. Before the advent of hose and pump, items were cleaned with water obtained by

drawbucket over the side. While going to and from the fishing grounds this gear was lashed down.

13. The small barrel up in front of the wheelhouse is probably a mark or spot buoy. This was thrown over to see which way the tide was going. Trawls were set from this buoy.

14. At the base of the foremast was the companionway to the forecastle where most of the crew ate and slept. Flour, potatoes, sugar, molasses, salt beef, fresh fish, beans, rolled oats, bangbellies, buns and bread made up most of the menus. Beans, rolled oats or hard bread (brewis) with tea were breakfast foods. Dinners were often potatoes with peas pudding and salt beef; for supper, hash or leftovers were served. Day after day meals were routine. Fresh meat or eggs were not affordable or available.

In early years on South Coast schooners there was no sugar, only molasses. When a schooner came into a port the flies that were attracted to the fish were so thick they were even in the molasses, but the men pushed them aside and went on eating. The cook baked bread every day for the crew which usually numbered between twenty and twenty-five. Schooner owners rarely supplied other vegetables beside potato. Tinned milk for tea did not become common until the 1940s; even then it was considered a luxury item and had to be bought by the crew. To make a tin of milk last all day, often the cook poured it into the large kettle of tea steeping on the galley stove; thus, milk lasted longer and each man got an equal share.

Between twenty to twenty-six barrels of drinking water were carried on a typical banker stored in iron or wooden tanks usually stored below deck. This was barely enough water for twenty or so men gone on a three week trip and had to be rationed. There wasn't enough to wash hands and face. Fish and fish offal handled daily could only be wiped off if a mitt was dipped overboard and used as a cloth. In cold weather any water stored in barrels on deck froze solid; while in hot weather the water became flat and often matted and stringy.

Each crewman supplied his own bed clothes and eating utensils (fork, knife, spoon, mug and plate). Up to the mid-1940s mattresses were home made of calico and often stuffed with wood shavings.

Each man carried his clothes bag aboard. It contained at least two changes of clothes, several pairs of mitts, socks. Most crewmen also had a little better change of clothes in case the vessel harboured away from home for a night or two.

Often, after a trip was over and results were poor, destitute bank fisherman were often heard saying, "All I brought home from this trip was a bag of dirty clothes."

By the summer of 1957, *Harold Guy* was employed in the coasting trade. On June 28 she loaded coal in Sydney destined for Footes in Grand Bank. As the vessel neared the Newfoundland coast on the next day, she crept along through thick fog. A buoy near the western side of St. Pierre was thought to be the guide through Langlade Reach. With the tide and fog, it was impossible to determine if it was the right buoy, and course was not changed.

Outside Savoyard, *Harold Guy* touched a reef and grounded. Her rudder post was driven up through the bottom; her propeller and shaft smashed. The crew — Captain Harvey Banfield and engineer Charlie Follett of Grand Bank; mate Willy Elias Anstey, cook Randell Grandy, and Garfield Anstey of Garnish — tried to lighten the schooner by shovelling most of the deck coal off the after quarter.

Harold Guy, under her weight of coal and seawater, fell off the rock and sank. The crew and three male passengers, who by this time had the dory over the side, clambered aboard. With little wind to hinder them, they rowed around Cape Noir, through the South East Passage and into St. Pierre harbour. One of the last South Coast schooners left her bones, as had scores of others before her, on the rocky environs of St. Pierre.

Getting Back Home from the Wrecked *Laverna*

Several years prior to the loss of *Harold Guy*, another Grand Bank schooner, *Laverna*, was wrecked on the Labrador coast. Although the schooner grounded relatively gently in daylight hours, the crew were lucky to escape with their lives on the voyage home.

In the fall of 1936, the Grand Bank schooner *Laverna* fished off Labrador. Unlike voyages to the Grand Banks when schooners stayed out for two to three weeks, South Coast fishing vessels on the Labrador grounds came into harbour each evening.

Before daylight on September 7, Captain Frank Thornhill, determined to get an early start to the day's fishing, sailed *Laverna* from Round Hill in Salmon Bight Passage, Labrador, toward the grounds. As the schooner rounded the point she hit a ledge of rock, driving the rudder post up through the bottom. Captain John Thornhill in *D.J. Thornhill*, a schooner with power, agreed to tow *Laverna* back to Salmon Bight.

Built in the James and Tarr yards in Essex, Massachusetts, in 1911, *Laverna*'s model was taken from the schooner *Valerie*. At 106 feet long with a bowsprit measuring twenty-two feet, *Laverna* had a net tonnage of ninety-five.

Gordon Thomas in his book *Fast and Able* (1973) says, "*Laverna* carried a great spread of canvas, was able, and as for looks few vessels surpassed her. Captain Alan Larkin (of Essex) claimed she was the fastest craft he had ever commanded."

In 1920 Samuel Harris of Grand Bank purchased the productive banker and by 1936 her registry was changed to Grand Bank Fisheries firm. She had three Grand Bank captains in her day: Charles Rose, Charles Anstey and Frank Thornhill, her last. While *Laverna* was under the command of Charles Rose, one of her crewmen died in Domino, Labrador. James Elms of Stone's Cove, Fortune Bay, passed away aboard ship on October 4, 1931. He was twenty-one and the son of Arthur Elms and nephew of Captain Reuben Elms.

As an indication of the size of schooners like *Laverna*, compare her mast height to the height of an average Grand Bank waterfront store. The Grand Bank Lumber building (Samuel Piercy's store in the 1930s) from wharf to peak is approximately thirty feet high; *Laverna*'s mainmast from the deck to the cap was seventy-seven feet high and the main topmast was another forty-six feet, for a total of 123 feet from deck to topmast — four times higher than most waterfront buildings.

Considering the 1920-30s were the years when South Coast towns like Grand Bank had many two and three masted schooners, the waterfront and harbour was a forest of spars, booms and rigging. If one stood on Church Street facing east toward the waterfront, the sight of tall ships with their masts towering above buildings, was very impressive.

At the time of her loss, *Laverna* was twenty-five years old, well past her prime and her timbers may have been in need of repair. In Salmon Bight, the aged vessel filled with water and no amount of pumping nor temporary repairs could keep her free. *Laverna* was run ashore at Black Tickle, near Salmon Bight. Eventually she broke apart on the Labrador coast.

In essence, the twenty-three crew were stranded until a passage home could be found. There were three possibilities: the coastal steamer *Kyle* which made runs every two or three weeks; other Grand Bank schooners, each due to remain fishing until mid-October; or another privately-owned vessel hired especially to bring them home.

Howell's of Carbonear had a small business in Black Tickle and he gave the crew an unused store loft to stay in. All the men brought their duffel bags and sacks to their temporary home for a two week stay. Nearby was a small shed with a stove and during the extended wait, *Laverna*'s cook, Elias Francis, prepared their meals with food brought up from the wrecked schooner.

The men removed as much of the ship's supplies and equipment as possible — masts, spars, canvas, deck engine, fishing gear. A little salvage was to be brought down on other South Coast bankers, some on the schooner sent to bring the stranded men home, and what could not be transported was left behind. *Laverna's* timbers, large gaffs, and booms — her main boom measured seventy-four feet long, main gaff, forty-five feet — most likely became firewood for Labrador stoves.

Captain Frank Thornhill asked a man from the Labrador coast to take *Laverna*'s grub supply — potatoes, flour, beans, dried peas, salt beef and other food — to Battle Harbour. It would be picked up later. Thornhill assured him he would be paid for his work, but once the food was aboard the small skiff, the man sailed off and neither he nor the food was seen again.

Sam Patten, Grand Bank's Wreck Commissioner, was sent to Black Tickle to access wreckage and potential salvage for Grand Bank Fisheries' manager Percy Carr. Carr had already hired the motor vessel *Gertrude Jean,* a speed boat captained by Thomas Fiander, of English Harbour West — Claude Fiander was engineer, and Frank Pine, mate — to take Patten up and to bring the stranded crew back to St. John's.

Laverna's twenty-three men were in cramped quarters on the smaller vessel, already overcrowded with her own seven crew and with items of salvage from the wrecked schooner — *Laverna*'s deck engine was stored below and her dories stacked on deck.

With a fair wind, within two days *Gertrude Jean* and her crew, carrying *Laverna*'s shipwrecked men arrived in St. John's. However, Fiander had to be paid extra to complete the journey to Grand Bank. In those days there was no long-range weather forecast by radio or newspaper, only innate weather lore and government posted storm flags. The flags had balls (circles) indicating wind directions and possible storms; Fiander's boat was too small and overcrowded to be at sea during inclement weather.

South Coast fishermen called vessels like *Gertrude Jean* "a speed boat" — she was low in the water and built for speed. At one period in her long career she, like Grand Bank owned *Reo II* and *Administratrix,* was a rum running vessel transporting liquor illegally between St. Pierre and the United States.

On the day *Gertrude Jean* left St. John's, the storm warning balls were up, but Fiander steamed on. As the little vessel rounded Cape Ballard, the labouring engine quit and no amount of coaxing would make it start.

Fiander now had no recourse but anchor the schooner to keep her from drifting onto the rugged rocks of Cape Ballard. The crew of *Gertrude Jean* tied two ropes together, lashed one end to an anchor and threw it overboard, but the rope slipped off and the anchor was lost. Captain Frank whispered a grim warning to his men below deck, "Boys, we may have survived the *Laverna*, but we could meet our end right here on this one."

So close was the little schooner to hitting the base of the towering cliffs and rocky ledges that white froth from the rocks was flung back over her quarter. *Laverna*'s crew could see it was a most dangerous situation; there were dories enough for all but neither the open ocean nor the rugged landfall offered much refuge. Then just as it seemed the vessel would strike, the stalled engine caught and Fiander steamed off ten miles.

Eventually all reached home safely. *Laverna* carried twenty dorymen, a captain, cook and kedgie. Several of her crew are recorded: Captain Thornhill, cook Francis, Foote Lee, Jim Penwell, Garfield Rogers, Gord Tibbo, Ambrose Saunders, Jim Rogers, Charlie Fizzard, Matt English, William Riggs, Joe Lawrence, Grand Bank; brothers Mike and Jim Joe Hackett, English Harbour East; brothers Garfield, Frank and Jim Osbourne, Bay L'Argent; Bill Mitchell, Burin and four from Garnish: Bob Legge, Sam White, Fred Cluett and Harvey Banfield who later resided in Grand Bank.

Other Misadventures on the Labrador

Later that same fall another schooner, *Paloma*, Captain Wilbert Moulton of Garnish, also owned by Grand Bank Fisheries, burned on the Labrador coast. Unlike the adversity and danger faced by *Laverna*'s men, her banking crew returned without incident on *Freda M*, Captain George Follett.

The harsh Labrador conditions were especially hard on South Coast schooners. *W.L. Mckenzie King*, owned by Foote's business, fished in the fall of 1936 near Seal Island. During a fall storm, her captain, Sam Ridgley of Harbour Breton, took shelter in Bolster's Rock, ordered both anchors out and had two dory ropes ashore to hold *W.L. Mckenzie King* into the wind.

Bolster's Rock, Labrador, a community which had a little over 40 people in 1936, had a unique feature that came through for this schooner. Located on a small island in the mouth of an inlet a little north of Hawke Harbour in southern Labrador, the name Bolster's Rock refers to a large rock in the harbour. The rock had a heavy iron rod driven down into it and *Mckenzie King*'s lines were tied to that.

Ridgley, an experienced banking captain born in Little Bay West, had at least three Grand Bankers among his crew that fall: Igol Green, cook; Waterfield Green and Hector Rose. Veteran seamen claimed *Mckenzie King* had an unusual shape, but she weathered many storms in her long years of service. A saying about her claimed:

> *Mckenzie King* is pretty low;
> Her head is hanging down.
> But Am Foote says she's safe on deck
> And she is really sound.

In the 1940s Foote's sold her to Steers Company, St. John's, and the schooner was later managed by John Reeves of Englee.

When the Essex-built *Antoine C. Santos* was owned in Belleoram and commanded by Captain Harry Pope, the schooner weathered a rough storm off Labrador. While going into Batteau, *Santos* was pushed by gale force winds over a reef called Farmer's Ridge, outside Batteau harbour.

As the schooner went over, a sea broke on the reef causing *Antoine C. Santos* to touch momentarily. The same sea washed splitting tables, buoys, barrels and every tub of gear which were all filled with trawl lines, over the side. The topmast broke completely off leaving the schooner's rigging in shambles. In time, temporary repairs enabled *Santos* to sail back to Belleoram — her voyage over for that year.

A Ride on *Ria*

In the 1920s, a trip overseas to Europe on a tern schooner was the thrill of a lifetime for an eleven-year-old Grand Bank youth. He had seen the three-masters with their tall sea-bleached sails leave for exotic ports of call: Cadiz, Pernambuco, Maceio, Gibraltar and Magala; his father often sailed on "foreign-going" voyages as a seaman and as captain.

John Douglas of Grand Bank made this trip in 1926 and can

still recall the event vividly. Tern schooners last sailed out of Newfoundland ports over fifty years ago and their memory is but a fleeting vision in the minds of a few. The ranks of those who have the knowledge and impressions of life on sailing vessels, especially in the era when many South Coast ports were frequented by tern schooners, are getting thinner with every passing day. But Douglas remembers conditions on the tern schooners.

Born on Brunette Island, his father was George Douglas who came to Grand Bank with his family seeking employment on the banking vessels and worked his way up through the ranks until he took charge of large schooners himself.

He was a dory fisherman under Captain Alex Smith and later a deckhand with Captain Edwin Vallis. Not content with his lot in life, he learned navigation from Vallis and thus qualified himself to take command and to sail to foreign ports.

Once when his schooner was in Burgeo, Vallis heard the tern schooner *Catherine M. Moulton* — owned by Moulton's firm of Burgeo — needed a skipper and recommended George Douglas. Douglas was in charge of *Catharine M. Moulton* until October 1925 when she sprang a leak and sank. He and his crew were rescued by a passing steamer.

G & A Buffett of Grand Bank saw the potential of the young man and asked him to take command of their tern schooner *Ria*. One hundred feet long and twenty-seven feet wide, the 154-ton *Ria* had been built on Stapleton's Point, Marystown, in 1920 by master builder James Forsey of Grand Bank and was named for Buffett's daughter.

After the Grand Bank school closed in June 1926 John Douglas, sensing the attraction of life on the sea and hearing the talk of distant ports of call, asked his father if he could sail with him on *Ria*, about to embark for Oporto, Portugal. By September his schooner would be back in Grand Bank — in time for school opening.

It was a 5500 mile trip, from Grand Bank to Oporto and back, and even with good weather the round trip would take over two months. Summer crossings were relatively danger free; unlike the treacherous fall and winter trips when many Newfoundland schooners had disappeared in the stormy Atlantic, often ravaged by northwesterly gales.

Young Douglas had to clear permission with three people: his father, his mother and the vessel's owner. His father agreed to let him go, but asked him to see Aaron Buffett, owner and manager of the salt fish procuring and exporting business of G & A Buffett.

"If you go down to the *Ria* and help stow fish in the holds, then work your passage across, it's allright with us," Douglas remembers Buffett saying.

He watched the men bringing load after load of the salt dry fish out from Buffett's three-storey fish store on "draft bars." Two men, one at each end of the draft bar would walk out the plank over the hold, dump the two quintals (224 pounds) of fish into the hold and return for more.

Stowing the fish in the hold and sealing the hatches was Douglas' first taste of work. *Ria*'s hatch covers were single boards with cracks and openings between each board. These had to be tightly sealed. Cracks were caulked with oakum; then the oakum was rubbed with Sunlight soap and further sealed. Then the heavy tarpaulin was stretched over the entire hatch and wedged in place. Then the dry fish stored loose, not in casks, was safe from sea water leaking down.

When the work was finished he heard his father tell the crew to go home for an hour, relax and bring down their suitcases or duffel bags. The tern schooner was about to sail. But that morning, unseen by anyone, the young seaman had put his suitcase aboard. "Let's go home and see your mother," said his father.

"I have my clothes down," said the boy. "If I go home mother will surely say no. I'll stay here."

He waited aboard ship. Soon her crew returned: mate George Sam Welsh; cook John Hickman; William Keating; Joe English of Grand Bank and John Hiscock of Grand Beach. Captain George Douglas needed no navigator, as did many other foreign-going captains, for he had learned that skill and knowledge many years before.

The crew unshipped the mooring lines, raised a small sail and slowing slipped past the Grand Bank lighthouse. As the wind caught *Ria*'s mainsail, foresail, mizzen, jib and jumbo, the tern schooner headed eastward.

John Douglas' shipboard duties were light, but he recalls steering quite a bit while standing on a wooden box so as he could see the compass in the binnacle. *Ria*'s crewmen steered, kept the schooner ship-shape, painted the deck, bulwarks and the cabin house. Cook Hickman came on deck at noon and around 4:00 p.m. to relieve the crew when dinner and supper had been prepared.

The young sailor slept in the captain's after cabin and ate the "rough food" with the crew: pork, beef, beans, peas, soup, bread — the cook baked every second or third day. Water, used primarily for drinking or cooking, was carried in three large puncheons, or butts, on deck and was dipped up in a large can tied on near the butts. On a long ocean voyage water could not be wasted on washing the body or clothes.

In two weeks *Ria* arrived in Oporto, a city which South Coast sailors had visited often since the 1900s. It was the second largest city in Portugal, located on the Douro River. Three main railway lines met in Oporto and the main river is spanned by great iron bridges. The mouth of the river leading into Oporto is blocked with a sand spit and usually Newfoundland schooners anchored off the bar until a tug towed them into the city. Or, as was the case with *Ria*, barcos rabello, flat bottom barges with huge rudders conveyed the fish into Oporto.

By 1926, Oporto's population was over a quarter million. The beauty and size of the busy city must have been amazing to a boy from a tiny Newfoundland fishing port: Oporto's river front streets rise in terraces up from the bank, many streets and homes were made of granite overlaid with plaster giving the city a glistening white appearance. Palm and orange trees grew along the streets; opera houses, bull rings, Roman Catholic cathedrals with high granite towers, museums and libraries were common structures. Older sections in the eastern part of

Oporto were and still are overcrowded and have narrow streets overshadowed by high balconied houses.

If John (accompanied by his father) or the crew wished to visit Oporto city, they hired a boatman. As a passenger or taxi service, Portuguese boatmen waited near foreign ships or hung around the harbour entrance and ferried crew ashore. Oporto and Cadiz, the next city on *Ria*'s journey, would be a topic of conversation with Grand Bank friends for years to come.

When the cargo was discharged, *Ria* took on a load of salt at Cadiz, Spain, and headed for home. The westward voyage took two or three weeks longer than expected. Adverse winds and occasional storms buffeted *Ria*; some days she lost headway and ran back many miles. Around mid-September she sailed into Fortune Bay and Grand Bank harbour, everyone aboard safe and sound.

Schooners like *Ria* sailed wherever their work took them or required them to go and turned down no paying cargo. In April of 1924 *Ria* left Harbour Grace for Sydney and to return to Newfoundland via Grand Bank. Since the tern was entering Sydney, a foreign port custom's clearance papers had to be signed stating each crewman's name, age, work, previous vessel and wages. *Ria*'s papers for 1924 show the following crew, all of Grand Bank except White who may have been a passenger, signed on:

Name	**Age**	**Position on Vessel**	**Wages**
Thomas Belbin	34	Captain	Salaried
Charlie Poole	40	Mate	$40.00
James Belbin	60	Cook	$40.00
Robert Gilliard	19	Seaman	$35.00
James Whiteway	19	Seaman	$35.00
Charlie Belbin	22	Seaman	$35.00
Charles White	62	——	——

In February of 1929 Samuel Harris' business chartered *Ria* to collect a load of herring from various Fortune Bay communities and to deliver the cargo to Gloucester, Massachusetts. Thomas Belbin stayed on as captain, but a few crew changed from 1924: cook Charlie Belbin; Bob Gilliard; James Moore and George Sam

Welsh. Also making the trip was an employee of Harris, Clarence Griffen, who supervised cargo quantity and quality.

At Anderson's Cove, Stone's Cove and two or three other small settlements *Ria* loaded 1250 barrels of loose herring which were stored in the holds. The Fortune Bay fishermen were paid tweny-five cents a barrel for the loose herring. *Ria* also had 350 barrels of pickled herring and 1530 boxes of smoked herring. Packed twelve fish to a small wooden box, the smoked herring were stored in the forecastle and in the after cabin.

Author's collection

Tern schooner under sail

Business manager Percy Carr planned to get the fish to the American markets in time for the church Lenten season when traditional diets called for fish. *Ria*'s cargo arrived in Gloucester in mid-March and although the cargo did not get the anticipated profit, it did well.

Tern schooner *Ria* lasted several profitable years in the North American-European trade routes, but on November 16, 1931, after a battering by Atlantic gales, the tern schooner sprang a leak and was abandoned. The crew was rescued by a passing steamer and carried to Boston. Captain George Douglas had practically the same men as five years previously with the exception of John Hiscock and the cook who had been replaced by Augusta Almeda, a Portuguese seaman living in Grand Bank.

In time John Douglas, like his father, made a career of the sea; first working as a dory fisherman on the banking schooners like *Pauline C. Winters* with Captain Sid Harris. He sailed with his father on a four-dory schooner, *Eva King*, a twenty-eight-ton schooner built in Garnish in 1934-35. Registered to Eva King, Lamaline, the little schooner procured fish for Fred King's small business in Lamaline.

For a short while, George Douglas skippered *Eva King* with George Lee of Grand Bank, Billy Tuff and Jim Haley of Lamaline as crewmen. In 1949 she was sold to Henry Dibbon of Port au Bras — her eventual fate is obscure, but she was involved in the rum running trade from St. Pierre to Nova Scotia for awhile.

Author's collection

In the 1940s John Douglas went coasting on the schooner *Robert Max* and was a crewman on this schooner when she was shelled by a German submarine on August 4, 1941.

For awhile in the 1960s he ferried *Rodco* (above) on her daily run from Grand Bank to St. Pierre and return. Owned by Robert Stoodley of Grand Bank, *Rodco* was captained by Edwin Vallis and manned at that time by John Douglas, Tom Evans, and Bob Thornhill. Later Douglas found employment on a government icebreaker.

***Alhambia*'s Story**

In April 1940, seamen Waterfield Green, his cousin John Green and William Baker, all of Grand Bank, were deckhands of the auxiliary schooner *James and Stanley*, owned by Grand Bank Fisheries. As regular crew of *James and Stanley* they were given any work available on the schooner. Now they had orders to take a load of salt bulk fish to Greece. She was tied on near Grand Bank Fisheries premises and her crew had loaded about five or six hundred quintals of fish when Percy L. Carr, the general manager of Fisheries, came to the waterfront. He ordered the crew to take the fish out of *James and Stanley* and to load *Alhambia* instead.

James and Stanley was termed an auxiliary/sail vessel, since two years before the owners had had an engine installed, an International truck engine capable of driving her six or seven knots per hour. Her mainsail was taken off and her masts were cut down. Thus *James and Stanley* could sail when the wind was fair, but was usually engine driven on long trips. Yet in Depression years, when there was little money, owners opted for the most economical method of transportation and engine-driven schooners lay idle.

James and Stanley was reassigned to Barbados. She went in rock ballast, that is, mainly rocks to keep her deep and steady on a long ocean voyage. Carr gave her a reduced cargo of thirty-six four-quintal casks of fish. She brought back a load of molasses.

The vessel that replaced *James and Stanley* for the overseas trip was the 115-foot auxiliary schooner *Alhambia* which Grand Bank Fisheries had purchased from Dixon's of Fortune. Built in 1919 at Bridgewater, Nova Scotia, she had originally carried the name *Bertha L. Walters*. Now her name bore some similarity to Alhambra, a thirteenth-century fortress palace of the Moorish kings of Spain.

By the time she plied her trade on the South Coast she was twenty-two years old — past the average age for wooden schooners. Schooners like *Alhambia*, built of soft wood, were not designed to endure the rigours of winter storms and years of strained timbers caused by heavy cargoes of coal, salt bulk cod and salt from Europe. Crewmen who sailed on *Alhambia* claimed she didn't like her new name. In heavy seas the nameplate often became dislodged or hung by one nail to be replaced again and again.

Now *Alhambia* was due to cross 3000 miles of the storm-tossed Atlantic which by 1940 was patrolled by enemy submarines. Manager Carr hired her five crew although they were chosen by her captain, Thomas E. Evans: his half-brother Stan Grandy (Sr.); Charlie Thomas; Ben Hiscock all of Grand Bank.

Many skippers like Evans had excellent knowledge of the North American coastline and could take a schooner to any port on the eastern seaboard, but on foreign-going voyages they required a certified navigator. Navigators had formal school training, could read a sextant and could do the necessary calculations to determine position. Fisheries hired George Ayres of Fortune to navigate *Alhambia.*

Captain Evans, at age thirty-five, was a veteran seaman. He had sailed with Captain Charles Anstey on *Partanna* some years before *Partanna* was lost with crew, and he had been a seaman on *R.L. Borden* when she was abandoned at sea in 1936. He, Captain Charles Rose, Willoughby Mullins, Sammy White, Clar Grandy and cook Charles Thomas were rescued by a passing ship.

Grand Bank Fisheries held Evans' ability as captain in high esteem, not only for his knowledge of sea and ships, but from his eight years of employment with Fisheries on foreign-going voyages to Nova Scotia, New York and the West Indies. They remembered the time Captain Evans had refused to take command of an unseaworthy schooner and valued his advice.

Alhambia's crew were well-experienced, except for Stan Grandy, age twenty-two, who was a seaman for only a few years. His father, Captain Joe Grandy, had suffered an appendix attack while at sea on the banker schooner, *Lillian M. Richards* and died a few days later. Captain Grandy's story is related in chapter fifteen.

Charlie Thomas experienced several shipwrecks in his long sea career — the most notable on the tern schooner *Mary D.*

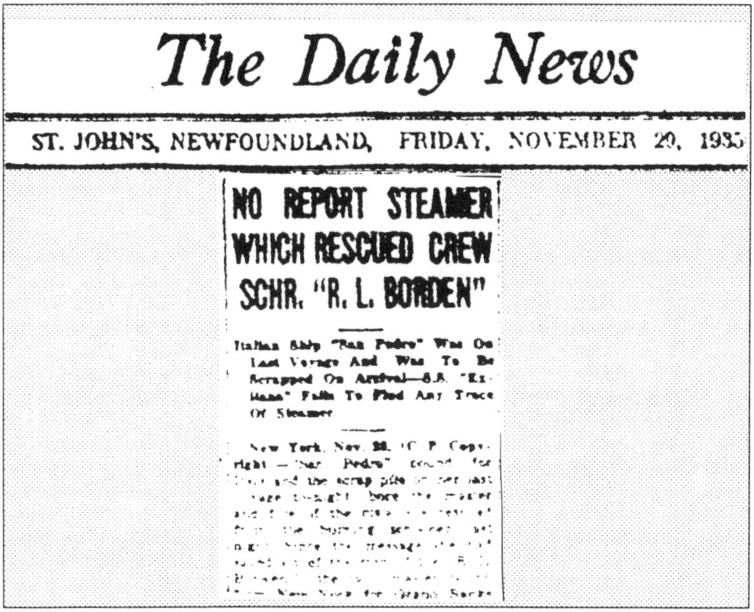

The Daily News

ST. JOHN'S, NEWFOUNDLAND, FRIDAY, NOVEMBER 29, 1935

NO REPORT STEAMER WHICH RESCUED CREW SCHR. "R. L. BORDEN"

Italian Ship "San Pedro" Was On Last Voyage And Was To Be Scrapped On Arrival—S.S. "Ex-[illegible]" Fails To Find Any Trace Of Steamer

New York, Nov. 28. (C P Copyright)— "San Pedro" [illegible]

Abandonment of Grand Bank schooner *R.L. Borden* as acknowledged by a November 29, 1935, paper. At the time it was not known which steamer plucked 5 Grand Bank seamen from a watery grave. Later news reports identified it as *San Pedro*, bound for Italy.

Young wrecked in St. Pierre harbour in 1918. Thomas and his shipmate, Charlie Parsons, spent fourteen hours on the wreck before they were rescued. Thomas and his other crewmates abandoned *J.E. Conrad* in the mid-Atlantic in December 1940, only a few months after his trial on *Alhambia*. They had rowed eighteen hours in a violent storm before reaching the Azores.

Alhambia was leaky; her owners probably knew that before the vessel left port. Within a few days after leaving Captain Evans brought her back for some caulking around her chain plates. Undaunted Evans and his crew headed overseas on an old and unfit ship. Work was hard to come by and pay was regular on foreign-going or coasting schooners — $30 a month by the late 1930s.

A few days out, *Alhambia's* seams opened up. Evans ordered the men to the pumps and for nine days there was no let up with pumping; yet water steadily rose higher.

Several ships passed, but were not signalled for fear it might prove to be a German warship. On the ninth day of pumping, the situation grew desperate. The old workhorse was settling fast and would sink at any hour. Finally on May 9, the exhausted crew signalled to and stopped a steamer, S.S. *Examiner*, heading to Gibraltar, a British protectorate. *Alhambia* slipped to the Atlantic floor at latitude 40.39, longitude 35.11.

Several days later, the weary crew were landed at Gibraltar. At least one, Stan Grandy, had his picture taken while there.

Eventually they were transferred to England and while there, the crew saw the impact the ravages of war had on British soldiers. In England at this time, late May/June 1940, British forces were being evacuated from the beaches of Dunkirk and *Alhambia*'s crew rode the trains with some of the 335,000 young soldiers, battle weary and wounded, just rescued. In time the Newfoundlanders found a passage home and were landed in St. John's.

Captain Evans stayed in Grand Bank for a short time, but found employment on *Edwin T. Douglas* and in September 1940, he signed on the British merchant ship *Claudius Magnus*. A short while after joining this vessel, Evans became the first mate, but died of heart failure while writing his first mate's logbook on December 5, 1942. Evans is buried in Blythe, England. He was survived by his wife and four children: Janet, Thomas, Margaret and John.

Dozens of young British school children knew of Evans although neither he nor they had ever met. It was the custom of British schools to "adopt" or make friends with an Allied ship during the war. The children would write letters, words of encouragement, send memorabilia and small gifts to ships like *Claudius Magnus*. This was their adopted ship and when tragedy struck, they responded. When Evans was buried several British school children attended his funeral.

As for the schooner *James and Stanley*, she completed her journey south without incident, but was wrecked two years later on a rocky point near Pennant Bay, twelve miles southwest of Halifax. Captain Hughie Grandy, mate Gordon Hollett, engineer Russ Thornhill, cook Eli Pardy, and seamen Len Grandy and Bernard Foote, all of Grand Bank, safely escaped the wreck.

South Coast Schooners Sold "Down North"

A considerable number of schooners used on Newfoundland's northeast coast were built in Nova Scotia or on the South Coast. When merchants in Fortune, Burin, Grand Bank, English Harbour West and Harbour Buffett considered their banking vessels too small or too old to endure the North Atlantic's beatings, the schooners were sold to northeast coast fishermen. The ex-bankers served their new owners, who fished closer to shore, well. Between 1920 and 1950 several of the South Coast schooners sold to Bonavista Bay or Trinity Bay were: *Helen Vair, Mac Lake, Passport, Tishy, Catherine B, Ornate, Winnifred Lee, Kitty Clyde, Smuggler, Flora Nickerson, Marion Elizabeth, Marjorie Inkpen, Watersprite, Olive Evans, Saladin, Archie F. Mackenzie, Grace Boehner, Maxwell Corkum, Lillian M. Richards* and *Helene.*

Courtesy of Gerald Loveridge, Twillingate

In the mid-1930s Captain Josh Winsor bought *Winnifred Lee* — a 77-ton banking schooner built in 1916 — from Buffetts of Grand Bank. Winsor fished in her for one year before she was chartered by the government to provide services to the people on the Labrador coast. *Winnifred Lee* exploded and burned in Twillingate harbour on September 5, 1955, and thus passed from our sight a schooner well-known on three fronts — South Coast, Northeast Coast and the Labrador Coast.

One of these came to a particularly tragic end: *Passport,* a 69-ton schooner once owned by Thomas Foote of Grand Bank. Sometime before 1920 Foote sold his seventy-four-foot long schooner to a business in Greenspond.

On December 5, 1921, *Passport* in company with several other schooners including a Carbonear schooner *Pet,* left St. John's laden with winter freight and Christmas supplies. A light southerly wind blew in St. John's, but off Cape St. Francis the wind veered to a strong southeasterly with snow.

Captain Art Osmond's *Pet* made it to Bristol's Hope; *Passport* tried to make Carbonear, but was wrecked at Caplin Cove with a loss of several Greenspond lives: Captain Lewis Bragg who was married with three children; Joseph Stratton, single; Pierce Burry, married; William Peckford, married with one child; Christopher Rogers, married with three children; Thomas Button, married with one child. In addition to these 6 crew, *Passport* carried an unidentified lady passenger.

On the opposite side of the island, the same December storm pushed a schooner belonging to S.J. Young and Brothers of St. Jacques onto the rocks. *Natoma,* Captain Frank Tibbo, was a total wreck at Connaigre Head near Harbour Breton. Unlike the ill-fated *Passport, Natoma*'s crew escaped unscathed.

Often when a veteran South Coast sailor is asked about a schooner he sailed on in the 1930s or 1940s, occasionally the answer is that the schooner had been sold "down north" and he doesn't know what happened to her after that. Down north meant Newfoundland's northeast coast, a geographic area that extended roughly from Trinity Bay to Twillingate. At times a story, however brief or vague, of a ship's loss or fate appears in a family diary, scrapbook, obscure magazine or old newspaper from the northeast coast. *Olivia May*'s wreck is thus recorded.

The wreck of *Olivia May* was written by Captain Carl Barbour in his history of the Barbour family of Newtown, Bonavista Bay. It serves well to illustrate the loss of a South Coast schooner on a rocky coast far from the port where she was built.

Olivia May, a seventy-seven ton schooner built in 1889 at Mahone Bay, Nova Scotia, for Footes business of Grand Bank, was sold around 1920; her registry went to Captain Walter Barbour of Newtown, Bonavista Bay. On November 14, 1923, while returning from St. John's laden with winter food and supplies, *Olivia May* ran into a storm in Conception Bay. Barbour and his crew ran up the bay hoping to anchor in Carbonear. The lights of homes in Crocker's Cove were mistaken for those of Carbonear. Once in behind the headland of Crocker's Cove *Olivia May* was caught there due to head winds and heavy sea.

Barbour ordered the anchor out, but it slipped and the schooner struck the rocks to become a total loss. Whitfield Vincent and his brother Samuel were aboard. Whitfield later related they could hear the planks being broken by the rocks. Before the crew could get the small lifeboat in the water, *Olivia*

Courtesy Jack Keeping

Athena, built in 1908 in Essex. In 1928 a consortium of Fortune businessmen, G.T. Dixon, Arch Elford, Gordon and George "Ki" Noseworthy purchased this 94 net-ton schooner for $2800.00. She was used in bank fishing and then put in the foreign trade.

Athena was sold to Genge Brothers of Flower's Cove on the Great Northern Peninsula. Genge had also owned *Cote Nord*, a tern schooner once operated and sailed by Fortune men. *Cote Nord* was lost at Petty Harbour on June 23, 1932.

As seen in the photo, *Athena*'s sails have been patched considerably. Canvas was torn off during violent Atlantic storms and, since owners often could not afford an entire new sail, they were repaired with pieces. Those sails were functional in moderate weather while going from harbour to harbour, but could be "blown away" during mid-Atlantic gales.

May was slipping under. All Barbour's crew, which hailed from Bonavista Bay, escaped safely.

The next day Whitfield Vincent found his keg of molasses on the beach. One barrel of salt beef and a few vegetables drifted ashore, but the salvage was minimal. The crew reached home thankful for their lives; however their supply of food was gone and they were faced with a long and hungry winter for their families.

Archie F. Mackenzie on the Gerald S. Doyle Bulletin

The radio program *Gerald S. Doyle Bulletin,* a Newfoundland institution that lasted more than thirty years, was first broadcast from St. John's VONF radio in 1932. The daily show, hosted by Gerald S. Doyle, earned the loyalty of rural Newfoundlanders by being a notice board for government statements, news, weather and shipping reports. But most fishermen and wives religiously listened to the bulletin for "messages" — health and birth announcements, deaths, jobs, and goods for sale. The captain of various railway steamers returning from Labrador during the fishing season brought reports of the Labrador fishery which were relayed over VONF. According to the *Evening Telegram* (May 22, 1994) the Bulletin aired more than one million messages in its years of operation.

It was through the Doyle Bulletin in the spring of 1947 that Chesley Forsey of Grand Bank advertised the sale of his ninety-four-foot schooner *Archie F. Mackenzie.* His aging schooner, built in Shelburne, Nova Scotia in 1924, had been employed in the South Coast fishery and in the coasting trade for several years. Now the workhorse was in need of repairs; since Forsey was closing out his involvement in the fishery and in coasting business, he was selling *Archie F.*

Captain Michael Croke of St. Brendan's in Bonavista Bay heard the "For Sale" message for two schooners, *Archie F. Mackenzie* and Kearley's *Audrey Bartlett* of Belleoram, on the Gerald S. Doyle Bulletin and wired to Grand Bank for details. Croke was already familiar with most South Coast schooners that fished the Labrador and traded in St. John's. Although he had not seen Forsey's vessel, Captain Croke knew the capabilities of South Coast banking schooners; if the price was right this was what he wanted. As Captain Croke remembers:

> We (Croke and his father John) wired Grand Bank to say we were interested and needed price and particulars. Forsey wrote a letter back with specific details on the *Archie F. Mackenzie*, dimensions, age, when and where built. His letter said she was for sale, but the engines were in poor condition and would be too expensive for Forsey to replace or repair. But the schooner could be bought without the engine for $6000.
>
> In the next few weeks, letters from Chesley Forsey related the condition of her deck engine and that her sails were practically useless. I agreed that to close the deal we would have to see the *Archie* first and then, if we bought her, to arrange to have her towed to St. John's.

Forsey agreed to pay for half the towage fee. Now all Croke had to do was see the schooner. Forsey wired to say Buffett's *Reo II* would be in St. John's on a certain date and Captain Croke could come to Grand Bank on her. Croke and three other St. Brendan's men — his father, brother Louis, and Joe Mackey — travelled to St. John's by train. There they joined *Reo II*, captained at that time by Heber Keeping, and came to Grand Bank. As Croke recalls:

> At Grand Bank we made the deal, arranged payment and spent 3 days preparing *Archie F. Mackenzie* for her towage to St. John's. We lived aboard the *Archie F.*
>
> *Reo II* was headed for St. John's for freight and would do double duty by towing us. When we left Fortune Bay there was good fresh breeze of northwest wind. We told the crew of *Reo II* to keep a lookout for us in case there was any problem.
>
> When we got halfway to St. John's, off Cape St. Mary's, the tow line burst. This was a hundred fathom wire cable with a chain on the end of it; the tow line had been bucking and plucking and finally the chain burst. We drifted on almost out

of sight of the *Reo* because it took a long time to warp in the tow cable.

Luckily we had a chain aboard we bought in Grand Bank from J.B. Patten's store. While we waited for the *Reo* we got our chain ready and secured it around the windlass and

Courtesy of Capt. Croke

As seen here on the St. John's dry dock, *Archie F. Mackenzie* underwent repairs in 1970. For twenty-seven years she served Captain Croke both in the coasting and in the Labrador fishery.

The year after he sold *Archie F.* Captain Chesley Forsey disappeared with four other Grand Bank crew — George Sam Welsh, Arch Rose, Harvey Keating and Robert Lee — off Cape Race when his vessel *Administratrix* was cut down by a larger ship.

> foremast. When Heber Keeping got her alongside, we got the tow chain aboard and had no more problem after. You see, there were no more plucks and heavy strain because the weight of the chain had more give to it.

About 9 o'clock the next morning both vessels were off Cape Spear. Captain Croke and his crew stayed in St. John's for a week, but found it difficult to locate an engine, either new or second-hand, to fit *Archie F. Mackenzie*. Finally they learned of an agent in Conception Bay who had an engine brought in for Croke's schooner.

Captain Croke fondly recalled one incident that had happened while he was in Grand Bank. While they were repairing *Archie F*'s windlass, several Grand Bank seamen helped out:

> Our newly-bought schooner had a poor fit out for mooring. After we bought a chain from Patten, we set out to fix up the windlass. After we got it working, a piece of rust flicked out and went into Joe Mackey's eye. It was painful and he had no way to get it out.
>
> Skipper Ben Snook was on deck, yarning and helping out where he could. He grabbed Joe, wrapped his two arms around him so as Joe couldn't move. Snook stuck his tongue into Mackey's eye and licked out the piece of rust. It happened so quickly Joe never had a chance to move or blink. I never forgot that and told Skipper Ben about it in later years. He came north (Bonavista Bay) often especially in the *Nina W. Corkum*.

Captain Michael Croke and his brothers used *Archie F. Mackenzie* in the Labrador fishery until 1951 when declining fish prices forced many schooners out of business. After several years in the coasting trade out of St. Brendan's, she was sold to Quebec. Today she's still afloat in Quebec City, engine house removed, bowsprit and topmasts added and is used in the tourist trade.

Chapter 14

Harbour Breton: Feats of Seamanship

HARBOUR BRETON, with its present day population of about 2400, is located around a deep, land locked and ice-free harbour near the southern end of the Connaigre Peninsula which juts out for 10 miles into Fortune Bay's north side. One of the oldest and largest fishing centres on the South Coast, Harbour Breton saw hundreds of her men sailed on the great banking schooners.

Originally called Havre Bertrand, Harbour Breton was first occupied by the Bretons of France whose headquarters were at Plaisance (Placentia). When the English established settlements along the South Coast in the eighteenth and nineteenth century, Harbour Breton became the base of the English fishing fleet. Several English firms — Waldren, Spurrier, Young and Clarke — established themselves at Harbour Breton, but toward the end of the 1790s Newman and Company became the dominant merchant house. Harbour Breton then had one of the highest populations on the South Coast and was a service centre for the head of Fortune Bay.

In his 1776 survey Captain Cook described Harbour Breton as "the principal harbour in Fortune Bay" and wrote that it had "room for a great Number of Mercht. Ships, & many convenient places, for building of stages, landing & drying fish."

In July 1848 Bishop Edward Field, while visiting Harbour Breton on the church ship *Hawk*, wrote: "(I was) refreshing my admirable recollection of this picturesque harbour, so completely land-locked that a stranger could hardly guess the passage to the sea, and surrounded by hills of bold and fantastic outline."

Earliest known permanent settlers of Harbour Breton were Benjamin Chapman (1824), Samuel Hutchings (1835), James

Courtesy of Marine Archives

Harbour Breton plant. Tied up in front of the Fisheries Products fish plant are deep sea draggers *Zaley* (left) and *Zebrula* (right). Some longliner fishing vessels are moored to the right. The plant is built on the old Newman premises. In the centre background is Coady's Store and warehouse, today torn down.

Taylor (1851), Richard Longmead (granted land at Back Arm, 1851), John Strickland, James Stone, George Rideout, James Hunt, James Holley, William Herritt, George Burns, William Tibbo(e) and James Hardy, a storekeeper in 1859. Lovell's *Newfoundland Directory* of 1871 listed J. Molloy, A. Skinner and W.J. Gallop as merchants of Harbour Breton with John Hearn and John Simms as resident traders. In 1851 its population was about three hundred.

Around 1900 Newman and Hunt's Company declined and a succession of Bank fishery based businesses grew. Many men found employment in Nova Scotia or on schooners based in Harbour Breton and other Fortune Bay ports. At the end of the bank fishing era, around 1945, its population numbered nine hundred. One of Newfoundland's first fresh fish freezing plants was built there in the 1950s by B.C. Packers.

During the Newfoundland government's resettlement program of the 1960s, Harbour Breton was designated "a growth centre" absorbing many people from other, now-abandoned communities: Jersey Harbour, Stone Valley, Red Cove, Muddy Hole, Piccaire, Grole, Sagona, Miller's Passage, Little Bay West.

But it was during the years of the schooner fishery that the

Author's collection

Mabel Dorothy, dories nested on deck, stopped in the mouth of Grand Bank harbour as a man from the dory prepares to climb aboard. When this vessel was lost with crew, Thomas Jensen of Harbour Breton was listed among the missing.

When a schooner harboured in Grand Bank with her catch of cod, dory loads of salt bulk fish were taken from the harbour to the eastern side of the brook or past the lighthouse to Trimm's Beach. There it was washed out in fish pounds and then carried to the beaches to dry.

Even the harbour's close confines posed a danger to seamen. James Keeping of Harbour Breton drowned when his overloaded dory sank in Grand Bank harbour as he was carrying salt bulk fish to the pounds. Keeping was married to Maggie (Rose) Keeping of Great Harbour near Harbour Breton.

Keeping's fatal accident in Grand Bank harbour was not the first to happen there: on August 2, 1921, Luke Thornhill and George Patten upset a dory near the harbour and drowned. Several years previously two Grand Bank men, John Francis and John Beavis, disappeared off Grand Bank Cape when their punt, full of fish, apparently capsized.

town saw its greatest tragedies — shipwrecks, banking schooners reported "Lost with Crew"; and frail two-man dories missing in the treacherous Atlantic. One of the most devastating blows occurred in the emerging community in March 1935, when the schooner *Alsatian* disappeared with 25 crewmen.

Alsatian, a ten-dory banker owned by J.B. Patten's firm of Grand Bank, had left Harbour Breton for the Banks on March 3, but failed to report. Several crew hailed from Harbour Breton: Captain Jim Lawrence, aged forty-eight; mate Phil Herritt, forty-three; John Herritt, twenty-two; cook John Perry, thirty-three; John Henry Myles, fifty-eight; Hubert Pardy, thirty; brothers Arthur and Cecil Martin; Sandy Hynes; Steve Mallay. Three Bond brothers, George aged thirty-seven; Josiah, thirty-five; and John, twenty-seven belonged to Great Harbour near Harbour Breton.

Although Harbour Breton did not have an extensive banking schooner fleet, its men were hard working fishermen on vessels from Grand Bank, English Harbour West and Jersey Harbour. On May 24, 1926, Joseph Day and Sam Tibbo of Harbour Breton, two dory men of *Christie and Eleanor*, disappeared on the Grand Banks. They had gone to set trawls and were never seen again. When the coasting schooner *Mabel Dorothy* out of Grand Bank was lost with crew in early November 1955, Thomas Jensen was one of the crew. Appendix D lists several marine accidents which claimed Harbour Breton seamen.

Extraordinary Feat of Harbour Breton Seamanship

John J. Stone of Harbour Breton and his dorymate from Jersey Harbour, Thomas Mullins, experienced what the newspaper *Evening Telegram* of May 16, 1940, called an "extraordinary feat of seamanship." The captain of the schooner who found the two said that, "with the heavy seas running and the high wind, the two men would have been lost in short order if they had lost their head or their nerve."

In mid-May 1940, *Autauga*, a banker owned by Joseph Rose of Jersey Harbour, and commanded by John Rose began fishing on Saturday, May 11, near the Virgin Rocks, about 120 miles from St. John's. The crew caught about a hundred quintals on Saturday. As was the usual custom in bank fishing days, Sunday was a day of rest. No schooner captain would order his men to the dories on Sunday no matter how good the fishing was.

John Stone, aged thirty-nine, and Tommy Mullins, twenty-nine, left *Autauga* about 4:30 am on Monday, May 13, to set their fishing gear. At the time there was light fog but no wind. After they had rowed about a mile from the schooner and set the hook and line trawl, the wind came up.

Fog and wind combined to throw off their calculations and they could not find their schooner. Mullins and Stone rowed around for six or seven hours until about twelve o'clock, trying

Courtesy Parks Canada Poster

The dory is a flat-bottomed boat originally developed for the inshore fishery. Dories were ideal for the bank fishery because they could be stacked one inside the other to save space on the crowded deck of a schooner. They could also carry large loads of fish and were exceptionally seaworthy.

1. stem
2. painter
3. cap rail or gunnel
4. roller cleat
5. thole pins
6. frame
7. riser
8. thwart
9. Bulkheading
10. transom or tombstone

every possible course. With the wind blowing up much harder and no prospect of locating *Autauga*, they set their course for land.

South Coast banking dories were well-equipped: two sets of dory oars; a small mast, spar and a triangular sail called the "goose sail"; a tin of water; a box of hard bread or hard tack as it was called; a dory compass; fish gaffs; trawl tubs; gob stick; gurdy wheel and other fishing gear.

Putting up their small goose sail, the Fortune Bay fishermen kept as close to their course as straight as possible even in the storm of wind which was now raging. Three times during the night their banking dory filled with water. Both men were near exhaustion from bailing and keeping the dory's head to the seas to avoid another swamping.

At 10:30 p.m. a large wave swept over the small dory and the compass disappeared. For one hour they looked for it, for without being able to determine direction on a stormy night, chances of survival were slim. Fortunately the compass had not washed overboard, but was lodged undamaged between the rising and the side of the dory. Soon they were back on course.

Sometime between 10:30 and twelve o'clock, John Stone was washed over the side by a particularly heavy sea, but he was able to grab the side of the boat and haul himself aboard.

About midnight, the gale-force wind broke off the spar and carried away part of the goose sail as well as three of the four oars.

Left with only one oar, Stone and Mullins improvised another from a piece of board with a fish fork handle. They could not hoist their sail because of the broken spar. But courage, skill and ingenuity was a strong trait in these hardy men from Harbour Breton and, undaunted by the lack of proper sailing gear, they cut the large sail in two parts and rigged up the two smaller sections fore and aft on the broken stick.

Tuesday morning at daylight they were still being driven along on course toward land. At 10:30 a.m. they sighted land. Tommy Mullins and John Stone talked over their possible route and speed and guessed they had reached Bay Bulls.

An offshore breeze kept them from making land, so they headed toward Cape Spear. A mile off St. John's harbour they sighted a schooner which turned out to be *James Strong*, Captain Wiseman. Wiseman described how his vessel was sailing under storm sail when someone sighted the dory. It was around 6:00 p.m., as it was getting dark.

When the men in the dory began to wave a single paddle, the captain realized something was amiss and slowed to investigate. In Captain Wiseman's account of the perilous trip of *Autauga*'s men and his sighting of them, he said that:

> They were driving out to sea once again with the wind. It was blowing a gale at the time and with the dory bobbing around like a cork on the heavy seas, it was only with the greatest difficulty that the schooner was manoeuvred so as to get the dory to leeward.
>
> With the heavy seas running and the high wind, the two men would have been lost in short order if they had lost their heads or their nerve.

Stone and Mullins had come 120 miles in heavy seas and

high winds rowing and sailing for thirty-eight hours to reach safety. When they were picked up, what food was in the dory was spoiled by the seas that came in over the craft. In almost two days, they had not touched their can of water as they did not know how long they would be at sea. They would not drink the precious water until absolutely forced to.

A doctor in St. John's examined them and pronounced John Stone and Tommy Mullins none the worst for the trying experience. Both were anxious to get back home or to resume fishing on *Autauga*. To allay the fear of their shipmates, Stone and Mullins broadcast a message over the Doyle news bulletin to their captain, Johnnie Rose aboard *Autauga*, to say that they were safe at St. John's and awaiting his arrival to rejoin their vessel.

Loss of the *Knock*

A historic vessel and a familiar sight to many South Coast towns came to a fiery end on November 23, 1958, when *W.E. Knock* burned about five miles off Cape St. Francis. Her crew hailed from Harbour Breton: Captain Reginald Augot, mate Ronald Rose; chief engineer Martin Parrott; second engineer Hubert Short; cook Ches Rose, sailors George Jim Day and John Joe Hunt.

Built in 1923 in Lunenburg, Nova Scotia, *W.E. Knock*'s long career out of Fortune as Lake and Lake's banker was over and the schooner had been purchased for the coasting trade by St. John's lawyer P. J. Lewis. Captain Augot, the son of a banking captain Michael Augot (see chapter fifteen), had been a fisherman, engineer and captain all his life on such vessels as *Ray M*, *Josephine K* and *Sen Sen*. He had survived one shipwreck when *Autauga* stranded and sank in August 1951.

When a fire broke out in the engine room — the fate of many a Newfoundland schooner — Augot, seeing nothing could be done to extinguish the flames or to reach land, told the crew to abandon ship. After rowing for three hours in twenty to thirty mile an hour winds and snow flurries, they finally reached

Courtesy of John Hackett, Terrenceville

W.E. Knock at Harbour Breton. Rose's general store is at near left. Behind the schooner's mainmast is businessman John B. Stewart's home, today designated a heritage structure. To its right above the white shed is the Anglican school.

Pouch Cove. No one saved any clothes or oil skins except what they stood in.

The people of Pouch Cove were more than generous to the stranded sailors, offering them warm food, shelter. Mr. Parrot brought them to St. John's. While waiting for the steamer *Bar Haven* to reach Argentia where they would connect with her by train, the Harbour Breton men stayed in the Cochrane Hotel for a week. Each man picked up new clothes from the clothing store London, New York and Paris, all paid for by the insurance on the vessel.

Chapter 15

Harbour Mille Sea Disaster

By September 4, 1924, the banker *Lillian M. Richards* had almost finished her final trip for the year. She fished on the western Grand Banks — Quero Bank. A storm came up and Captain Michael (Mik) Augot, of Harbour Breton, had let the schooner lie to under a jumbo and foresail heading to the northwest. Cook Igol Green of Grand Bank, an experienced seaman, confronted the captain saying, "Skipper, I know you're young and new at this, but if were you, I wouldn't jog to the north'rd. I'd jog southern; you'll have the tide more or less going with you than you would jogging this way and it's not so rough."

Captain Augot agreed, but for some reason did not change his ship's position right away. *Richards* had weathered many storms worse than this; in fact, she was well-known to sail and to ride rough water well. Short verses and humorous sayings helped veteran seamen remember their favourite schooners. One skipper, when told *Richards* with full canvas on was driving her head under in a heavy wind storm, replied, "Grumble you may, *Lil*; but go it you must."

By six or seven o'clock, the day's fish catch had been split and put below in salt. After a long day's work, the watch, or helmsman, was reduced to one man taking a half hour watch and being relieved by another throughout the night. Everyone else went below for a well-deserved sleep. Work came early. At 4:00 a.m. Skipper Augot would have his twenty-three dorymen on deck, baiting hooks and preparing trawl tubs for the day's fishing.

In 1915 Patten and Forsey of Grand Bank had purchased *Lillian M. Richards*, an eleven-dory banker built in Lunenburg in 1911. She measured 108 feet long and carried eleven dories. Patten and Forsey had put her under Captain Joe Grandy of Grand Bank with a very capable second hand or mate: Michael "Mik" Augot of Harbour Breton. Then twice in one year, 1924, tragedy struck the schooner.

While fishing on the Grand Banks in May, two or three days' sail from land, Captain Grandy had an attack of appendicitis. Mate Augot took command but before he made port, Grandy's conditioned worsened. Unless he could reach emergency care, death was imminent. But by the time *Lillian Richards* reached Grand Bank and Captain Grandy was carried to Garnish, then overland to Burin, he was in serious condition. He was put on board the S.S. *Home*, the coastal boat crossing Placentia Bay, and then joined the train at Argentia going to St. John's. Grandy died in the hospital on May 18 from a ruptured appendix.

Patten and Forsey gave Augot command of the productive *Lillian Richards* and he did well with his crew of Fortune Bay men. Two crewmen were from Harbour Mille: brothers Sam and Tom Pardy. Tom, aged nineteen, had been married only a month previously to a young lady from Fortune.

Like all towns in Fortune Bay, Harbour Mille depended on the sea for its existence. It is located in a well-protected harbour on the west side of a narrow peninsula of East Bay, at the head of Fortune Bay. At one time the town might have been called Harbour Millay or Millais, probably named for a family name or place name of the Jersey Islands, off the South Coast of England.

Some of the first residents recorded were Jonathan Baker and Thomas Pardy listed as the families of Shelter Point in 1835. George Sunders was a planter there in 1858. Thomas Barnes was the earliest recorded resident of Harbour Mille proper and according to family traditions, he was a native of Dorset, England, and a veteran of the Battle of Waterloo, 1815.

Early settlers of Shelter Point most likely moved to Harbour Mille which would account for its population growth around 1857. Harbour Mille had been reported in the Census of 1836

Grand Bank harbour in the heyday of bankers like *Lillian M. Richards*. By 1915-1920 the harbour had been dredged and could accommodate more schooners wintering over. But there was not enough room for the whole fleet and many captains and owners still preferred to moor schooners in the off-season in spacious sheltered Fortune Bay harbours, like Jersey Harbour and Rencontre East.

According to the traditional family information of Captain Joe Grandy, *Richards* has her white sails up, perhaps tied on near Patten and Forsey's premises well up in the harbour.

and 1845 as Mulier Harbour with six Protestant Episcopalian families numbering thirty-seven people.

But the sea gave Harbour Mille, situated near many fishing grounds, its greatest population boost — the rise of the herring fishery in Fortune Bay brought the numbers up to 152 by 1891. When Archbishop Edward Wix visited the head of Fortune Bay in 1836, he had this to say:

> The thrifty people of this bay endure, perhaps, greater hardships and privations than any in this trying island. They continue catching fish till Christmas and, when the fish generally failing for a season, they avail themselves of this respite, to do their winter's work in making boats.... It is exceedingly deep water in which they fish... I have myself seen the fish as soon as they have been taken out of the water, turn up from the cold and die immediately.

Salmon and lobster fishing berths are situated west from Harbour Mille to Yellow Cove. Good cod fishing grounds were located beyond the shoreline lobster and salmon berths. The herring fishery boom provided employment until the late 1800s and within the next decade lobster factories were profitable. A little mining was carried on; as Lovell says in his *Newfoundland Directory* (1871): "One of the first copper (and silver) mines in the country was worked here but without much success."

In the era of the schooner fishery, 1920-1950, the population stayed around three hundred and fifty and after that era the pattern of employment changed: a few men were engaged in the local inshore and long liner fishery; several found employment in fish processing in Sydney, and later Marystown; in the 1940s and 50s many had seasonal jobs in Argentia, Stephenville and Gander.

Fortune Bay towns like Harbour Mille depended on schooners for employment; yet the sea exacted a great sacrifice of human lives. Older established family names like Barnes, Saunders, Baker and Pardy knew the pangs of sorrow ships like *Lillian M. Richards* brought.

Man Missing

About eight or eight-thirty Sam Pardy had finished his watch and, according to an agreement worked out between them, his brother Tom went up to do his shift. In the relative comfort of the forecastle, Sam joined in with some of men softly singing an old Sanky, or Salvation Army hymn; "On the resurrection morning, Soul and body meet again." A fateful prophecy — for within five minutes a huge wave swept the vessel, not from forward back but from stern to stem. Cold sea water half-filled the cabin putting loose boxes, and boards afloat. Most men jumped out of bunk thinking *Lillian Richards* had struck something and was sinking.

The first reaction was to go on deck to see what had happened or to assess damage. Everything moveable on deck was gone or smashed, including the chainbox, most of the windlass, blubber barrels, trawl tubs, buoys and all other gear. The heavy cable about three hundred fathom long was washed off deck. Of the eleven dories securely lashed down for the wind storm, only the stem of one remained. The mainsail and mainboom were carried away. Nothing remained only a few loose ropes and rigging where the sturdy boom had been a few minutes before.

Before temporary repairs were made, the immediate question was who was on watch? Sam Pardy knew. His brother had relieved him on his watch a few minutes before. Only the doomed man's mitt was found, entangled in a rope near the mainmast. Tom Pardy was nowhere in sight, apparently washed overboard and lost.

There was nothing that could be done: no dories could be put over in the wind storm to search, and within a minute or two he had been carried hundreds of yards behind the schooner. *Richards* could not be turned around without proper rigging and the crew would not know where to search in the vast, dark ocean that had taken a shipmate.

Augot immediately gave orders. The schooner was somehow leaking from the deck. The crew discovered holes where the blubber butts — the 100 gallon puncheons standing on deck and used to hold raw liver — had been. The sea had torn the ring bolts from the decks and water poured through these holes. Junks of wood used for stove fuel in the galley were fitted and driven into the holes to stop the water.

Lillian Richards, her fishing voyage prematurely over, slowly sailed back toward Fortune Bay under foresail and jumbo and wearing a black flag at half mast signifying a man lost. On the way she was met by another schooner which relayed a message of trouble to Grand Bank. Another of Patten and Forsey's schooners came out to meet *Richards* and towed the maimed and disfigured workhorse back to port.

Another veteran fisherman, who was on the schooner at the time, claims that when he and several others rushed on deck to assess the damage, he saw his shipmate, Tom Pardy, a few minutes after the accident several feet from the side of the schooner. From his position he couldn't see who it was, but soon learned that it was the man on watch. Instantly word spread it was Tom. Although it was dark and the whitecaps obscured his view, from the glow of the riding light when *Lillian Richards*

Grand Bank Schooner

DAMAGED IN STORM--SEAMAN WASHED OVERBOARD.

A message received yesterday by the Deputy Minister of Customs from the Sub Collector at Grand Bank that the schr. Lillian M. Richards had arrived there from the Banks with her bulwarks damaged and everything moveable on deck washed away. The vessel was caught in the storm of Thursday last and lost one man overboard. The following is the message received:—"Lillian M. Richards arrived here this morning from the Banks, reports loss of Thomas Pardy, washed overboard, storm Sept. 4th. Dories smashed, bulwarks damaged, everything moveable gone."

According to an *Evening Telegram* clipping, she arrived on September 9th as documented by this all-too-brief report of the tragedy.

rolled down, he was clinging to the wreckage of the main boom. He thought the doomed man signalled or waved before the boom was swept out of sight.

Whatever the circumstances, Mik Augot was faced with the difficult task of reporting the death to Tom Pardy's family or to Grand Bank authorities who in turn notified his family and his young wife at Harbour Mille.

Repaired and refitted, *Richards* fished out of Grand Bank for many more productive years until she was sold to Fishery Products. Captain Hubert Grandy of Garnish took charge of her for several years. For a while in the early forties *Lillian Richards* was under the command of Captain Jacob Thornhill of Grand Bank. By then the schooner had an engine installed. While entering Sydney Harbour in the night she ran over the rope and cable gate protecting the harbour from possible enemy attack. It took several hours to free her. One of her last owners was Stewart Hounsell of Jackson's Arm, White Bay. Several years later a fire consumed *Lillian Richards*.

Sam, the brother of the drowned fisherman, worked on the banking schooners for another twenty years and became a schooner captain around 1940. The schooners he commanded were:

1940	*Mary Michael*
1941-46	*Hattie T. Monks*
1947-48	*Ruby and Nellie*
1951	*Dantzig*
1951-54	*Miss Glenburnie*
1954-59	*Belgrave*
1959-61	*Gladys Wiscombe*
1961-63	*L.A. Dunton*
1963-66	*Harry W. Adams*

He survived two shipwrecks. On April 23, 1948, *Ruby and Nellie* caught fire. Pardy was badly burned fighting the blaze before *Rex Perry,* Captain Gord Evans, rescued the crew. In 1954 *Miss Glenburnie* was cut down in thick fog off Halifax. Pardy and his crew rowed seven hours before another vessel picked them up. He died in 1987.

Chapter 16

A Jersey Harbour Workhorse

Dauntless had been built in the James and Tarr yards in Essex, Massachusetts in 1899. She netted seventy-seven tons, was ninety-one feet long and twenty-four feet wide. While under American registry she fished for halibut and herring, landing her catches in Gloucester. Early in her career she often sailed to Newfoundland's Bay of Islands for cargoes of herring destined for American markets.

In March 1912, *Dauntless* was sold to Samuel Harris' business of Grand Bank; Captain Morgan Handrigan sailed her down and remained skipper for one year. Some years after she went through a number of owners including Felix Tibbo and Tom Murphy, Grand Bank, and Orlando Bungay, Jersey Harbour. In 1935 she had her masts and rigging cut down and an engine installed. By the time she was owned in Jersey Harbour, *Dauntless* was already thirty-three years old, and well-known around the South Coast as a worn but reliable workhorse.

Jersey Harbour, like many Newfoundland outports, has succumbed to resettlement. First known as Jerseyman's Harbour, it is located three kilometres northeast of Harbour Breton in Fortune Bay. Early Europeans arrived in the area around the early 1500s when French, Spanish, Portuguese and English migrator fishermen were attracted by excellent fishing grounds and a well-protected harbour.

Captain James Cook in his 1765 survey noted of Jersey Harbour: "It was safe & commodious & sufficient to contain, a great Number of Ships sheltered from all Winds..." Beginning in the 1780s many English firms, including Nicholle and Company, set up fish exporting businesses, but each in time

Courtesy of Jack Hackett, Terrenceville

Jersey Harbour in the mid-1950s showing the area called the Bottom; the hills behind are the Scrape and Bugger's Hill. Moored in the center is *Mary Pauline* owned by the Hardy's of Jersey Harbour; on the right is the wreck of coastal steamer S.S. *Home*, stranded in Jersey Harbour in October 1952. Anchored to the left is Chesley Boyce's *Jennie Elizabeth*.

On May 2, 1947, one of Chesley Boyce's schooners *Norma and Marilyn*, hit a ledge at St. Shott's. Captain Moulton and his crew landed safely, but the schooner was a total wreck. *Norma and Marilyn*, of seventy-seven-net tons, was powered by a Diesel engine.

declined. In the 1930-40s three remained — Chesley Boyce, Norman Boyce and Joseph Rose — owned and operated by Jersey Harbour residents.

At its highest peak its population reached two hundred and ten. By then principal family names were Boyce, Bungay, Griffin, Hardy, Mayo, Myles, Osmond, Rose, Stoodley, Tibbo and White. Jersey Harbour people have paid the price for their livelihood from the sea. On May 24, 1922, Albert Myles drowned while dory fishing from the schooner *Ornate*, a schooner owned by the Boyce's of Jersey Harbour.

On May 27, 1932, Captain Jim Lawrence of *Coral Spray*, registered to Patten's of Grand Bank, arrived in North Sydney to report the loss of two men of Jersey Harbour: John Hooper, aged twenty-seven and John Bungay, thirty-three, both married. They were shipmates on the schooner *Admiral Dewey* and had been fishing in dense fog off Flat Point in Sydney Bight, Nova Scotia, when their dory became separated from the schooner. They were never seen again. Hooper was born on

Newfoundland's northwest coast, but had married a girl from Jersey Harbour.

Tricks and Trials on *Dauntless*

In 1932, when *Dauntless* was owned by Orlando Bungay of Jersey Harbour, her main work was freighting fish offal from the herring plant at Bay of Islands. In the fall the old workhorse freighted produce from Prince Edward Island to Newfoundland's South Coast.

One particular trip to PEI has been documented. Owner Orlando Bungay who skippered *Dauntless,* had a very capable mate, his nephew Len Bungay. Although only seventeen, Len learned the skills of navigation and before he was twenty he had navigated *Dauntless* across to Oporto with a load of salt dry fish. Other crewmen were: Clayton Moore and Tom Rob Snook of Jersey Harbour; two men from Grand Bank, Waterfield Green and Allen Snook, Captain Ben Snook's brother.

Orlando Bungay had no problem getting a well-experienced crew. Steady work and regular wages in the 1930s, the Depression Years, was hard to come by and wages for a schooner deckhand were $16 a month.

Seaman Waterfield Green remembered that trip for several reasons: an elderly gentleman he met, and the jokes and tricks seamen played on each other while on long voyages. As he recalled:

> One fall the *Dauntless* was up in PEI and we were bringing down potatoes for St. Pierre. We had 30 or 40 sheep on deck, so many pigs and hens. When the time came to leave port, this fellow came down, came aboard and we were talking away to him. He told us he was on a schooner once with a load of produce and got wrecked near Grand Bank harbour. He went by the name of Captain Bushy (probably Boucher). So I said, 'Captain Bushy, what schooner would that be?' and he said, "The *Ariminta.*"

Green recalled the wreck of *Ariminta.* Early in October 1925, *Ariminta* left Prince Edward Island with general cargo and several head of livestock destined for the French Islands of St. Pierre and Miquelon. Although owned in Nova Scotia, she was commanded by Chesley Walters and his mate Chas Grandy, both of Garnish. Before Captain Walters reached the French Islands, a gale of wind pushed his schooner past St. Pierre.

Driven before the storm, Walters had guided *Ariminta* into the familiar waters of Fortune Bay, hoping to escape the ferocity of wind and waves under a lee shore. At daybreak, October 30, 1925, the schooner drifted unrestrained past Fortune in seas so high that when *Ariminta* dipped into the trough only the tops of her mastheads could be seen.

With her mainsail torn to ribbons and foresail stripped, Walters ran his ship under bare poles, with no sail, and attempted anchorage near the mouth of Grand Bank harbour. *Ariminta*'s crew, knowing the ship was lost, attempted to save some of the livestock, if possible. Cows, pigs and sheep were thrown overboard in the hope many would swim to shore and safety. Green recalled his conversation with supercargo Captain Bushy about *Ariminta*'s wreck:

> This Captain Bushy, now on the *Dauntless* and taking a trip to St. Pierre, was the old guy that was aboard *Ariminta*, seven years before. He had been supercargo (owner and manager of a ship's cargo) on the *Ariminta*. Walters was bringing his produce and animals to St. Pierre and came down north of Miquleon Head. When she ran ashore here she was under bare poles. She had no sail. Perhaps he could have run her up into Fortune Bay. Chances are if he got up there all around Little Bay East, there were good harbours and he could have anchored.
>
> After she broke apart near Grand Bank, people picked up potatoes, cabbage and turnip for the next two weeks after, right from Eastern Pier right down to Lance aux Loup. And the cows instead of swimming to shore, swam off to sea. She had 30-40 animals aboard. Many of the cattle drowned, or later drove in the beach.
>
> She was a big schooner, perhaps around 140-150 ton. Her nameboard with A R I M I N T A wrote on it was up on John Hickman Matthews' store and was nailed up there for a long time. Matthews was working for insurance or was the local Wreck Commissioner at the time.

Several Grand Bankers benefitted from the wreck of *Ariminta*, especially Captain John Thornhill who helped remove the planks and salvageable wood from the schooner. With much of *Ariminta*'s timber, Thornhill built a wharf in the southern end of Grand Bank harbour behind the old Co-op store.

Green recalled the tricks played on Captain Bushy and related how some of his livestock went missing during *Dauntless*' long trip to the South Coast:

> On the way down (from PEI) the cook Tom Rob Snook said, "My goodness, what I wouldn't give for a bit of chicken, now when we are having our supper."
>
> The chicken crates were nailed and tied on the cabin house and every now and then the spray would be going over them. You could hear it lashing on the cabin roof.
>
> Clayton Moore and I were on watch together. We had relieved the other watch, Al Snook and Len Bungay. Skipper and cook ware keeping the third watch.
>
> That night Clayton Moore said to me, "Here, you take the wheel. I'm going out on deck." He got back of the cabin house, crouched down and you could hear the hens going cluck, cluck.
>
> When he came back I said, "Clayton, were the hens laying?"
>
> "Ah," he said, "I don't think this one will lay any more." He got them, twisted their necks see.
>
> Next morning someone said to old Captain Bushy, "Captain, couple of hens got drowned last night in their box. There was a awful lot of water, spray going over the schooner."
>
> "Oh well," said Bushy, "you can expect anything in heavy seas with water going over them."
>
> Anyway cook had the two chicken that day and the old fellow sat down with us and had a good feed of chicken.

Clayton Moore, a veteran of the sea, had had his share of misadventures and liked to relate his story of shipwreck of three years previous when Captain George W. Winsor, mate William Penney, Robert Penney, all of Carbonear; Norman Monster and Bert Thornhill of Fortune were his shipmates on *George A. Wood*. Early in December 1929, she made a quick fish-laden voyage to Barbados, loaded 123 puncheons of molasses and set sail for St. John's.

Built in Nova Scotia, this two-masted schooner netted 120 tons. At one time she was skippered by Harry Brushett of Burin.

George A. Wood followed the American seaboard until December 29-30 when Moore and his crew encountered heavy south east winds off Nova Scotia. On the thirtieth, the schooner struck a sandbar off Sable Island about two miles from the island lighthouse. The crew abandoned ship, rowed to the island and after a short wait there, they were taken from Sable Island to Halifax and then carried to St. John's.

Moore also told how he and the crew of *Admiral Dewey* escaped with their lives when a vicious northeast gale pushed *Dewey* and two other schooners onto the beach in St. Pierre harbour on September 10, 1932. Captain Thomas Hardy, Moore and three other men, all Jersey Harbour residents, with the help of rescuers on shore rigged a line from the mast to the beach and each man shimmied to safety. The Hardy business had purchased the 111-gross ton *Admiral Dewey* from Forward & Tibbo of Grand Bank.

Such were the stories of wreck and rescue told on sea voyages when the wind whistled through the rigging, but the forecastle and after cabin provided a refuge from the gales.

S. (Sydney) T. (Thomas) Jones' business at Little Bay Islands bought *Dauntless* in 1938 and used her for fifteen years in the coasting trade. Jones sold her to Mercer and Green in Clarenville; eventually after other registry changes South East Fisheries, Harbour Grace acquired her. In 1957 *Dauntless,* a well-remembered schooner which had laboured long and hard under several skippers, was finally hauled up on a beach near Harbour Grace to die.

Her bones today lie in the Conception Bay bottom silt; perhaps an unfitting end to a schooner which had often fished the productive banks, plied the overseas routes to Europe, sniffed many harbours large and small along America's east coast while in the coasting trade and had often anchored in ports like Boston, Gloucester, Sydney, Halifax, St. Pierre, Grand Bank and Jersey Harbour.

Chapter 17

Rencontre East's Safe Anchorage

BECAUSE HARBOURS like Grand Bank and Fortune had limited space and were exposed to northerly winter winds, schooners like *Dauntless* were often moored for the winter in sheltered inlets on the western side of Fortune Bay: Jersey Harbour and Rencontre East. For example, in the fall of 1938 Captain Will Thornhill of *Eva U. Colp* and Captain Reuben Thornhill, *Nina W. Corkum* sailed into the head of Fortune Bay dropping off dory fishermen. The men, with their winter supply of food, if they had any after settling up, were returning to their homes in Bay L'Argent, Little Bay East, Little Harbour East, English Harbour East, Grand Le Pierre, Bay de L'Eau, Anderson's Cove, Femme and Stone's Cove. After making the last stop at Rencontre East, where both schooners were then moored for the winter. The Grand Bank seamen returned home via J.B. Patten's schooner, *Florence,* with a temporary crew of Gerald Patten, the son of J.B. Patten; John Douglas; Don Baker and Joseph Price.

Today Rencontre East is an isolated community of a little over two hundred people. According to local sources, French fishermen who fished there so named the harbour as a gathering place for ships sheltered from wind and American privateers. Although fishing was the mainstay, at one time a molybdenum mine operated at Rencontre Lake and in later years a freezing unit for fish was located on Rencontre Island.

At the turn of the century, as the South Coast bank fishery fleet grew, the number of schooners winter anchoring at Rencontre increased. The herring fishery stimulated the economy between 1890-1920 and Rencontre East inshore herring seiners did well.

One of the first official accounts of the town's prominence in supplying herring bait was contained in the Newfoundland Fisheries Report of 1903. Inspector Donnelly, who travelled by S.S. *Fiona* enforcing the Bait Act enacted in 1886-87, touched in at various ports in Placentia Bay and Fortune Bay in April 1903.

At St. Jacques, Inspector Donnelly found a large number of vessels including local schooners and American bankers baiting for halibut. He reported Rencontre East as a busy harbour and that:

> ...all the way along the ports were full of vessels. At Rencontre East there were seventeen, some loaded, others not. The vessels included: *Nightingale, Maritime Electra, Olive, Orient* and *Clyde* of Burin; *Blanche M. Rose* of Harbour Breton; from Grand Bank *Orion, Occident, Passport, Chester (Harris), Sentinel, Cora, Mary F. Harris* and *Pleidias.*
>
> All the vessels baiting at Rencontre East paid $13 a dory load for their herring. Well over a hundred loads were taken for a sum of over $1500. The Hartigan brothers of Rencontre

Courtesy Marine Archives, Memorial University

Rencontre East. With such a long and rich history of the sea, Rencontre East resisted the government's resettlement programs of the 1960s. People held on to their roots and today, with services provided by Marine Atlantic, bi-weekly medical visits and a good school, the harbour is still a busy place although the size, style and function of its fishing craft have changed.

baited two American vessels at eight dory loads apiece for $12 a load.

When South Coast schooners went to Rencontre to be moored for the winter, captains ordered out the big bow anchor to hold the vessels into the prevailing winter wind and the stern lines would be tied ashore. This would keep them in one position. The vessels were cleaned, usually by local women, and during the winter were looked after by one man.

With so many craft, large and small, moving in and out of the harbour, stories of their mishaps abound. In Rencontre East, up in Rencontre Brook, where many boats moored, there was one home built out over the water, as indeed were many houses in an earlier era. In the winter of 1922, when Captain John Thornhill of Grand Bank was manoeuvring *Vera P. Thornhill* close to shore to get her situated for winter mooring, her bowsprit went in through the kitchen window on the side of the house.

Luckily there were no injuries. The woman of the home, while knitting in her kitchen, was rocking the baby in the cradle with her foot. *Vera P. Thornhill*'s bowsprit went over the top of the kitchen stove.

Her daughter, who planned to go up the coast on the steamer, had her money for a ticket laid on the window ledge. The money disappeared in the shambles of the house. John Thornhill's cook, Igol Green, rushed on deck and had a good laugh over Captain John's embarrassment. The skipper reluctantly repaid her money.

Grand Bank and Rencontre East seamen had a verse about *Vera P. Thornhill:*

'First come in was the *Vera P*
Second come in was the *Dazzle*
Third come in was the *Winnifred Lee*
And now comes Harry Thornhill'

Chapter 18

Marystown Coasting Vessels

IN EARLY DECEMBER 1964, schooner *J.W. Wiscombe* left Marystown for North Sydney to load coal and general produce. Midwinter weather was typically rough along the South Coast. To get out of the bad weather *Wiscombe*'s skipper, Captain Bernard Whiffen of Rushoon, went up along the southwest coast, hugging the shoreline, but was forced to harbour at LaPoile. Three times *J.W. Wiscombe* attempted to leave Lapoile, but storm conditions forced her to return.

Finally on the fourth attempt the old schooner made it across to Sydney, but the pounding opened old seams. *Wiscombe* had quite a wait to load coal, but she was leaking so badly Captain Whiffen enquired around for time on dock. With no docking time available at the Halifax, LaHave or Sydney facilities, he eventually hired a diver to go down to assess the bottom and to do any necessary repairs.

The diver caulked *J.W. Wiscombe* under the waterline, patched her seams and tightened the schooner somewhat. Built in Monroe, Trinity Bay in 1938 and christened *Trinity North,* she netted seventy-three tons and was eighty-two point nine feet long and twenty-one feet wide.

On January 6, Old Christmas Day, Whiffen and his crew — his brother Patrick Whiffen, engineer; Arch Moore, mate; and James Norman, all Rushoon seamen; the cook James Mallay, hailed from Marystown — left North Sydney for Marystown. The vessel's holds were full of coal. General produce, cases of oranges, apples and other fruit were stacked in every available space in the forecastle and cabin.

Due to high winds, Whiffen again followed the coast and, as

he neared the French islands, kept well inside Langlade Reach. The schooner was leaking badly, but home port, Marystown, was only a few hours away. Hopefully, manning the pumps would get *J.W. Wiscombe* to port and later to dock in Burin. Captain Whiffen recalled:

> I had been up all night because we were pumping and everything. When I got coming along Miquelon, I went down to get in bunk. When I put my feet out in the bunk, I put them out in the water. I got my feet wet.
>
> I went back on deck and I said, "Now boys, there's Green

Courtesy of Marine Archives

J.W. Wiscombe, with potential salvors tying up alongside and a few men on her deck, was doomed. Part of her cargo fell into the sea; but much coal and cases of fruit became winter supplies for several families all along the shore: Point May, Lories, Wreck Cove, Point Crewe, Lamaline and as far down as Lord's Cove.

Wiscombe's wreckage was visible up into the seventies with her weather-scrubbed nameplate attached. Her sunken stern washed into a small cove near the wreck site; today nothing but a few iron bolts mark the spot.

> Island Light. Don't change the course until you get out there off the light and then call me."
>
> So I went down and I got in my brother's bunk and lay down. I wasn't in there any more than a hour when I heard her thump on the bottom.

In a confusion over the location of lights, course was changed. The light on Miquelon was thought to be Green Island light and the vessel ploughed into an underwater rock locally called Bank Boat, near Point Crewe Head.

James Norman was the first to report the accident. He jumped down the gangway and told Captain Whiffen, "Skipper we're after losing the schooner." When the captain arrived on deck a minute later, *J.W. Wiscombe* was in on her side, firmly wedged between two ledges of rock.

It was about 4:00 a.m. on January 7, when the five men threw the dory over the side and rowed ashore abandoning the stranded *J.W. Wiscombe*. Not knowing how far they had to walk nor how long, they carried oranges and other items of food from the schooner's galley with them. According to Captain Whiffen:

> We hauled the dory up on the beach and we walked. The first house we came to was (Joe) Stacey in Point May. I knocked on the door and someone put their head out through the window and asked us what we wanted. I told them we were shipwrecked. It wasn't long before they were down. So the missus that belonged to the house and her husband came down and got us hot tea and something to eat. And then I got to phone Wiscombes.

By the next morning *J.W. Wiscombe*'s crew went back to where their vessel was stranded. Within two days, she broke in two pieces. The old planking and wood from the stern stayed on the rock or sank and the new wood drifted ashore.

By that time, the crew of the wrecked schooner had arrived in Marystown.

Situated on the eastern side of the Burin Peninsula, Marystown is the commercial hub for much of the Burin Peninsula. Early settlers were attracted to the deep, protected Mortier Bay and its proximity to the prolific Placentia Bay fishing grounds. The narrow land-locked harbours of Mooring Cove, Mortier Bay, Little Bay, Creston North and Creston South — once considered separate communities, but today part of Marystown — provided excellent shelter for small fishing craft and coasting schooners.

In the 1960s at least two local firms, Murleys and Wiscombes, were engaged in the coasting trade sending schooners to the mainland for produce. Each owned several vessels which in time were lost or stranded on Newfoundland's rocky shores. *J.T. Murley*, a small 64-ton schooner, brought general cargo from Nova Scotia to Murley's Marystown business. Built in 1948 at Marystown by shipwright George Brown, she was 93.3 foot long and 23.6 feet wide.

In mid-October 1958 *Murley* grounded at Savoyard, St. Pierre. Three men — Captain Charles Butler of Port Elizabeth; William Power, Marystown; and Roy Reid, Baine Harbour — lost their lives; Charles Hodder, Wesley Harding of Creston and wreck in *J.T. Murley*'s small dory.

Marystown, according to local knowledge, is thought to have been settled in the early 1800s when an Englishman, Joseph Cleal, put down roots in Creston South. He was followed by families of Farewell, Mayo and Wiscombe. By 1890, fish merchants Joseph Baker, Michael Flynn and Hugh Reddy were involved in the bank fishery. These men persuaded the government to open a telegraph office in 1908, which further established the town's status as a mercantile centre.

By 1907 both G & A Buffett business and Samuel Harris of Grand Bank operated schooners and fish exporting businesses in Marystown; Harris' known as the Marystown Trading Company with its premises in nearby Little Bay.

In 1907 a major schooner disaster, the first of its kind for the small community, hit Marystown. *Orion*, a banking schooner owned by Buffetts but operated out of its Marystown branch, disappeared while on a voyage from Labrador to Marystown. From debris found later, it was concluded the schooner was wrecked on October 7 in the Strait of Belle Isle. The men were from Mortier Bay, a smaller town near Marystown: Michael Power, married with six children; Thomas Roff, married, five children; George Spencer, married, two children; John Spencer, George's brother, married with six children; William Drake, married, two children; Samuel Murley, married, three children; Michael Farrell, married, no children and four single men, William R. Hodder, Thomas and Michael Ducey, and Michael Kelly. Twenty-four children were orphaned.

It was not to be the last marine hardship the emerging town had to face. During a great storm on August 24-25, 1935, two fishing schooners based in Marystown were claimed by the angry seas: *Annie Anita*, skippered by Patrick Walsh and *Mary Bernice*, under the command of Walsh's son, James. A day after the storm abated, the wreck of *Annie Anita* drifted in at Hazel Cove near St. Shott's. Two bodies — twelve-year-old Frank Walsh, who with his brother Jerome had gone with his father for a trip, and Thomas Reid — were found on the derelict. The others, Captain Walsh, Dominic Walsh, John Brinton, Charles Hanrahan, George Mitchell and the captain's fourteen-year-old son Jerome were never found. *Mary Bernice* was a smaller vessel and carried six men: Captain James Walsh, Billy Reid, Dick Hanrahan, Michael Farrell, all of Marystown and Dennis Long, Fox Cove, P.B.

After the end of World War One when fish prices declined, Buffetts phased out and the Marystown Trading Company went bankrupt. With the collapse of world fish markets Marystown's sole dependence on the bank fishery declined. However, ship building had had some prominence there throughout the 1800s. *E.G. Reddy*, a seventy-two foot-long, sixty-ton banker was built in 1911 by Thomas Palfrey and later sold to the Kemp Brothers of Placentia. Hugh Reddy built banking schooners in Marystown and in the post war boom five tern schooners were constructed at Stapleton's Point:

Schooner	Net Tonnage	Length	Year Built
General Byng	196	113.1′	1918
Jean & Mary	194	114.5′	1918
Violet Buffett	174	108.6′	1919
General Rawlinson	140	106.9′	1920
Ria	154	100.7′	1920

In 1941, on the site where the Marystown shipyard now stands, four warships were built — *Merasheen, Jude, Maricot* and *Oderin* — each were magnetic mine sweepers and each vessel bore the name of a Placentia Bay island.

At eighty-three tons net, *Meracheen* was launched in late 1941 and then delivered to Hull, England; the crew who carried her across the sub-infested Atlantic were: Captain Harry Thomasen, first mate Lawson Fox, second mate Charlie Thomas, cook Luke Rogers, Gabriel Vincent of Grand Bank; chief engineer Fred Blackmore, Catalina; Raymond Morgan, Grand Falls; John Moulton, Richard Gosling and another Gosling of Burin.

In 1949 the provincial government established a centre for the building of longliners on a shipbuilding area known in Marystown as The Beach. That same year shipwright Thomas J. Hodder built the largest wooden fishing schooner ever to be constructed on the Atlantic seaboard, *Alberto Wareham,* at 243 gross tons and 134 feet in length. Throughout the 1960s, the community went through a development stage when a fish plant and shipbuilding/repair facility were built on Marystown's north side.

Today Marystown's population hovers around 7000. With a population absorbed from many Placentia Bay and Fortune Bay towns, the historic town recalls its roots based in the fishing and shipbuilding industry.

By 1960 banking schooners were all but obsolete in towns like Marystown, Grand Bank, Burin and Burgeo. Many bankers had been converted to coasting schooners, but their days were numbered. With the completion of the TransCanada Highway across Newfoundland and improvements to the Burin Penin-

Courtesy Jack Keeping

The rocky shoreline of St. Pierre claims another vessel bringing food and supplies from Canada to Newfoundland. *Isabel H*, an ex-rum running vessel, ran aground on May 5, 1955. Captain Bill Norman of Catalina and his crew escaped without incident but the ship was wrecked.

sula highway, the trucking industry supplanted the coasting schooner.

Aging vessels seldom underwent the necessary repairs to keep them fit for rigorous winter runs to mainland Canada. Those schooners lost were not replaced. *Lucy Melinda*, owned by John Power of Little Bay, plied the coasting trade routes until she ran aground in St. Pierre harbour in 1955. Captain Gus Power stopped at St. Pierre but when the schooner stranded off Pointe aux Canon, he abandoned ship. Successfully refloated by St. Pierre salvers, *Lucy Melinda* continued coasting under the French flag for a number of years.

Gladys Wiscombe Crossing the Angry Seas

The year previous to his ordeal in *J.W. Wiscombe* Captain Bernard Whiffen of Rushoon commanded another of Marystown's schooners, *Gladys Wiscombe*.

Built at Argentia in 1935, fifty-four-ton *Gladys Wiscombe* once carried the name *John Theresa Smith*. In 1947 she ran ashore on the Brandy Rocks off Burin and was refloated. In 1959, after she was purchased by J.W. Wiscombe's business, *Gladys Wiscombe* was rebuilt in the Marystown shipyard.

On Wednesday, December 20, 1963, she left Sydney in company with *Invasion* and three other South Coast schooners. Heavily laden with coal and buffeted by a gale *Gladys Wiscombe* made slow headway. Captain Whiffen had with him a veteran, hardworking crew from the Marystown area: engineer Thomas Walsh, Little Bay; cook Melvin Mayo and Mackey Brinston, Creston and Charles Cleal, Marystown.

In the Gulf seas and winds increased. Off Newfoundland's South Coast her engine died when seawater, rolling over her deck and seeping down into the engine room, contaminated the fuel. The engine stopped running three times and each time the engineer fired it up. Twenty-five miles from Cape Coupe, off St. Pierre, the engine stopped again, for the last time.

Captain Whiffen ordered the foresail put out. *Wiscombe* hove to and that night, Thursday, about 3:00 a.m. a sea swept her deck. The foresail blew away and one of the water butts washed off the deck. More seriously, the dory which was lashed across one of the hatches, beat up. This deprived the five crew of any chance of self-rescue in case they had to abandon ship. Captain Whiffen recalled:

> We drove then broadside to the wind because we couldn't get the engine going. After this sea took her and beat up the dory and she went on a list, a twenty-five degree list where the coal shifted in the hold.
>
> *Gladys Wiscombe* had two Kelvins in her and I had gas to start the engine figuring if we could get it going we could keep her head to the gale. The foresail was gone, tore up in bits. We went down below. There were two batteries to start her engine and in the storm they were broken up. Now we had nothing to start her with.
>
> So we got two batteries together. The two-gallon can which had gas for priming the engine was upset when she listed out. We used a can of lighter fluid which I had below my bunk. The engine turned over four or five times, but refused to catch.

Gladys Wiscombe drove broadside until Sunday morning. Each man thought the schooner with a heavy list would roll over at any time. Although the crew were of different religious faiths, according to Captain Whiffen, each man appealed to his inner spiritual belief in the darkest hours:

> Tom Walsh got up with the crucifix to the porthole in the wheelhouse. He got up there and that's where he spent the night crossing the seas with the crucifix. Somewhere in the night Brinston said to me, "What about having a few prayers, skipper."
>
> "Well boy," I said, "I don't know your prayers, but if you want to listen to mine, we'll have the prayers."
>
> But whatever happened we never had any. I suppose we must have been working so hard to keep afloat. In the way it was going every fellow was saying his own.
>
> We survived that night and the next day I asked to Charlie Cleal to have a good look around. There's something going to be looking for us this morning because we are overdue.

Whiffen was right. The schooner had been reported missing and sometime that day, Sunday, three days after they should have arrived in Marystown, a search plane passed over. All five crew were out on deck, but the low-flying plane reported only four men. By this time *Gladys Wiscombe* had drifted off Cape St. Mary's.

To loved ones and relatives waiting in Rushoon, Creston and Marystown, anxious moments grew more tense. During the 40 hours *Gladys Wiscombe* was missing, families feared for the life of Captain Whiffen and his crew. Although it was two days before Christmas Eve, no one in Rushoon celebrated the festive season or decorated the Christmas tree. On December 24, the news came through to Rushoon the schooner was sighted, but only four crew were accounted for.

Sometime Sunday evening a steamer, using the co-ordinates given by the search plane, approached the beleaguered *Gladys Wiscombe* offering a tow to Trepassey. Knowing through his ship-to-shore radio, which was receiving signals but not transmitting, that dragger *Zinnia* from Burin was on the way,

Whiffen declined the tow to Trepassey. Just before dark, Captain Curt Mitchell manoeuvred *Zinnia* into position, attached a cable and towed the wallowing schooner into Burin. Relatives anxiously waiting news on *Gladys Wiscombe* breathed a sign of relief when all crew were reported safe and well.

During the height of the gale, Whiffen had a close call when he went out on deck to secure the hatch covers. He remembered:

> She was pretty low in the water. I was stood up in the wheelhouse and the water coming over the deck filled my rubber pants three times. When I looked out the dory was broken up and the battings (wooden cleats) were going off the hatches. I had a rope there so I tied it around me and cook Melvin Mayo took the turn of the rope around the exhaust pipe from the engines. They weren't hot on account of the engines not going.
>
> When I got to the hatches, I tore some boards off the dory where she was beat up. I had three inch nails with me and nailed boards on the battings. Just as I had the last nail drove, away I went. A sea took me and put me overboard. I grabbed the lanyards. Mayo was hauling on the rope. Only for that I suppose...I says that's what saved me that time, Mayo. He was holding the rope and keeping it tight. I climbed in over the rail and got in the cabin again.

Gladys Wiscombe arrived home Christmas Eve. In each home town Christmas was more special for five men delivered from the furious seas off the South Coast.

Later in her career, *Gladys Wiscombe,* one of the last schooners out of Marystown, was destroyed by fire off St. Pierre, July 15, 1970.

Another of Wiscombe's schooners, *Mary Wiscombe,* went ashore two miles east of Cape Coupe while sailing from Fortune to North Sydney. Wrecked on December 26, 1962, with the loss of three lives were Charles Scott, Albert Hillier and George Brushett. Captain William Farewell of Little Bay and Thomas Walsh, who had gone through four days of hardship on *Gladys Wiscombe* four years previously, survived.

Marystown has changed considerably since the early 60s.

There is no indication in the many smaller harbours that at one time they sent many schooners to the Placentia Bay fishing grounds, the Cape Shore, and the Grand Banks. The old wooden slipways on Stapleton's Point that produced the little vessels have been replaced by the ultra-modern shipyard. While schooners like *J.T. Murley* may never again be stranded on rocky shores far from home, a little over a generation ago seamen on coasting vessels and the people of Mortier Bay paid their forfeit to the demanding sea.

Chapter 19

Schooners of Little Bay, Placentia Bay

TODAY LITTLE BAY IS PART OF MARYSTOWN, but in the years of the bank fishery it was a separate community. Basque and French fished there in the sixteenth century; English settlers appeared in the early 1800s.

Little Bay's first families were Dober, Hanrahan and Kilfoy. In the Newfoundland *Census* of 1836, Little Bay had fifty-four inhabitants; all engaged in the fishery. Samuel Harris of Grand Bank had established a branch business, the Marystown Trading Company, in Little Bay around 1908 and several of his schooners operated from that port.

On May 23, 1910, the men of Little Bay employed on Harris' banker *Ruby* were wrecked on Nova Scotia's shores. *Ruby,* captained by Josiah Hiscock of Grand Bank, had been fishing on Quero Bank and ran out of bait. While attempting to enter Louisbourg harbour, the 71-ton banker ran ashore on Fourshu Point, near Louisbourg, Nova Scotia. Her cargo of nine hundred quintals of fish was not insured, but the vessel itself, worth $4000, was covered by the Grand Bank Mutual Insurance Company.

Paddy Dober of Little Bay was one of the crew and his younger brother Jim was in dory with him. Jim was not ready when the dory was hove off after *Ruby* struck the rocks. Someone must have grabbed him and thrown him aboard the dory, injuring his knee. Hiscock, the Dobers and the remaining crew reached Louisbourg safely, but Harris' schooner broke up on Nova Scotian shores.

After the loss of one banker Dober found employment on another — *Garfield,* owned by the Marystown Trading Company. In 1923 when Harris closed out his Marystown branch, he sold several schooners, including the seventy-five-ton *Garfield*.

Dober had some money put away to buy a schooner for he had the felt the urge to become an independent vessel owner and he knew Harris' business was declining. Harris wanted $6000 for his eight-dory banker, but Dober intended to pay no more than $4500.

In July of 1923, when Dober arrived in port with a trip of fish, news came that Harris had gotten word from the bank that his business had gone bankrupt. The branch manager at Little Bay called Paddy in and asked if he still wanted the *Garfield*. The asking price was $6000, but at that time Harris was in no position to haggle and Dober settled the deal at $4000.

Dober finished up the season's fishing voyage, but the bottom had dropped out of the salt fish market and *Garfield* was mainly used in the coasting trade. Like all schooners plying the treacherous ocean highways, *Garfield* had several narrow escapes. Appendix E tells the story in song of one incident.

Dober used *Garfield* for around a decade, both at fishing and in the coasting trade in the fall to spring. Eventually Captain Dober sold her to a business near Bras d'Or Lake, Nova Scotia.

Another familiar Little Bay schooner was the *Saval* which was later sold to Bairds of St. John's who had a branch business in Baldwin's Cove, near Marystown and the vessel fished out of there. In the fall when the fishing season was over, *Saval* was engaged until March in the coasting trade — produce from Murray's Harbour, PEI, to Marystown and other Placentia Bay ports; coal from Sydney, Nova Scotia, to the South Coast.

In the late 1940s her crew was: Captain Martin Hanrahan, his brother Michael and two other deckhands from Little Bay; and three Grand Bank crew: Fred Green, engineer; his son George, second engineer; and Caleb 'Kip' Penwell.

After *Saval* was sold to Hollett's business of Burin, the engine was taken out by Fred Green and John Dolimount and replaced with another. The old engine was rebuilt, perhaps to be installed in another vessel, but for years it lay idle in Buffett's old store on the Grand Bank waterfront.

Courtesy of George Green, Grand Bank

First owned by a partnership of Captain Tom Harris and J.B.Foote's of Grand Bank, *Saval* (above) was an auxiliary/sail banking schooner built in Head of Bay d'Espoir in 1944 by master builder Morgan Roberts. She was eighty-five net tons when built and measured ninety-nine feet long and twenty-four feet wide.

One of her last owners was Lewisporte Wholesalers who painted *Saval* white and built a large cabin house on her deck, possibly to carry supplies along the northeast coast and Labrador.

Saval was high on the bow, but could steam along well at nine knots; when necessary the sail would be raised. Switching from engine to sail was a great asset when putting out from St. Pierre while en route to PEI. When vessels like *Saval* illegally carrying St. Pierre goods to ports in PEI, encountered *Shulamite* and *Marvita,* two government cutters anxious to apprehend smugglers, the latter two would be left behind in the fog when *Saval* shut off its engine to sail away, unseen and unheard.

Saval had a close encounter with disaster while leaving a Nova Scotian port. On his wireless radio, Hanrahan called Captain Ben Snook on M.V. *Icehunter* asking about the weather in the Gulf. In those years, around 1946, Captain Snook carried a Grand Bank crew: mate Isaac Thornhill; bosun John Moulton; second engineer Waterfield Green; seamen Frank Snook and Percy Trimm. George Pomeroy of Brigus was first engineer. *Icehunter,* owned by Steers and operated out of St. John's, travelled the coasting/Gulf run bringing supplies from the mainland to Newfoundland. In the winter months *Icehunter* went to the ice in search of seals.

Snook, a veteran skipper and well-experienced in any weather the Gulf could throw at him, replied to say it would be a fine time down to Newfoundland. When *Saval* was out, a sudden storm overwhelmed the schooner and gave the crew some anxious hours.

On September 28, 1974, *Saval* grounded off Caribou Island, Labrador, to total loss.

Chapter 20

Ramea: Three Disasters

THE LAST PEOPLE to see the Ramea schooner John Cabot were some residents of Burnt Islands, sixty miles or so west of Ramea. From the vantage of a high hill they observed a ship, presumably the missing schooner, standing off from the land. A November snow squall lasting for about an hour engulfed the craft and she was lost from view — forever.

Built in Ship Cove, Ramea, four years previously the twenty-two-ton *John Cabot* left her home port on Thursday, October 17, 1901. On board were three Ramea men: Captain (and part owner) George Drew, married with five children; his brother-in-law James Vatcher, married with one child; and George Drew's father, Henry. The crew were to sail for Sydney to load coal for John Penny & Sons of Ramea.

Early morning on the nineteenth, the weather looked threatening and *John Cabot* put into Rose Blanche. There Reverend Doctor Camelius O'Regan, the Roman Catholic priest, joined the schooner. Rev. O'Regan intended to visit parishioners along the coast.

When the storm abated on Monday *John Cabot* left Rose Blanche for Channel, about seventeen miles away. At 4:30 the same evening, several fishermen of Burnt Islands, six miles from Channel, saw the schooner standing off from the land between Black Rock and Gull Rock. The wind at the time was not heavy. Perhaps a sudden and intense snowstorm upset the schooner, but that could not be proven. When the storm cleared the vessel was nowhere to be seen.

Several veteran mariners in Ramea were inclined to believe the schooner was run down by some passing steamer; others

RAMEA NEWS

Full Details of "Cabot" Disaster—The New Light-House—Shipping Fish to Market, &c.

HAVING observed the varied, and in some respects, misleading accounts that have appeared in the press respecting the marine tragedy that recently occurred on this part of the coast, will you permit me, through the columns of your widely-circulated paper, to give the full details of the sad occurrence, as far as they can be known?

In its November 15, 1901 edition, this is how the *Evening Telegram* reported the loss of Ramea's *John Cabot.*

thought the freak storm upset *John Cabot*. She carried a good dory lashed to the deck. If the schooner was thrown on her beam ends in a gale there would not have been time to free it. No bodies nor wreckage was ever found.

O'Regan's, a farming community on the north side of the Grand Codroy River and once named Backlands, is named after the unfortunate priest who disappeared on a Ramea schooner.

Today Ramea is a community of over twelve hundred people situated on the shores of Ship Cove, on the southeast side of Northwest Island, one island of a group. Other islands which once had viable communities — Big Island, Southwest Island, Harbour Island and Fox Island — are now uninhabited.

Ramea's name may be an anglicized version of *rameau* (branches), referring the area's many waterways and arms of the sea. The islands were known to Europeans as early as the 1500s — Portuguese fishermen called them Ilos Santa Anna. The first English families were Keeping and Moore, with Kendall, Payne, Giles, McDonald, Marsh, Eavis and Hatcher coming later.

Penny & Sons, established in 1874 by John and George Penny became the dominant business in Ramea. In time Pennys acquired a fleet of schooners to be employed in the bank fishery. Around the turn of the century several schooners were built at Ship Cove: *John Cabot, Maris Stella, Izette, Rattler, Shamrock, Little Jewel, Vignette, Venus* and *Maple. John Cabot* became the first shipping tragedy of Ramea, but not the last.

Courtesy of Marine Archives, Memorial University

Rameaux II, a wooden dragger owned by John Penny & Sons, aground. Later in her career, when she burst into flames off Gloucester, Massachusetts, on March 30, 1962, her eight Ramea crewmembers were forced to abandon ship. Under the command on Henry Tibbo, she had left the Ramea fish plant several days previous laden with frozen cod fillets. A United States coast guard vessel came by and rescued her crew; Samuel Fiander of Ramea, age 52, was treated for burns.

Faustina and *Annie Young*: Two Disasters

In the 1920s Ramea, like most South Coast ports, built up a fleet of foreign-going schooners including *Minnie J. Smith; A. G. Isnor; Edith M. Cavell; Allan F. Rose* and *Faustina*. The latter tern schooner was shipwrecked twice: while en route from Ramea to St. Anthony, *Faustina* was found floating bottom up south of Cape Spear. Although the wreck was towed ashore, refloated and refitted, her Ramea crew — Captain Jesse Sibley; Isaac Payne; John Joe Chambers; James Porter; Harry Warren and Ambrose Morris — was never seen again. *Faustina* continued to ply the foreign trade until 1930 when she was abandoned at sea, this time all crew were rescued.

In the 1930s Penny's business entered into the Labrador fall fishery when the firm purchased three schooners: *Mary F. Hyde* from Grand Bank; *Annie Young* and *Frank M. Young*, both built in Grey River by Frank Young. The latter schooner lasted six years when a fall gale wrecked *Frank M. Young* on September 30, 1936.

Annie Young had a more tragic ending. During an August 1935 gale, while bound for the Labrador grounds, she disappeared with all her crew.

George Hayman was skipper and he carried seven men: cook Bennie Hayman and six men for *Annie Young*'s three dories, John McDonald, John Warren, John Marks and three men named Coley from Fox Island near Ramea. On August 24, *Annie Young* and another vessel *Man Alone* travelled near each other about fifteen miles off Newfoundland's west coast. During frequent storms the relatively shallow waters of the Gulf of St. Lawrence build up mountainous seas. Small schooners caught in its roiling seas need sheltered harbours; but there was no haven for the twenty-two-ton *Annie Young*.

When the sudden gale flew in their faces in the evening, both schooners attempted to lie to in order to ride out the gale until it abated. In the morning hours during the gale Captain George Warren of *Man Alone* saw the distressed schooner's mainsail torn off. Later Warren lost sight of *Annie Young* and the next morning *Man Alone* made it to harbour to report the Ramea schooner would probably not survive the storm.

Courtesy George Green

In 1947 John Penny & Sons of Ramea, which owned and operated a fish plant in the town, purchased their first dragger, *Pennyson I* (above) to catch redfish. With the arrival of modern draggers, the era of wooden schooner using dories, hook and line for cod quickly declined in Ramea.

Built in Maine, *Pennyson I* was the first dragger on the south coast. Her first captain was Walter Carter. On October 19, 1958, she sprang a leak and sank en route to the St. Pierre banks. She had to be abandoned, but her crew escaped safely.

Penny's enterprises purchased *Senator Penny* in 1959 and used her for fishing until 1970 when she was converted to a passenger ferry to operate between Ramea, Burgeo and Grey River.

On November 1, 1991, she drifted out of Grand Bank harbour where she had been tied up for two or three years. Above, *Senator Penny* lies beached near Dunford's Rock on the western side of Grand Bank. Successfully refloated, today the old ferry lies a derelict at Little Bay near Bay L'Argent.

Warren's dire prediction proved correct. According to a *Daily News* report of September 11, 1935, one of *Annie Young*'s dories was picked up at Cow Head — the vessel and her crew disappeared. After the storm another schooner, *Geneva Ethel*, arrived at Pushthrough to report a seaman, Abram Tibbo, had been washed overboard in the heavy seas.

Not all sea stories of Ramea schooners ended tragically; as with the crew of *Stanley Joseph*, rescued in mid-ocean and brought to Saint John, New Brunswick, on December 17, 1921. They were: Captain Hubert Vallis; mate Stanley Vallis; cook Martin Keeping; deckhands Edward Dicks and John Sibley, all of Ramea.

Nearly ten years later another Ramea schooner was abandoned at sea — Penny's *Edith Dawson*, a large tern built in 1918. On December 1, 1932, while on a foreign-going voyage Captain Stephen White and his son, George Kendall, William Grant and Joseph Davis, all of Ramea and Arthur Wambuck of LaHave, Nova Scotia, were rescued by the United States tanker *Sylvan Arrow*.

Chapter 21

Red Island: From Out of the Jaws of Death

CAPTAIN JAMES MCCARTHY'S SCHOONER *Annie* left St. John's on Monday, November 8, 1915, headed for Red Island, Placentia Bay. With him were William Rogers and Jeremiah Whalen. Over two weeks later, after battling the furious Atlantic off the southeast Avalon and without ever reaching Red Island, *Annie* went down, but not without a fight.

Annie, a boat of thirty tons, was deeply laden with food, shop goods and general supplies for an isolated island town in Placentia Bay. Red Island is the third largest (behind Merasheen and Long Island) and the most southwesterly of the group of islands occupying the head of Placentia Bay. Now abandoned except for occasional summer fishermen, the island once had at least three communities: Red Island Harbour, Margaree Cove and Wild Cove.

Local tradition claims that in the early 1800s the first settlers were two Irishmen, Tobin and McCarthy, the latter perhaps a forebear of *Annie*'s captain. The *Newfoundland Census* of 1936 records eighty-three residents, and for nearly a century the population rose steadily. When the population peaked in 1921 (around 484 people) it was a prominent fishing settlement serviced by a packet or supply boat every two weeks.

It was to this Placentia Bay island *Annie* was bound, but because of high winds, she had to harbour three times, first at Bay Bulls; then Cape Broyle and finally Fermeuse. On the final leg of the journey around Cape Ballard the wind veered to the south. Fully a week after leaving St. John's she attempted to make Trepassey.

Courtesy of Newfoundland Reference room

Red Island as it appeared in the 1930s. Lovell's *Newfoundland Directory* listed Red Island as a prominent fishing settlement with "the cod fishing... carried on in large boats." Common family names in the Directory included Barry, Carroll, Doody, Dunphy, Kerrivan, Lamb, Mulrooney, Norman, Reddy, Rose, Ryan and Walsh. Around 1921 the population peaked at 484, but by 1968, because of government-sponsored resettlement programs, most people had left the island community, migrating mostly to Placentia and area.

When the wind hauled around to a strong west northwesterly with heavy rain and dense fog, McCarthy was forced to run back for Fermeuse. About 3:00 p.m. on November 16, the crew saw a large steamer which when she bore down alongside proved to be *Seniac*. *Seniac*'s captain saw that the hurricane force winds were driving the little schooner out to sea.

The steamer ran up to the windward and put a lifebuoy on the end of a line to drift back. For over an hour *Seniac* tried to get the lifebuoy to drift near the schooner and finally *Annie*'s men snared it with a codfish jigger. A three-inch hawser was pulled aboard, tied to the schooner's foremast and the steamer began to tow *Annie* toward Aquaforte.

Not long after the tow line parted and for three hours attempts were made to re-attach it. The steamer left the scene and according to the story told about *Annie*'s crew in the local paper:

> It was an awful night of weather, very dark and the men (*Annie*'s crew) realized they would drive off the shore, but they did not worry, believing the ship would follow and stand by them. She, however, went on to Aquaforte and lay there all night. They say they will never forget that terrible night. The little schooner was constantly swept by the seas and they spend a night on deck watching for the ship's lights to heave in sight, but looking in vain.

Next morning they were about fifteen miles off Ferryland drifting before a wind which had increased in violence. McCarthy, Rogers and Whalen concluded the vessel could not live through the night.

With seas making a clean breach over *Annie* the men prepared for death late that night. Kneeling together they implored the mercy of God and recited the Rosary together. Each man was drenched and pierced with cold. They could not get warm food or drink and were worn out from lack of sleep.

On noon Thursday, November 17, breaking seas smashed the dory lashed on deck sweeping the pieces over the side. Captain McCarthy was washed over the side into the seething waters. *Annie* was drifting, and although McCarthy was heavily clad, he swam as hard as he could for the schooner.

According to McCarthy's story told later, he had a crucifix in his hand and a current or wave swept him toward the schooner. Suddenly the rope thrown by his shipmate Rogers fell near him. The skipper managed to grab it and put a turn under his armpits. Both Rogers and Whalen slowly pulled him over the side, exhausted and chilled.

McCarthy realized that in his excitement he lost his crucifix while grabbing the line. Still he heartily thanked God for deliverance from death. All three now knew it was dangerous to walk on deck and tied lines around themselves securing the rope to the spars. Later, the crew described the vessel's condition as:

> ...in a bad state, with the jib and bowsprit gone. The pumps were tried, but the vessel made no water. The wind abated

somewhat and more canvas was put on to keep the schooner's head into the wind.

At 8:00 a.m. the next day a steamer was sighted passing in the distance, evidently headed for Cape Race.

Seeing the steamer had a wireless, *Annie*'s crew signalled her with a flag, not for the purpose of abandoning ship but to ask to be reported to shore. The crew intended, seeing the weather was abating, to try and save schooner and cargo, if at all possible. The steamer altered course, but to the crew's consternation, she crossed behind, slowed for a while and then steamed away. The steamer was not near enough to see the name, but she was large with a black funnel.

All that day, the 19th, *Annie* laboured heavily. The crew raised some sail and reckoned, since they were eighty miles off Ferryland, they could make land. Luck was not with them, nor were the elements. Gradually seas and winds increased. Rain fell in torrents and the crew thought their schooner would founder.

Two am on Monday, November 21, Whalen heard the sound of a whistle; so faint at first it was thought to be the Cape Race whistle. At daylight they saw it was a steamer which, when signalled, came close. It was S.S. *Monadnock* from New York to London. Captain McCarthy attached *Monadnock*'s steel hawser to the foremast; no doubt hoping to be successful with a tow to land. After an hour of towing, the foremast was pulled loose. And this was the final wound for the Placentia Bay schooner.

Monadnock's captain agreed to take them off. With sixty feet of iron and steel ship towering above them, *Annie*'s crew first sent up their clothing tied up with a rope; then climbed a rope ladder up the side of the steamer. McCarthy was the last to leave.

To sink his schooner, he tried to chop a hole in the side but hadn't enough time to complete the work. Grabbing an armful of blankets, he saturated them with oil and set them afire.

As *Monadnock* steamed away *Annie* was burning fiercely. One hour into the journey toward London, the Newfoundland vessel *Cabot* came in sight. McCarthy knew she had been sent to search for them and asked *Monadnock*'s Captain Blackmore to allow them to transfer. Finally, at 4:30 pm, McCarthy, Whalen and Rogers set foot on land at Fermeuse. Their ordeal lasted two weeks.

At Fermeuse Captain McCarthy stayed at Mrs. Green's and a Mr. Walsh accommodated Rogers and Whalen. The government vessel *Cabot* had been searching for three missing schooners: *Swallow*; *Blanche M. Rose* of Harbour Breton; and *Annie*.

Remote and relatively inaccessible even in good sailing weather, Red Island must have been severely affected by the loss of supplies during that winter of 1915.

Chapter 22

The Ancient Harbour of Port aux Basques

OFTEN CALLED THE "Gateway to Newfoundland," Channel-Port aux Basques, a town of over 5500 people on Newfoundland's southwest corner, once earned dubious distinction as a graveyard of ships. As its name implies, it was founded by the Basques fishermen of southwestern France. Because of its proximity to Cape Breton Island and mainland Canada, the deep water ice-free port has seen numerous ships of all nations in its four hundred years of existence.

Scores of vessels have been lost near Port aux Basques; many wrecks are documented in the town's Gulf Museum, administered by the Southwest Coast Heritage Society. In 1892, according to records at the museum, it was reported that up to that year forty ships were wrecked off the area's shores — four of these were lost with complete crews. A profusion of underwater reefs and shoals offshore claimed many.

In era of sailing vessels, dense fog off the South Coast posed the greatest danger. To account for the great number of ships lost along the coast one theory suggests the method of navigation used by the captains. Position was determined by dead reckoning, an educated guess to a ship's location. Ships sailing from Europe to the Gulf of St. Lawrence would pass through Cabot Strait. Two main lighthouses flank the entrance to the Gulf: one on St. Paul's Island north of Cape Breton Island, Nova Scotia and the other at Cape Ray, located on the southwestern tip of Newfoundland, near Port aux Basques.

Generally ships navigating this area during dense fog and

heavy weather would mistake the Cape Ray light for the beacon on St. Paul's Island. In error, navigators would believe their ships further south and in trying to avoid St. Paul's Island altered their course to the north — a deadly navigational error.

Before the captain realized what he had done, it was too late. The ship probably struck one of the many clusters of reefs and hidden sunkers lying off the southwestern end of Newfoundland.

The loss of life was staggering; grave sites of unidentified sailors can be found along the coast in isolated areas and near towns. Today, improved navigational aids help the thousands of ships passing by headed for the Gulf of St. Lawrence.

By 1871 Port aux Basques was described as "the most westerly settlement of importance in Newfoundland... a place of considerable trade." It was often the last port of call for Newfoundland's South Coast sailing schooners going to Canada and it was the nearest port on the return voyage across the stormy, treacherous Cabot Strait and Gulf of St. Lawrence.

In early 1898 the port was chosen as the western terminus of the Newfoundland railway and by 1913 it was linked by gulf ferry to the Canadian rail network.

Ships Go Down off Port aux Basques

Western Baldwin Shoals proved treacherous to a thirty-three-ton schooner out of Belleoram, *Eva Gertrude*. On May 30, 1925, she ran upon the Western Baldwin to total loss. Captain Cluett and his Belleoram crew were safe.

Twenty years later another local two-masted schooner came to grief. *Robert Frampton*, owned in Port aux Basques, sailed out of her home port and into the stormy Gulf in late November 1945 with a crew of four. Neither the schooner nor its men were ever seen again: Robert Frampton, married with seven children; Charles Osmond, married, five children; Emmanuel Lawrence, married, three children. Robert Frampton's fourteen-year-old brother was also on the schooner.

On November 30, 1951, Spencer's business of Fortune lost their coasting schooner *Lloyd Hounsell* when she grounded on

Rhode Island Reef near Port aux Basques. Built in Pound Cove in 1935, the seventy-five foot long schooner was en route from Sydney to Port aux Basques. Captain Walter B. Spencer and his crew escaped safely.

One of Port aux Basques' worst marine disasters happened during World War II when the Gulf ferry S.S. *Caribou* was hit by a German torpedo on October 13, 1942 — a mere forty miles off Port aux Basques. Of 237 passengers and crew only 101 survived. The 265 foot long vessel had left North Sydney accompanied by an armed escort ship to protect *Caribou* from enemy attack.

A tremendous explosion ripped into the ferry's starboard beam, killing most workers and passengers below deck. Within a few minutes she went to the bottom; in the darkness and "lights out" wartime regulation many passengers could not find lifeboats. Most of her thirty-one crew lost were from the Port aux Basques/Channel area.

Her crew:

Name	**Position on Ship**	**Age**	**Born**
Ben Tavernor	Captain	62	Trinity
Stanley Tavernor	1st Officer	34	Port aux Basques
Harold Tavernor	3rd Officer	24	Port aux Basques
James Prosper	2nd Officer	54	Bonne Bay
John Skeard	Oiler	61	Channel
Charles Ford	4th Engineer	55	Port aux Basques
Howard Cutler	Mail Officer	45	St. Georges
Harry Hann	Chief Steward	34	Lewisporte
Bridget Fitzpatrick	Stewardess	60	Bay Roberts
William Hogan	Assistant Purser	22	Carbonear
Clarence Hann	Donkeyman	43	Channel
George Gale	Oiler	45	Cape Ray
Garfield Strickland	Fireman	52	Port aux Basques
Arthur Thomas	Fireman	37	Halifax, N.S.
George Thomas	Fireman	32	Port aux Basques
James Pike	Chief Engineer	55	St. John's
Victor Lomond	Trimmer	28	Channel
Elias Coffin	Bosun	53	Port aux Basques
Israel Barritt	Seaman	51	Brigus

Produced to commemorate the loss of S.S. *Caribou* and her crew, this poster was first published in 1944 by H. Thornhill of Corner Brook. In the Port aux Basques/Channel area twenty-one widows with fifty-one orphans were left without a breadwinner.

Combined with the disappearance of *Robert Frampton* in 1945 in which fifteen children were left fatherless, Port aux Basques had paid heavily for its dependence on the sea.

Richard Feltham	Seaman	38	Port aux Basques
Bert Coffin	Seaman	26	Channel
Albert Strickland	Seaman	19	Port aux Basques
Max French	2nd Steward	34	Bay Roberts
Charles Humphries	Ass't Steward	34	Greenspond
Lewis Carter	Ass't Steward	24	Port aux Basques
Jerome Gale	Ass't Steward	21	Port aux Basques
Thomas Moyst	2nd Engineer	66	St. John's
William Samms	Fireman	39	Codroy
Charles Piercey	3rd Engineer	31	St. John's
Joseph Richards	Fireman	42	Channel
Israel Sheaves	Oiler	62	Channel

Not far from Port aux Basques is the town of Isle aux Morts which over the years had seen many wrecks. As a mute testimony to volume of sea traffic that passed in and near Isle aux Morts for over four hundred years, an ancient astrolabe dated 1628 was recently found in the harbour. It was from the many

Courtesy of Jack Keeping

Edith Emery, a cutwater schooner built in 1883 at Essex, USA, was owned in Channel by William Mills. She sank in Port aux Basques harbour in 1903. Crews of other schooners headed for Port aux Basques were not so lucky: *Magno*, Captain Levi Baggs left Sydney in mid-August for Port aux Basques, but he and his 4 crew never reported and probably went down during an August gale, 1924.

wrecks that the town earned its name — Island of the Dead. Tucked away through a maze of rocks and headlands, the sea entrance to the town has to be navigated carefully.

Wreck on Codroy Island

Codroy Island, an uninhabited crag off Port aux Basques with only a single fishing shack on it, became the refuge of six crew of *Mary H. Hirtle*. For eighteen hours they waited for a storm to abate before rescue. John Osborne, forty-one-year-old captain of 196-ton motor vessel *Mary H. Hirtle*, was carried eighty-eight miles off course.

Built in Lunenburg, *Hirtle* belonged to Captain Job Blackwood and on her final journey in the winter of 1950, she carried Sydney coal to Wesleyville, Bonavista Bay. Osborne, a resident of Adelaide Street, St. John's, had as his crew: Abraham Lake and Jeddes Fudge, both of St. John's; Ernest Matthews, Wesleyville; Edward Hefferan, Placentia and Gordon Buffett of Burgeo.

When a winter storm hit on December 19, she was sixty miles northwest of St. Pierre — wind velocity reached ninety miles an hour. Osborne's original route was to go around the Avalon Peninsula to Wesleyville, but the storm forced the ship up the Gulf of St. Lawrence, the opposite direction to her intended route.

During the run, the bulwarks and dories were smashed; the cold and weary crew spent seventeen hours at the pumps. Seas broke over *Mary H. Hirtle* from stem to stern.

Off Cape Ray, Captain Osborne and his crew had their worst moments. He brought the schooner around to the wind in the hope of reaching Port aux Basques. With the weight of 200 tons of soft coal, she ploughed under the waves and would not rise until brought before the wind again.

Making Port aux Basques harbour was impossible; so Osborne steered the schooner for Codroy Island. It was necessary to navigate through a very narrow passage. *Mary H. Hirtle* went through, despite adverse winds and heavy seas.

In his report made the day after the wreck, Hubert Ridgley,

Justice of the Peace and local schoolteacher said, "I was amazed at the expert navigation which brought the men to safety under such conditions. It was a feat of great seamanship."

When the wind abated somewhat, the crew nailed together a dory to try and reach the island. With two men rowing and one bailing water with a bucket, they made land. Securing a rope from the schooner to the shore, a rough breeches buoy was rigged and the remaining three dragged themselves to Codroy Island.

Fortunately, there was a small shack on the island where they waited for rescue, sheltered from the freezing wind and spray. Eighteen hours later three men from the Port aux Basques area — Morgan Giles, the lighthouse keeper; Henry Fiander; and a man named Evans — rowed out and brought them ashore. Two vessels, *Western Explorer* and *Terra Nova*, left for Codroy Island to assist in taking the men off, but when a message came from the Halifax tug *Foundation Lillian* saying the men were safe, both returned to port.

Mary H. Hirtle, full of water, grounded near shore and was a total loss. A little gear was taken off, but the coal could not be salvaged. An old saying, "It's an ill wind that doesn't blow some good" proved true for the residents of Codroy, a small community near Port aux Basques. Many were busy plying back and forth with doryloads of Sydney coal taken from the broken back of *Mary H. Hirtle*.

Disappearance of *Barracudina*

In the 1960s Port aux Basques, like other South Coast towns, witnessed the end of the wooden schooner. The steel-hulled craft that replaced them were equipped with newer technology: radar, improved charts, lighting and modern communication devices which meant safer ocean voyages. Although marine disasters were not as frequent, the sea was no less treacherous. This became all too evident in December of 1978 when T.J. Hardy's vessel *Barracudina*, a 64-foot steel trawler, disappeared en route from Sydney to Port aux Basques.

Barracudina was last heard from when her captain James

Chaulk radioed the fish plant at Port aux Basques on December 26, about seventy miles southwest of home port. Built in Marystown in 1975, the trawler was bought by Hardy's business in 1978. Her crew were from the southwest corner of Newfoundland: Captain Chaulk, aged fifty-six, Isle aux Morts; mate Earl Lawrence, thirty-three, Burnt Islands; engineer Emmanuel Caines, forty-four, Isle aux Morts; cook Chesley Spencer, fifty-three, Rose Blanche and Olman Hefferman, twenty-seven, Port aux Basques.

Appendix F lists many vessels lost in the Port aux Basques area.

Chapter 23

Rose Blanche Marine Disasters

ABOUT THIRTY MILES EAST OF PORT AUX BASQUES are the towns of Rose Blanche and Harbour Le Cou. Early settlers there saw many wrecks, but one of the most memorable was that of a Cunard cruise liner *Ascania*.

During the First War the 9000-ton *Ascania* transported troops returning home from Liverpool, England, to Montreal when she ran aground on Gull Island. Several steamers went to her assistance, but with her bottom ripped open she quickly filled with water, rolled over and sank. Newfoundland steamship *Kyle* carried the troops to Newfoundland from the stricken vessel. Today a few homes in Rose Blanche have relics and mementos obtained from the wreck.

As a reminder that the early French fishermen used both harbours, Rose Blanche's name is a corruption of *roche blanche* (white rock). While most business activity in Rose Blanche has been concentrated in the safe anchorage on the east side of the narrow bay, other smaller towns nearby were Crow Cove, Big Bottom, Caines Island and Rose Blanche Pointe. The sheltered waters of Harbour le Cou, French for 'the neck,' opens to the southwest. When cartographer Captain James Cook visited the area in 1765, he found one fishing stage at Harbour le Cou.

The first permanent settlers in Rose Blanche — Buffett, Caines, Currie, Payne, Rose and Shears — probably came between 1810 and 1850. After the English firm of Newman's was set up, the population of Rose Blanche-Harbour le Cou tripled. Lovell's *Newfoundland Directory* of 1871 describes Rose Blanche as a "flourishing settlement... with a large mercantile establishment." Other families, such as the Anderson, Best, Hardy,

Courtesy of Marine Archives

Rose Blanche around the 1920-1930s. The structure in the foreground is probably the government building which housed the telegraph and post office. To the far right on the hill overlooking the town are the church, school and Orange Hall. The harbour and the principal merchants premises can be seen center right. Some business that grew and eventually declined over the years were Moultons of Burgeo, Job Rideout and William Horwood. Noted Newfoundland author Cassie (Horwood) Brown was born in Rose Blanche.

Parsons and Skinner at Rose Blanche and Buckland, Clarke and Rideout at Harbour le Cou came from eastern settlements.

The winter fishery out of Rose Blanche, which had its beginnings in the late 1800s, took a heavy toll of men and ships over the years. During one storm on January 23, 1925, an intense gale lasting for three or four days drove many vessels from Rose Blanche and Petites to sea. First news reports trickling into St. John's newspapers indicated Walter Blagdon's vessel of Rose Blanche, struck Point Platte, St. Pierre and the crew made it safely to land. Other boats drifted out of control south of Miqueleon.

Such were the terrible weather conditions — southeast winds and heavy snow — that for several days, coastal steamer *Prospero* was held up at English Harbour West. *Glencoe* left Harbour Breton for ports west to Burgeo, but had to return. She was later directed to pick up Blagdon's crew at St. Pierre and to search the waters off the French Island for the missing boats.

Courtesy of Marine Archives

A four dory schooner, *Mom and Allister* off Rose Blanche. Up to the 1940s, the Rose Blanche banks remained one of the most prolific fishing areas on the southwest coast. Built in Morrisville, Bay d'Espoir in 1946, this twenty-two-ton schooner was first owned by Robert Newman, Petites and later by Edward Cutler, Ramea.

Schooners like *Mom and Allister* phased out after T.J. Hardy opened a fresh fish plant in Rose Blanche in 1960. The next year Rose Blanche-Harbour le Cou were connected by road to Port aux Basques. Since 1994 population has stabilized at around nine hundred.

Within a week F. Vatcher, a Justice of the Peace on the South Coast, reported hope was abandoned for another vessel from Rose Blanche and that three other boats, each valued at $850, moored in Rose Blanche harbour were wrecked.

One body had been found: James Hayward of Captain Hanham's boat which was lost at Rose Blanche. Charles Buffett, his three brothers and a fourth crewman, all of Rose Blanche were driven off to sea in the hurricane and were never seen again.

The little town of Petites, with a population of just over one hundred at this time, was hardest hit. Two fishing craft and crews disappeared — Ephriam Hann with his three brothers in one and Herbert Groves and three crewmen in another. Four other boats were abandoned with no loss of life. At Isle aux

Morts, Nelson Lillington and Andrew Coleman lost a boat and all fishing gear. At Burgeo, Angus Ransome and his crew were missing, presumed swallowed up by the January hurricane.

When the steamer *Glencoe* returned to Rose Blanche with Blagdon and his six crew, one of them, John Ingram, was suffering from severe frostbite. It was thought he may have needed his hand and toes amputated and was transferred to a St. John's hospital.

When the storm abated and the toll of the sea was counted, four schooners with crews totalling eighteen men were missing.

Chapter 24

Rushoon Schooner Disappears in the August Gales

TRADITIONALLY, several small towns on the western side of Placentia Bay held "Ladies' Day" on August 15, the Catholic Feast of the Assumption. Ladies and young girls would don their finest dresses and hats. The men of the community were treated to a social and dance sponsored by the ladies and the church. Sailing craft gathered in the harbour: fishing crews in their western boats, inshore fishermen in their dories, and an especially welcome sight would be the tall sails of the schooners. Crews of the western boats and schooners would be gone for longer time periods for they fished off Cape St. Mary's and faced more danger on the perilous seas.

But in August 1927, the four-dory schooner *Hilda Gertrude* was in Rushoon and was due to sail before August 15th. To accommodate them Ladies' Day was held a day or so before its customary date.

After the celebrations and banqueting were over, Danny Cheeseman and his young crew hoisted sail and *Hilda Gertrude* slipped quietly away, bound for the productive grounds off Cape St. Mary's. Her crew: Captain Cheeseman, aged around thirty; Michael Norman, twenty-two, and Michael Hann, twenty-two, all of Rushoon; John Murphy of Parker's Cove; cook Oliver Dicks, Baine Harbour; and three men from St. Joseph's — Thomas Keating, Patrick (Paddy) Gaulton and Tommy Hawco. Hawco, in his fifties, was the eldest. Except for Michael Norman, all were married and several had small children. Captain Cheeseman had previously sailed with his brother Joe for years in *Western Annie* until he purchased his own vessel, *Hilda Gertrude*.

Cheeseman and his crew failed to return to their home port of Rushoon — a twist of nature originating much further south near the Tropic of Cancer saw to that. In this area late summer hurricanes are born. Like the recent Hurricane Andrew, they howl their way northward devastating parts of southern United States with winds often in excess of one hundred miles an hour.

By the time the violent tropical storms reach the Maritimes much of their fury is spent, but the final flick of the hurricane's dying tail often lashes the waters off Newfoundland. These wind storms, while lacking the intensity of a full-blown hurricane, were still powerful and dangerous to shipping. Around the island they were termed the 'August (or September) Gales.'

Such storms were weather phenomena well-respected by schooner captains and crews. Early coasting or banking vessels, ranging in size from twenty to sixty tons, were no match for the heavy winds and high seas which seemingly sprang from nowhere without warning. In those years of limited communication and inaccurate long range weather forecasting, boats caught miles from shelter met with devastating results.

For two and a half days in August 1927, from the 24th to the 27th, when several small schooners were on the fishing grounds, one of the most memorable "August Gales" to ravage the southern part of Newfoundland struck with destructive and deadly results.

Two Placentia Bay vessels fished near each other and were caught out in the storm: *Hilda Gertrude* and *M and J Hayden*, the latter a twenty-eight-ton schooner built in St. Joseph's in 1926. Jim Harris of St. Joseph's captained her for eight years.

The story of Captain Jim Harris and his last sighting of *Hilda Gertrude* is told in Andrew Horwood's fine and informative book *Newfoundland Ships and Men* (1971):

> Captain Harris in the *M and J Hayden* was about twelve miles off Long Island when one of the crew saw a vessel on her beam ends. On coming closer they saw that men were clinging to her side. Captain Harris attempted to manoeuvre his vessel

> alongside to attempt a rescue. The *Hayden* was wearing a jumbo, a reefed foresail and a storm trisail. When the helm was put down she wouldn't come around and fell off. In another attempt the helm was put up to wear her but at that moment the foresail blew away and it was utterly impossible to get to the distressed men.

One of Harris' crew was George Norman, twin brother of Michael Norman on *Hilda Gertrude.* George saw his brother and leaned out over the railing to shout something to him, but his words were lost in the roaring gale. Harris' crew could do no more; several went below into the forecastle to say a prayer for the souls of *Hilda Gertrude*'s men. Another foresail was bent on and *Hayden* made Clattice Harbour safely. Near Clattice Harbour — today an abandoned community northeast of Marystown — the August Gale claimed another victim: a small schooner, water-logged and sinking was drifting by, close to shore. Three men who made up the crew jumped for shore; two survived.

By the 1930s Rushoon's population was approaching 200 people. The town, located on the western side of Placentia Bay, has always depended on the fishery, but the lack of drying space for salted cod forced early settlers to keep premises on offshore islands and selling their catches to Baine Harbour or Oderin.

From the turn of the century many crews of Rushoon and St. Joseph's used larger "western boats," and sought the codfish across Placentia Bay at Cape St. Mary's or Cape Pine. Around 1913, one shipwright was Joseph Cheeseman who built several larger schooners at Rushoon, including *Western Annie.* According to local knowledge any kind of a stick, large and small, of many varieties of trees — spruce, pine, juniper, witch hazel — could be cut where the Rushoon town hall is presently located.

The community's name appears on early maps as Rashoon, probably a corruption of the French for brook (ruisseau). Early French settlers had a fishing station at Oderin and most likely cut firewood and timber in Rushoon River valley which runs through the town. According to community sources, Captain

Danny Cheeseman's forefathers were among the first settlers on the east side of the Rushoon River.

One of the most tragic shipwrecks in Placentia Bay happened near Oderin in 1915. Some years previously the Marystown Trading Company set up a salt fish collecting business which exchanged or bought fish for fishing gear, supplies and food with the populated islands of Placentia Bay. On November 1 while travelling from Marystown, *Madonna*, a small schooner owned in Ship Harbour and built in Fox Harbour in 1886, ran into a storm before she reached Oderin. She carried four men — Captain R. Tobin of St. Bride's, Placentia Bay; Mr. Sparrow, Mr. Dormody and his son Kevin.

Madonna stranded and broke up on Little Gull Rock near Jude Island, about eight miles east of Red Harbour. For two days and two nights the seas washed over the men who had managed to clamber onto the rock. In the cold spray lashing over them, the endurance of the older men ebbed. Kevin Dormody encouraged and held on to his father and Sparrow until his strength gave out and he could do no more. Both were washed off the ledge, but Kevin clung to the rock for several more hours.

Alphonsus Mullaley, a young man from Oderin Island, went up on the hill behind the small town. Hearing someone scream, he scanned the offshore rocks to see a person on Little Gull Rock. He ran to Magistrate McGrath who sent out a dory to pick the youth off the rock.

In the mists of time people came to the Placentia Bay islands and established homesteads like Oderin, but like other many communities that once dotted the Placentia Bay islands, Oderin is now only a memory, abandoned and silent. Fishermen seeking the elusive lobster which become scarcer each year, recreational sailors and home-coming returnees occasionally frequent its waters. Those of the older generation recognize each inlet, headland, cove and cliff, and point to places where tragedies and shipwreck have occurred.

Chapter 25

Rencontre West and the Story of *Effie May*

OFTEN LOCALIZED AND INTENSE, the lashing tails of fall hurricanes devastated areas within a hundred miles or so; yet occasionally their effects were felt all over Newfoundland. The 1927 Gale selected its victims from along the South Coast.

By 1927, the town of Rencontre West was one of the oldest and most prestigious communities west of Harbour Breton. Its name, French in origin, literally meant a 'meeting place' for the early French fishermen and settlers who had frequented the area prior to the mid-1700s.

The earliest English reference to Rencontre West comes from the diary of William Epps Cormack, a Scottish explorer who walked across Newfoundland from east to west in 1822. On his return journey to St. John's by schooner, he stopped in Rencontre West and noted there were four families.

People lived there to fish the quiet waters of Rencontre Bay, an inlet like many on the South Coast that runs deep—over 100 fathoms in some places. The inshore fishing areas were once prolific and the residents of Rencontre West had the best of two grounds at their doorstep with the shoal grounds fifteen miles out to sea and the waters of Rencontre Bay close at hand.

The community had a population of over 200 by the turn of the century and had become a frequent stop for American vessels looking for squid bait. From the 1890s William Webb and Sons was the chief merchant. Webb bought fish from other settlements and from his Rencontre base established a few branch businesses elsewhere on the coast. Older established families in Rencontre West included: Durnford, Ball, Buffett, Marsden, Goodridge, Stone, Simms, Cox, Parsons, Green and Spencer. Some family names indicate their Jersey Island origins: Durnford, Ball, Beauchamp, DeGruchy and Courtney.

Thomas Durnford, according to family tradition, was a planter or land owner who had moved to Rencontre West from the Jersey Islands sometime after 1850. He owned the small fishing schooner *Effie May*, but due to his advanced age, had given command of the schooner to his son Arthur.

In August 1927, some days before the intense gale swept along the South Coast, *Effie May* had been to St. Pierre on dock for repair. Because of its proximity to the South Coast, the St. Pierre dock saw many local vessels needing keel replacement, bottom planking or other major repairs. As an added bonus, crews like Durnford's could pick up food and supplies at St. Pierre for good prices.

When repairs were completed, Durnford's schooner left for Rencontre West on August 24. Somewhere in the fifty miles separating the French islands from her home port, *Effie May* disappeared. After anxious days of waiting and wondering, the families of Rencontre West realized Arthur Durnford and the five people aboard his schooner would never be seen again.

Making the trip with Arthur Durnford, married and aged 34, were his two brothers, George and John. John's two sons went to St. Pierre for the trip: Garfield, aged twelve and Frank, aged sixteen. The Durnfords had another man from Rencontre West with them, but his name is not recorded.

In time the traditional occupation associated with schooners, dory and trawl fishing of Rencontre West offered no attraction to young people and many moved away to work for regular, higher wages. Peak population of 248 was reached around 1935, but dropped steadily from that point on. By the early 1960s many people and homes were relocated and by 1969 Rencontre West was virtually abandoned. Most people — not only from Rencontre, but also those of nearby Richard's Harbour, Parsons Harbour, Cul de Sac East, Muddy Hole and

Mosquito — resettled in Francois, Burgeo, Fortune, Marystown or Port aux Basques.

So it was that a little more than forty years after *Effie May* and the other little schooners of the South Coast were swallowed by an all-too-frequent coastal storm, the schooner fishery that had its inception just prior to the 1890s, came to an end.

Today when descendants go back to visit the old home sites, they search for locations of family dwellings, gardens and other familiar haunts. Only the eldest will envision, in the sheltered waters of Rencontre Bay, schooners like *Effie May* that once spread their white wings to catch the wind. The names of stalwart seamen who manned them are now written on marble stones in lonely seaside graveyards.

Chapter 26

Red Harbour: Death on the Crosstrees

ONLY AFTER THE EVENING OF AUGUST 24, 1927, as reports of schooner losses from a sudden hurricane trickled into government agencies in St. John's, was the extent of loss of human lives realized. West of Rencontre, on the coast which Burin Peninsula schoonermen once called the 'Western Shore,' *Annie Jane* of Isle aux Morts with four men and *Vienna* of Burnt Islands with six men had disappeared. In Placentia Bay, *Annie Healey* of Fox Harbour was gone with seven men.

Twenty-eight young men of Newfoundland's South Coast from Isle aux Morts in the west to Fox Harbour in the east disappeared in the August Gale of 1927. In terms of human and economic loss, the disappearance of many hard-working breadwinners was a serious blow to towns like Isle aux Morts, Burnt Islands, Rencontre West, St. Joseph's and Rushoon — many were recently married with young families. But the trail of lost lives did not end with these communities; one more, Red Harbour, a small community on the western side of Placentia Bay, felt the effects of the sudden storm. The vessel *John Loughlin* was wrecked in Placentia Bay during the August gale — none of her Red Harbour crew survived.

Red Harbour first appears the Newfoundland Census of 1857 with a population of twenty-eight. According to family and community tradition, James Loughlin brought his family from Ireland, first to Long Harbour, Placentia Bay. In his quest to better his circumstances on more productive fishing grounds he moved to Red Harbour and joined families of Clarkes,

Peaches and Hamiltons who were also original inhabitants of the sheltered inlet.

John Loughlin, a western boat owned by John Henry Loughlin of Red Harbour, had been fishing on the Cape Shore Grounds when the storm hit without warning. A broken, battered derelict, she drifted in near Ship Cove, Placentia Bay. In the booklet *Our Cultural Heritage: A Short History of the Cape Shore Area* edited by Ernestine Power and others, the story of the discovery of the wreck was related by Carrie Brennan:

> I remember one time my husband, Edward Brennan, took a walk around the cliff after a storm. It was in August 1927. The sea was still rough and hazy, but when he came home he told us he saw a ship far out on the sea and as far as he could ascertain, it seemed like a man hanging from the cross trees.
>
> Immediately he got the fishermen together and although it was still rough and blowing they launched a motor boat and went to the ship which was well out in the bay. They saw a man hanging from the crosstrees by the right arm. When the boat listed he would dip in the sea and they held the motor boat close enough to the ship's side for him to drop into her when the boat listed again.
>
> They noticed that the name of the boat was the *Loughlin*. The anchor went through a hole in her bow and held her there. They brought the dead man ashore and put dry clothing on him. Next day they brought his remains, coffined, to Placentia courthouse where he was identified as John C. Loughlin, the skipper of the craft.

According to a recent conversation with Mrs. Winnie Dicks, sister to three of the drowned crewmen, the man tied to the mast was not John C. Loughlin, but her brother, Captain William Albert Loughlin, the only body recovered from the wreck.

Although it happened almost seventy years previously, she vividly remembered the day the letter arrived from Placentia saying the wrecked vessel and one victim had been discovered. The letter went on to say that if the storm had abated sooner and had the Ship Cove men been able to get out to the wreck, possibly the man's life would have been saved. Apparently he had died a few hours before help arrived.

In hushed undertones out of respect for those feared drowned, William Ben Loughlin, a relative living in Red Harbour, gathered some men and prepared his small boat to bring the body home from Placentia.

Winnie (Loughlin) recalled the morning of August 24, the day the gale flew at them seemingly from nowhere — a beautiful dawning, no sea and a splendid day on the water. Some days before, *John Loughlin* had sailed for the Cape Shore Grounds and she saw her three brothers off: Albert, Charlie and Fred. Herman Peach of Red Harbour, aged twenty-five; Josiah Stacey, eighteen; Gordon Frampton, Flat Island, twenty-four; and Josiah Barrett of Woody Island, aged twenty-four and married to Eliza Loughlin completed *John Loughlin*'s fishing crew. A boy, Joshua Barrett, went with his father, Josiah, for one trip.

Social life in Red Harbour continued after the schooners sailed; on August 24 there was a wedding. Sometime throughout the celebrations, everyone was suddenly aware of the heavy pressure of the wind and before the evening was over, a storm engulfed Placentia Bay that was so intense no one had time to get the drying fish off the rapidly disintegrating flakes. Fish stores and sheds collapsed; supplies and drying fish tumbled before the gale like autumn leaves along the ground.

For days following the storm, Winnie Loughlin and the other womenfolk of Red Harbour waited for reports, good or bad, of *John Loughlin*. News came that *Effie Pike*, a vessel belonging to Albert Dicks of Flat Island had safely put in at Petite Forte. Her crew had not seen nor heard any report of the Loughlin schooner.

Then the letter arrived from Placentia telling the Loughlins of the coffined remains of one unidentified crewman resting at Placentia. When William Ben Loughlin arrived at Placentia he recognized the victim as Albert Loughlin — married with a wife expecting a child in September.

Winnie's brothers, Charlie and Fred, and the other crew were never found. Charlie's wife was also pregnant; Fred had been recently married. Josiah Barrett, a veteran of the Great War, was also married. In time a clothes bag was retrieved from the bottom where the derelict had come to rest; the contents were identified as those of Barrett's.

Built in Marystown some years before, the salvaged *John Loughlin* was refloated to sail and to fish on the eastern side of Placentia Bay again. Out of respect for the several widowed womenfolk, she never again put into Red Harbour. The father of the three missing men lost all strength of his legs and never walked again. For some years after, the Loughlins, according Winnie (Loughlin) Dicks, never forgetting the courage and reverence the Brennans felt for a cargo of tragedy on a derelict ship, corresponded with Carrie Brennan and her husband. In time the people of the islands erected a memorial stone which still stands overlooking the islands and the sea — it lists the seven crew, lost on August 29, 1927.

Today Red Harbour, accessible by road to the Burin Peninsula highway, is a viable community of over 250 people. It too resisted pressures to relocate in the 1960s, eventually became a "growth centre" and received many of the people and homes of Port Elizabeth in Placentia Bay.

Today when one stands on the hills behind Red Harbour and looks out across to the islands and vast expanses of Placentia Bay, it is easy to believe in the beauty and mystery of the ships and in the magic of the sea. Although the great enterprise of salt dry fish and the schooners has gone, the stories of shipwreck and tragedy remain with the older generation. A few tales still linger on in the memory, folksongs and stories of older seamen or their spouses.

Chapter 27

St. Bernard's Seaman Survives

FIVE SCHOONERS left Sydney, Nova Scotia, together: *Nina W. Corkum,* Captain Harvey Banfield; *Mary Pauline,* Captain Jack Mills; *Shirley Blanche* of Gaultois, Captain John Rose; *Gladys Wiscombe,* Captain Bernard Whiffen; Jensen's schooner from Harbour Breton; and another small schooner owned in Baine Harbour. On the evening they left, December 18, 1963, the forecast predicted good weather and all the skippers looked for a good time down.

Some of the schooners, including *Mary Pauline* and *Nina W. Corkum,* carried ship to shore communications and kept in touch with news on the weather and sailing conditions.

Nina W. Corkum, Mary Pauline and another schooner steered for Langlade Reach, a more direct course for the Burin Peninsula, while the other vessels went across to the Western shore to work their way down the coast from Burgeo and Rose Blanche.

Mary Pauline was an old schooner, built in 1920 at Lunenburg; she gone through several owners including the Hardy family of Jersey Harbour. By 1963 she was registered to Pierce Fudge of Corner Brook.

Her crew: Captain Jack Mills, born in Doctor's Harbour and had lived in English Harbour West, was a resident of Lunenburg, Nova Scotia. He had skippered vessels owned by J. Petite and Sons, like *Palitana* in 1935. Sylvester Hynes and Nicholas Whittle belonged to St. Bernard's; Walter Baldwin, Corner Brook; Aubrey Rice and Chesley Windsor of Triton; and engineer John Clark of Fortune Bay (probably Terrenceville) who resided in Halifax, Nova Scotia. It was to be *Mary Pauline*'s last

Courtesy of Alex Hardy

Mary Pauline tied on at the Irving Oil premises in Halifax harbour. After her engine was installed, she had her mastheads cut down or spiked. For years beyond her prime she worked the South Coast trade routine: coal from Sydney; oil in drums from Halifax; produce from Nova Scotia and PEI and salt bulk fish from Newfoundland to the mainland.

voyage for the year; Fudge had scheduled her to tie up in Grand Bank harbour for the winter.

Newfoundland weather patterns change quickly. An old saying claims, 'If you don't like the weather, wait a half hour and it will change.' About one am, when both *Nina W. Corkum* and *Mary Pauline* were well out into the Gulf, the forecast changed to winter storm warnings — that night the wind reached eighty miles per hour. Deep in water and over-burdened with coal destined for Foote's business in Grand Bank, *Mary Pauline* wallowed and laboured in mountainous seas.

By daylight, both vessels were practically in the eye of the wind and engulfed in a thick snow storm. By this time they were about ten miles from the French islands, but could not steam up, due to head winds and seas, through Langlade Reach into relative safety.

Built in 1922 in Lunenburg, *Nina W. Corkum* was purchased by G & A Buffett of Grand Bank in 1932. She had bank fished with her ten or twelve dories for several years, when Grand Bank business J.B. Foote purchased her. *Corkum*'s main work was freighting supplies from the mainland to Newfoundland ports. On this trip the old wooden schooner carried flour destined for Bonavista. Captain Harvey Banfield, born in Garnish

In more peaceful hours as evidenced in this photo taken from *National Geographic*, *Nina W. Corkum* is moored by the quay in St. Pierre unloading oil drums. During the war years when many South Coast schooners lay idle because of the enemy submarine threat, Captain Clarence Williams hired a crew to sail south to Martinique, a French island allied with Vichy (Fascist) government. He and his crew made the dash down and back safely: Williams, mate John Smith, engineer William Baker, cook Charles Thomas, deckhand Reg Matthews of Grand Bank and Stan Lawrence, Bay L'Argent.

and a resident of Grand Bank, had with him engineer Charlie Follett; mate Max Bungay; Philip Downey, all of Grand Bank; Herbert Day and Randell Grandy, Garnish.

Because of the force of the wind, it was difficult for *Nina W. Corkum* to hold her head to the windward and at times drifted back about a mile an hour. Both captains, Harvey Banfield and Jack Mills were a few miles apart and kept in contact on their wireless sets, but visibility was nil.

Listeners on shore in communities like Point au Gaul and Lamaline, could hear the conversations and the struggle for life and death on the high seas through the wireless sets in their warm, safe kitchens. Many sat near their radios all night listening to a drama, heard but unseen, played out on the high seas a few miles beyond their shoreline.

Late that evening *Mary Pauline* was in trouble. Mills' SOS told the skipper of *Nina W. Corkum* he was somewhere in Langlade Reach and leaking badly in the stern. Mills asked if *Nina W. Corkum* could find them, take the lead and *Mary Pauline* would follow into safety. Captain Banfield agreed to help although the weather jeopardized his own chances of staying afloat.

Mary Pauline stopped, probably from flooded engines, just as the wind dropped somewhat. It was the right time to abandon the leaking schooner. When the wind picked up again an hour or so after, *Nina W. Corkum* was forced to leave the scene.

Another vessel, Fisheries Products' dragger *Zeta*, captained by Byron Adams of Burin and lying to in Langlade Reach, heard the wireless messages from both schooners and left to help. *Zeta*'s radar was out, but he was guided through the blizzard by the messages sent by *Nina W. Corkum.*

During *Zeta*'s steam up, the wind shifted to the southwest further endangering the wooden schooner *Nina W. Corkum.* Now as evening of December 19 closed in, wireless messages indicated the latter vessel had to leave the scene or go under. One of the last communications from *Mary Pauline* was that the crew was abandoning ship in two dories and that Captain Mills had a broken leg.

Zeta, according to the radio transmissions, came as near to *Mary Pauline* as possible. There was no way they could manoeuvre within a few feet of the stricken schooner, so *Zeta* had to wait until the schooner's crew left and then Captain Adams would attempt to rescue them.

By the time *Mary Pauline* was abandoned, the wind had picked up again. Crew from *Zeta*, standing by about twenty yards away, saw Hynes, Clarke and Mills get in one dory and Whittle, Rice, Baldwin and Windsor push off in the other. Wind estimated at seventy miles per hour lashed up mountainous seas tossing both dories like corks. Both dories capsized, throwing the men into the boiling surf.

Zeta's men threw lines, but only one, Sylvester Hynes of St. Bernard's, managed to hang on. The other six disappeared. According to Captain Adams, when he left the scene the wallowing schooner was about to drive in on the island's sand dunes.

Banfield tried to navigate *Corkum* around Cape Coupe and enter the reach or channel into Fortune Bay but the wallowing vessel could not steam against the heavy wind. She had some problem with steering.

Corkum swung out, around the Seal Rocks (Vieux Marins) west of Miquelon and then in as close to Miquelon Head as possible. As *Nina W. Corkum* limped past the Seal Rocks, the message came over the set from *Zeta* that only Hynes had been rescued from *Mary Pauline*.

Banfield figured in the lee of Miquelon he could anchor or beach the schooner to escape the howling gale of wind and snow. It was too dangerous to run to Grand Bank or Fortune, so course was set for Harbour Breton. Freezing ice and snow clogged *Nina W. Corkum*'s radar and the run to Harbour Breton had to be made 'by God and by guess.'

By daylight, *Nina W. Corkum*'s crew were all gathered in the wheelhouse assessing their schooner's situation and looking out for land. The man at the wheel, Phil Downey, spoke to the skipper, "What land is that ahead? Do you see that red headland?" Banfield knew these were the cliffs near Harbour Breton. He tried the radar again; it came on perfectly and he could see the lie of the land to sail right up through to Harbour Breton's safety. *Nina W. Corkum* remained there for three days until the storm abated.

In the same storm the French vessel *Douala* also went down about 30 miles south of Burgeo/Ramea area; eleven of her twenty-three sailors survived. The Frenchmen were rescued by the government vessel *Sir Humphrey Gilbert* in command of Captain George Burdock, formerly of Belleoram.

Douala's crew, which been adrift in a lifeboat, were so exhausted that one man was too weak to climb the ladder from the small boat to the deck of *Gilbert* and fell from the ladder into the sea and drowned.

The storm claimed another South Coast seaman when Isaac Douglas, age 60, of Grand Bank was washed off the deck of the schooner *Philip E. Lake*. At the time the Fortune vessel was about 14 miles south of St. Lawrence, battling the elements to make port.

After the disastrous events of 1963, *Nina W. Corkum* sailed for many years. In time she was sold to S. T. Jones' business of Little Bay Island who transferred her ownership to a business in New York City. In the mid-seventies she sank in New York harbour, never to be refloated.

Seaman Sylvester Hynes survived to return to his family at St. Bernard's, a community whose heritage is based on the sea. Located on the eastern side of Fortune Bay, the town, with its fine landing beach for small craft, was known as Fox Cove until around 1915. The land northeast of the beach was originally settled by the Johnson family and, to the southeast, is a smaller valley; both areas were extensively used for pasture and gardens.

St. Bernard's first appears in the Newfoundland *Census* (1836) with a population of twenty-eight with family names of Johnson, Whelan, Power and Stewart. Based on a prosperous lobster and cod fishery and through supplying herring to banking schooners, the town grew slowly through the nineteenth century. After the turn of the century other families arrived: Hodder, Hackett, Banfield, Parrott and later, with the arrival of Whittle and Hynes families from the near-by settlement of Langue de Cerf, St. Bernard's population stabilized. Today its population is around 650 and, with road connections to the main highway, St. Bernard's remembers its historic ties with the treacherous ocean and recalls the days when seamen struggled to wrest a living from the deeps.

Chapter 28

Brunette Island and White's Shipwreck Map

It has been estimated that within Newfoundland's recorded history more than 10,000 ships have been wrecked around its shores. Very few maps have been produced to locate these wrecks, but in 1904, Mr. R. White, a St. John's resident, drew a shipwreck map of Newfoundland and wrote an accompanying 10-page pamphlet entitled: *A List of Wrecks on the Coast of Newfoundland to 31 December, 1903*. White's work was the first attempt to locate and map the wrecks of Newfoundland. He listed

Courtesy Jack Keeping

Two rust-streaked stern trawlers limp into Fortune; on the near side, *Fermeuse* escorting *Fame V* on the outside. Silhouetted in the background is Duck Island, Bird Island and the North West Head of Brunette Island some fifteen miles away.

Author's collection

Buried in beach are the ribs and engine of *Lucy and Carl*, a small vessel that burned in Brunette Harbour (Mercer's Cove) on October 15, 1961. Her crew — Captain Howard Lake, Frank Spencer, Clyde L. Douglas and Rodger Borotra — escaped safely.

Despite its strategic location at the mouth of Fortune Bay, only a few ships were wrecked on Brunette Island shores within this century: *Newsboy*, 1901; *Jessie*, April 6, 1907; *Vesta*, January 1909, *Fortune Bay*, destroyed by fire at Hatcher's Cove, August 16, 1961 and *Lucy and Carl*.

approximately five hundred; most of which were located on the Avalon and North East Coast.

Researchers and those interested in locating the many South Coast shipwrecks would do well to examine White's documentations. Today it is stored in the archives in the Centre for Newfoundland Studies at Memorial University, St. John's.

Brunette Island has ten wreck sites on White's map: one vessel on the eastern side of the island and 9 on the north. The earliest is *Royal Negro*, a British brigantine lost in 1859 and the more recent 1901 wreck of *Newsboy*, a schooner owned by Foote's, Grand Bank. Although White's map locates several shipwrecks in Fortune Bay, since the era of the banking schooner enterprise there have been others.*

* *Shipwrecks of the South Coast*, a 34 x 22" map showing the dates and sites of over 500 south coast vessels, was recently produced by the author and is available from most craft stores in Newfoundland.

Situated in the mouth of Fortune Bay, the island is some twenty kilometres long. Probably named by early French settlers, the triangular shaped island was ceded to England in 1763. In 1865 a large lighthouse was erected on Mercer's Head which was replaced by an iron structure in 1921. In the 1960s, the two main communities — Brunette (Mercer's Cove) and Forward's Cove — had succumbed to resettlement.

Graves showing another loss at sea. Alfred Rendell of Fogo was the only immediate casualty of the wreck of *Jessie*. A young man of Brunette, William John Douglass, aged eighteen, was injured while rescuing sailors and died of tuberculosis the following year. The two stones lie adjacent to each other. Rendell's inscription reads: In Loving Memory of Alfred Rendell beloved husband of Mary E. Rendell, a native of fogo who drowned from the Sch. *Jessie* April 7th 1907. Aged thirty-five years.

Chapter 29

Wrecks Around St. Lawrence Harbour

Author's collection

Two schooners — *L.A. Dunton* (left) and *Nina W. Corkum* (right) — unload coal into a truck near the government shed in St. Lawrence harbour in summer of 1963. In the background is St. Lawrence's east side with the Anglican church and school on the left.

After the turn of the century Farrell's became involved in the bank fishery. In March 1907 Captain Walter Kennedy of Holyrood brought down the ten-dory schooner *Hispanola* from the mainland for Farrells. Farrells also owned *Campanola*.

Author's collection

In 1987, this is all that remained of *Foundation Jupiter*, wrecked (along with *Rio Sama*) at Blue Beach near St. Lawrence on January 20, 1946. Other strandings and sinkings near St. Lawrence over the years were: S.S. *Hump*, August 24, 1916; *Angela Marie*, owned by Burke's at St. Jacques, stranded at St. Lawrence, November 1917; *Norman W. Strong*, wrecked at Castle Hyde on October 23, 1923.

Most memorable is the wreck of two American naval ships on February 18, 1942: U.S.S. *Pollux*, wrecked at Lawn Point and U.S.S. *Truxton* wrecked at Chamber's Cove, near St. Lawrence. In both accidents over 200 American sailors lost their lives. Residents of St. Lawrence and Lawn helped rescue 168 men.

Chapter 30

Day Book for a Typical Banker

IN THE ERA OF WOODEN VESSELS, scores of schooners were owned in dozens of towns along the South Coast. Considering the number of large and small businesses and the hundreds of schooners managed by each, the number of logbooks, diaries of sailors, and journals of owners in existence today is relatively few. No doubt some written accounts are still in private homes — a few will be preserved, many will be lost forever. Generally the personal records are discovered when someone purchases an old home or store. If the new owner is aware of his find or is heritage conscious, written history is possibly preserved, but more often than not, such artifacts are thrown out.

Not long ago the journal of a vessel owner, Howard Patten, became available. The Grand Bank business he managed had been in existence for over seventy years. His father, J.B. (John Benjamin) Patten in partnership with William Forsey, founded a codfish procuring and exporting business around 1900. In 1922 J.B. Patten separated from Forsey and, for the next forty years, sent his own bankers to the productive grounds and his coastal/trading schooners to the mainland.

In the 1940s J.B. Patten's firm, as managed by son Howard Patten, acquired two vessels: the eight-dory banker *A and R Martin* and *Arawana*, a converted mine-sweeper which he put into the coastal trade.

Built in Glovertown in 1938, the seventy-four net ton *Martin* measured eighty-one feet long and twenty-three feet wide. Patten acquired her from Crosbie Co. Ltd. of St. John's in early 1948 and sent her to the banks that spring.

Patten kept a day-book or daily account of *A and R Martin*'s catches, crew, fortunes and misfortunes writing that she left Grand Bank for her first trip to the banks on March 31, 1948. Her crew came from various communities in Fortune Bay:

Grand Bank	Jersey Harbour	Harbour Breton
Capt. Tom Bartlett, age 32	Maurice Myles, 41, cook	Orlando Stoodley, 43, mate
Freeman Rose, 31, engineer	John Lilly, 48	James Skinner, 28
Richard Newport, 32	Fred Moore, 28	
George Bungay, 21		
James Hunt		

Brunette	Grand La Pierre	Grand Beach
Clarence Hillier, 23	John Bolt, 26	William Hollett, 26
Clayton Hillier, 21	Charlie Kearley, 42	Stan Follett
Sim Hillier		Tony Follett

Dawson's Cove	Little Bay West	English Harbour East
Eric Wells, 28	Clyde Skinner, 26	William Clarke

A little over three weeks later, on April 24, *A and R Martin* arrived back in Grand Bank with 317 quintals of salt bulk fish. Three days after she left to collect bait in Fortune Bay, proceeded to the Banks and arrived back in port on May 21 with 569 quintals.

This pattern was repeated five times until her final voyage for the season ended on September 6, 1948. Her best trip yielded 796 quintals; lowest 248. The cook and engineer were paid a dollar fifty a day plus their share of fish while the dorymen accumulated credit for their fish at J.B. Patten's business. Several of *A and R Martin*'s men had to purchase fishing supplies which was debited against their earnings. For example, William Hollett "took up" or bought on credit: ten trawl lines and ten gross of hooks; Stanley Follett, twenty-four trawl lines; twenty-four sed lines and twenty gross of hooks.

In the fall of 1948 when the fishing season ended Patten, like many South Coast vessel owners, put his schooner in the coastal trade. Her five crew went on a monthly wage: Capt. Bartlett, $150.00; cook Ren Smith and engineer Freeman Rose, $90.00; mate Richard Newport, $85.00 and sailor Am Murphy, $80.00. The following shows the progress of *A and R Martin* for a two month period:

Sept. 20, left Grand Bank 3:45 p.m. for St. Pierre to dock
Sept. 21, docked St. Pierre this a.m.
Sept. 23, sailed this a.m. for Sydney
Sept. 25, arrived Sydney today
Oct. 2, left Sydney 130 tons coal for Grand Bank/Fortune
Oct. 3, arrived Burgeo stormbound
Oct. 5, arrived Grand Bank 9 p.m.
Oct. 9, left Grand Bank 10 a.m. for Sydney
Oct. 10, arrived Sydney this p.m. Big delay
Oct. 23, left Sydney, 2:00 p.m.
Oct. 24, arrived here 8:30 p.m. coal for Grand Bank/Fortune

A and R Martin made three more coal-laden trips until the coasting crew signed off on December 11 and Patten moored his schooner for the winter to await the spring fishery. Over 600 tons of coal had been delivered to Grand Bank, Fortune, Burin, Placentia and Burgeo. On her final voyage she brought fruit, vegetables, general produce as well as coal slated for Patten's own business in Grand Bank.

High turnover of crew from year to year was not unusual; thus by the next spring fishery, some fishermen had left; others joined: mate Clarence Grandy, Grand Bank; Richard Vallis, Harbour Breton; John S. Hackett and Michael T. Hackett of English Harbour East; Abram S. Skinner, St. John's Bay; Herb Hollett, George Anstey, James Follett, Wilbert Hiscock, Grand Beach; John Coombs, Terrenceville and George T. Snook of Sagona Island. With the addition of Harold Tibbo of Grand Beach as kedgie, or cook's helper, half the crew had changed!

Less than four years after Patten bought *A and R Martin*, her career ended. Like so many South Coast schooners, she was wrecked in the winter months when hazards were much greater

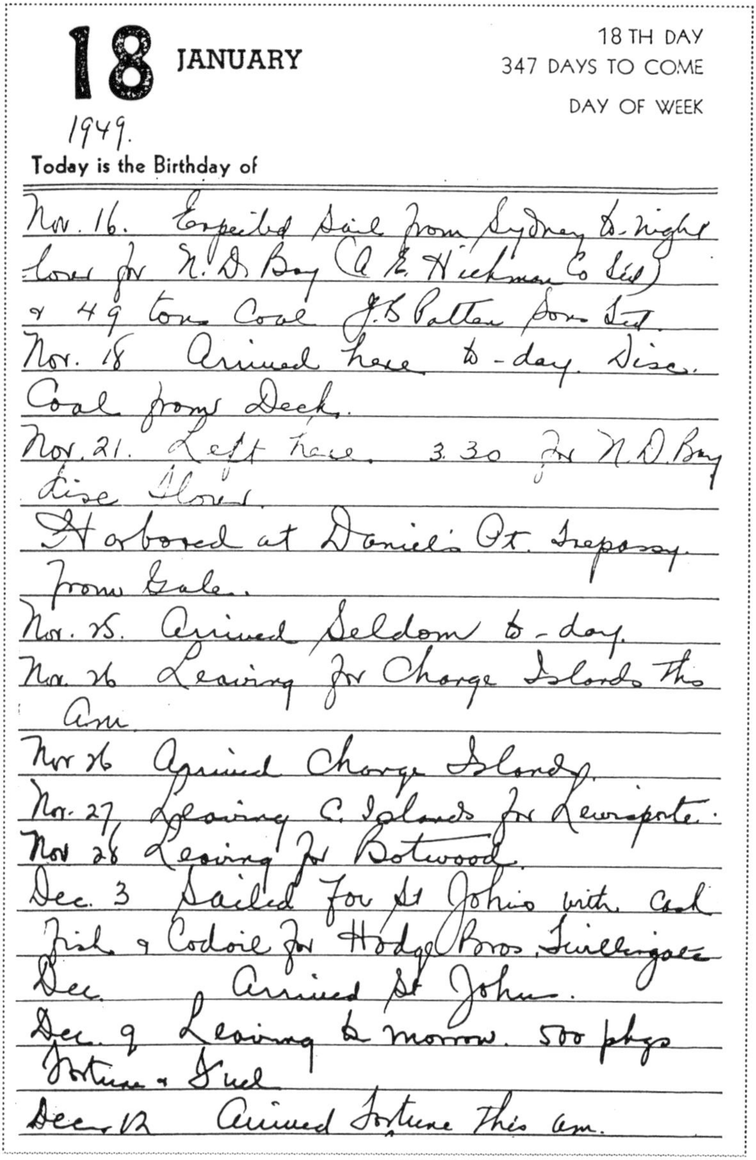

18 JANUARY

18 TH DAY
347 DAYS TO COME
DAY OF WEEK

1949.

Today is the Birthday of

Nov. 16. Expected Sail from Sydney to-night
flour for N. D. Bay (A. E. Hickman Co Ltd)
& 49 tons Coal J. B. Patten Sons Ltd.
Nov. 18 Arrived here to-day. Disc.
Coal from Deck.
Nov. 21. Left here. 3.30 for N. D. Bay
Disc. Flour.
Harbored at Daniel's Pt. Trepassey.
from Gale.
Nov. 25. Arrived Seldom to-day.
Nov. 26 Leaving for Change Islands this
am.
Nov 26 Arrived Change Islands.
Nov. 27 Leaving C. Islands for Lewisporte.
Nov 28 Leaving for Botwood.
Dec. 3 Sailed for St Johns with Coal
Fish & Codoil for Hodge Bros. Twillingate
Dec. Arrived St John.
Dec. 9 Leaving to morrow. 500 pkgs
Fortune & Fuel
Dec 12 Arrived Fortune this am.

A and R Martin's transactions from November 16 to December 24, 1949, shows various Newfoundland ports and cargoes: sailed from Sydney with flour for Notre Dame Bay and forty-nine tons of coal on deck for Grand Bank. After offloading coal left for N.D. Bay, but harboured at Daniel's Point near Trepassy for three days to wait out a gale.

19TH DAY
346 DAYS TO COME
DAY OF WEEK

JANUARY 19

Today is the Birthday of

Dec. 12. Something wrong with propeller.
Put on shoal. Nothing serious.
Dec 14. Refloated & ready sail
this p.m. (4 th)
Dec 15 Left here early am for Sydney.
Dec 16 Arrived Sydney to-day.
Dec 22 Expect load 50 tons to-day
Dec 23 Sailing to-day 119 tons Sydney
Screened. Left 1 pm. to-day.
Dec 24 ~~Left here~~ Arrived here
3.30 or 4 pm. to-day.

Courtesy Neil Locke

Between November 25 to December 3, *A and R Martin* arrived and discharged cargo at Change Islands, Lewisporte and Botwood. Emptied of flour, she brought fish and cod liver oil for Hodge Bros. of Twillingate to St. John's. To round off the trip the owner had 500 packages (possibly food) as well as fuel brought to Grand Bank/Fortune. The schooner arrived in her home port at 4:00 p.m. on Christmas Eve.

than the bank fishing voyages from March to September. On December 12, 1951, while on the coal run from Sydney to the Burin Peninsula, she hit a ledge off Lamaline harbour. Her crew Captain Ben Snook; mate Ambrose Murphy; engineer Maurice Snook; cook Charlie Fizzard, seaman Frank Barnes and passenger Clyde Warren were rescued by inshore fishermen of Allen's Island.

When some of her coal fell out and the tide rose, the abandoned *A and R Martin* drifted onto Point au Gaul point where residents made short work of her remaining coal. The insurance company arranged to have the engine removed from the wreck and then to be later fitted into a Fortune schooner, *Helen G. McLean*.

Chapter 31

"So Ends the Day"

FROM A PHYSICAL VIEWPOINT the harbours, headlands and islands from Placentia Bay to Port aux Basques have changed very little since the days of our seagoing forefathers. Several communities are now abandoned, but many others still cling to the shoreline. The grey-blue seas surrounding the coast have not changed at all. Northwesterlies still roil the brooding ocean; the same waves that destroyed ships and men two generations ago still pound the shore today. The seas and rocks of the South Coast are the final resting places of many beautiful ships and hard working pioneers.

As long as men sailed the coast, women waited home for their return or for news of safe arrival. In their homes perched on the rock-studded cummerbund between land and sea, they listened to the howl of storms and harkened to breakers falling ceaselessly on shore. They prayed their menfolk would escape the dangers of the Sunken Keys of Placentia Bay; the fog-bound ledges off Corbin Head; the Dune Sands, Miquelon; the Northwest Rocks off Ramea and that they had managed to navigate their schooners safely through Langlade Reach.

In the days of limited electronic communication, news of shipping accidents often came many hours, days or, as in the case of foreign-going vessels abandoned in the Atlantic, weeks after the event. In the loss of the Grand Bank motor vessel *Administratrix* off Cape Race in April 1948, Mrs. Chesley Forsey turned on her home radio for shipping news. She heard the initial reports that *Administratrix*, her husband's vessel, had been cut down by a steamer and five out of seven crewmen were missing. After hours of distressful waiting, she learned of two survivors — George Barnes and Charlie Fizzard — and that Chesley Forsey was presumed drowned.

Improved communications and paved highways now link the coastal towns to larger centres. There are no coasting schooners similar to *Gladys Wiscombe* or *Spencer II*, struggling to land food, coal and supplies to places like Port Elizabeth, Brunette Island, Pushthrough and Rencontre West.

Yet despite the horrendous claims made by the "waters dark and rude," so many of our pioneers were tenacious and were determined to make a go of it, even through hard times and failure. They survived to tell; they lived to a ripe old age to become the storytellers who told us what it was like in the olden days and reminded us once again what a rich and colourful place this island of ours is — especially so in the sea-faring traditions of the South Coast.

Courtesy Rosalind Downey

Zagreb aground on Grey River Rocks on November 6, 1990. The Fisheries Products International dragger left Harbour Breton bound for Ramea with 160,000 pounds of cod aboard; but through some malfunction of the automatic pilot she never made port. Her crew abandoned ship into a raft and were picked up one and a half hours later by a Canadian Coast Guard vessel from Burgeo. *Zagreb* took a beating from the seas, broke apart and slipped under a few days later.

Her crew at the time were all Ramea men: Captain Eric Skinner; first mate Guy Bowles; chief engineer John Rose; second engineer Gerald Poole and deckhands Rodney Fudge, Michael Kendall, Wilfred Young, Lloyd Fudge and Gordon Rose.

Appendix A

South Coast Bank Fishing Fleet, Late Spring 1935

Schooner	**Owner**	**Place**	**Qtls Caught on Herring Baiting**	**Eventual Fate**
W. E. Knock	Lake and Lake	Fortune	2,250	Burned off St. John's, Nov. 23, 1958
Dorothy P. Sarty	Lake and Lake	Fortune	1,300	Abandoned Off Nova Scotia, June 12, 1954
Alhambia	Geo & J. Dixon	Fortune	1,700	Abandoned Atlantic, May 1940
Beatrice & Grace	Geo & J. Dixon	Fortune	500	Abandoned off Nova Scotia, Sept. 2, 1955
Nina M. Conrad	Jerry Petite, Sr.	English Hr W.	1,550	Beached at St. Brendan's
Palitana	Jerry Petite, Sr.	English Hr W.	2,200	Burned Ming's Bight, NF, June 11, 1957
Robert Esdale	Jerry Petite, Sr.	English Hr W.	2,150	Abandoned in gulf en route Harbour Buffett
Jenny Elizabeth	Jerry Petite, Sr.	English Hr W.	2,150	Stranded Badger's Quay, July 18, 1959
Ethel M. Petite	Jerry Petite, Jr.	English Hr W.	——	Stranded off Halifax, Feb. 5, 1948
Francis Spindler	Clifford Shirley	English Hr W.	1,700	Abandoned off Labrador, Sept. 10, 1938
Laverna	G.B. Fisheries	Grand Bank	1,450	Stranded, Labrador, Sept. 7, 1936
James & Stanley	G.B. Fisheries	Grand Bank	1,400	Stranded off Halifax, Aug 19, 1942
Paloma	G.B. Fisheries	Grand Bank	1,200	Burned, Labrador, Sept. 28, 1936
Partanna	G.B. Fisheries	Grand Bank	1,700	Lost with crew, St. Mary's Keys, Apr. 27, 1936
Robert Max	G.B. Fisheries	Grand Bank	1,300	Shelled by enemy sub, Atlantic Aug. 4, 1941
Coral Spray	J.B. Patten	Grand Bank	1,550	Stranded St. Shott's, Sept. 15, 1937
J. E. Conrod	J.B. Patten	Grand Bank	1,300	Abandoned in Atlantic, Feb. 14, 1940
Irene Corkum	Forward & Tibbo	Grand Bank	1,700	Stranded Flint Island, N.S., Oct. 15, 1951
Eva U. Colp	Forward & Tibbo	Grand Bank	2,000	Run down off Sydney, N.S., July 13, 1942
W. L. McKenzie King	J.B. Foote & Sons	Grand Bank	1,300	Sold Englee, fate obscure
Antoine E. Santos	J.B. Foote & Sons	Grand Bank	1,650	Stranded Miquelon, April 15, 1942

Schooner	Owner	Place	Qtls Caught on Herring Baiting	Eventual Fate
Helen Forsey	William Forsey	Grand Bank	2,250	Shelled by enemy sub, 2 men killed, Sept. 6, 1942
Christie & Eleanor	William Forsey	Grand Bank	1,706	Stranded St. Georges Bay, Dec. 16, 1946
Freda M	G. & A. Buffett	Grand Bank	2,200	Run down off Burin Pen, Oct 7, 1961
Pauline C. Winters	G. & A. Buffett	Grand Bank	1,650	Sank on West Coast of NF, Nov. 1, 1963
Nina W. Corkum	G. & A. Buffett	Grand Bank	1,850	Derelict in New York Hr. 1975
L.A. Dunton	G. & A. Buffett	Grand Bank	1,900	Floating exhibit at Mystic, Connecticut
Flores	Sam Piercy	Grand Bank	550	Sank in Gulf, August 30, 1936
Ariel	Sam Piercy	Grand Bank	——	A floating exhibit at Magdalen Islands, Quebec
Josephine Walsh	Philip Walsh	Little Bay, P.B.	300	Abandoned Grand Bruit, July 5, 1952
Pauline Lohnes	Chesley Boyce	Jersey Hr.	2,100	Run down on Banks, July 17, 1937
Autauga	Joseph Rose	Jersey Hr.	2,000	Stranded Cape St. Lawrence, N.S., Sept. 8, 1951
Marion Spindler	J. Parrott	St. Bernard's	900	Stranded November 13, 1937
Myrtle L	J. Parrott	St. Bernard's	800	Abandoned off Point Rosie, Dec. 28, 1938
Ellen & Mary	Harvey & Co.	Belleoram	885	Stranded St. Lawrence River, July 18, 1942
Reading	Harvey & Co.	Belleoram	733	Stranded Rose Blanche, March 10, 1938
Florence	Harvey & Co.	Belleoram	890	Abandoned St. Pierre Bank, Sept. 30, 1940
Lucy Edwina	Harvey & Co.	Belleoram	976	Stranded Raleigh, NF May 24, 1953
Mary Ruth	Harvey & Co.	Belleoram	1,146	Beached at Southport, Trinity Bay
Ruth Adams	Harvey & Co.	Belleoram	970	Stranded near Point au Gaul, 1943
Dorothy O	Harvey & Co./J. Rose	Belleoram	1,212	Burned in Hermitage Bay
Rex Perry	Mrs. Harry Petite	Belleoram	1,650	Abandoned in Fortune Bay, Dec. 13, 1952
Jenny	J. Cluett	?	——	?

Schooner	Owner	Place	Qtls Caught on Herring Baiting	Eventual Fate
Joan Ella May	Thomas Hollett	Burin	600	Abandoned in Gulf, May 1, 1957
*James Young**	Hollett's Fisheries	Burin	150	Sold to Twillingate
Betty Zane	E. & M. Hollett	Burin	600	?
Carrie and Nellie	George A. Bartlett	Burin	1,300	Stranded Seal Island, Labrador, May 1945
Beatrice Vivian	Hollett's	Burin	——	Run down on banks, J une 12, 1936
Lottie Dunford	E. & M. Hollett	Burin	150	?
Andavaka	Jim Anstey/For'd Tibbo	Garnish	——	Cut down by a convoy on the banks during WW II
Jean & Mona	Thomas Grandy	Garnish	——	Burned at sea, Sept. 13, 1951
Mary Kemp	Thomas Kemp	Placentia	——	Burned off Labrador, Sept. 29, 1966
Nina Davis	Wareham	Harbour Buffett	——	?
Tweedsmuir	Wareham	Harbour Buffett	——	?

*Captain Harry Hollett disappeared from *James Young* while on a voyage from St. John's to Burin on April 29, 1945. No one knows exactly what happened, but he was probably washed off deck or knocked overboard by a swing boom.

Author's collection

Fortune harbour, facing south, in the 1940s. Two schooners shown are *Mary Ruth* and *Mary F. Hirtle*, both of which were at one time captained by Harold Ayres.

Appendix B
South Coast Schooners Sunk by Enemy Action in World War II

Schooner	Town	Date	Crew Killed
Robert Max	Grand Bank	August 4, 1941	None
Mildred Pauline	Fortune/Halifax	August 1942	All crew including Abe Thornhill, George Thornhill, Samuel Pierce; all of Fortune
Helen Forsey	Grand Bank	Sept 6, 1942	Arthur Bond, Frenchman's Cove, Leslie Rogers, Grand Bank
* *Angelus*	Halifax	May 19, 1943	Cecil Hardiman, Grand Bank; Alex Holmans, John Hillier, Clarence Mullins, Belleoram
Margaret K. Smith	Belleoram	August 1943	Horatio Kearley, Eric Bond, Charles Dominaux, Silas and Charles Savoury, Herbert Sheppard, Charles Blagdon
Beatrice Beck	Burgeo/W.Indies	January 1944	Arch Matthews, Elias Anderson, of Burgeo, Len Anderson, Otter's Point
** *Dixie*	Bay de L'Eau Is.	October 1944	Joseph Bullen, (Sr.), Joseph Bullen, Willie Jensen; Bay de L'Eau Is.

*The bark *Angelus* was owned in France or Canada and she was crewed by several South Coast seamen.

**Although *Dixie* disappeared during the war years, it is not likely she was sunk by the enemy since her route was deep in Fortune Bay.

Courtesy of Marine Archives, Memorial University

Mildred Pauline, a tern owned by Sainthills of Sydney, disappeared during World War II supposedly torpedoed by a German submarine. Captained by Abe Thornhill of Fortune and crewed by his son George, Samuel Pierce of Fortune and three others, the 325-ton *Mildred Pauline* (formerly named *Herbert Fearn* and *Jean F. McCrae*) was built in Placentia in 1919.

In this photo the top masts are cut down since she is powered by an engine.

Appendix C

Fortune Shipping Disasters

Schooner	Owned by	Date	Loss of Life
Sailor's Home	John Lake	Dec. 31, 1890	Two
**Weaver Belle*	Capt. Fred Smith	1892	Five
Joseph P. Johnson	John S. Bennett	Early Nov., 1918	Five
Harry Lewis	Philip BurtonM	Oct. 29, 1918	Five?
Gladys S.	Fred Bennett	Oct-Nov 1918	Five?
P.F.	George Mayo	Mid Nov., 1918	Two
***Russell Lake*	Lake Bros.	March 16, 1929	Five
Mark H. Gray	T. Douglas/Garlands	Oct./Nov., 1933	Five

*According to family history *Weaver Belle*, while on a foreign going voyage, perhaps in the Mediterranean or Gibraltar, was captured by pirates off the Algerian coast. Her crew may have been murdered.

**There was one survivor, George Day of Fortune.

Appendix D

Harbour Breton Vessel Disasters

Schooner	Owned By	Date	Loss of Life
Mary Smith	John Smith	Dec. 1912	Two
Martha E	Peter Mullins	1931?	Five
Alsatian	Patten, Grand Bank	March 3, 1935	Thirteen
Dixie	Joseph Bullen	Nov. 1944	Three

Appendix E

Song of Storm-Tossed *Garfield*

The story of *Garfield,* built in Grand Bank in 1903 for Samuel Harris' business, was written by John Dober. In 1923, when Harris went bankrupt and closed out his branch business in Change Islands and Little Bay, Placentia Bay, he sold the schooner to John Dober of Little Bay, the port where *Garfield* was based.

Her crew during the voyage described in this song was Captain Val Dober, Joseph Hanrahan and three others.

It was on the 6th of January
Well known as Christmas Day
When five hardy sons of Newfoundland
Set sail at Little Bay
They faced out on the ocean
With courage stout and bold
Bound to the port of Sydney,
To buy a load of coal.

The day it being a fine one,
The wind was rather light
When at the close of evening
Nearby the St. Lawrence light
We had a mind to harbour
But it would cause delay
We agreed with one another
To keep her on the way.

It was our skipper's intention
If the night held fine and clear
And nothing to prevent us,
We would call in at St. Pierre
To buy a drop of brandy
To cheer us on our way
Our skipper changed his mind again,
Said he, "We will go to sea."

So the snow began to fall
And the night got very dark
Our skipper he went to his room
For to consult the chart
His parallel rule soon told him
The course outside St. Pierre
The dividers told the distance
When all rocks and shoals were clear.

We shaped our course for Sydney
And ran her through the snow
About eight or nine o'clock that night
The wind came on to blow
We then took in our mainsail
It seemed to carry away
Under jumbo and reefed foresail
We ran her until break of day

The next day it was Wednesday
As you may plainly see
With the wind down from the west northeast
And headed us all day
We kept her in position
In hopes the wind would veer
We pulled in our log which told us
We were ten leagues from St. Pierre.

Early on Thursday morning
Gloomy looked the sky
The ocean was like snowdrifts
The sea ran mountains high
To pay your ship's regard, my boys
You know its your command
Ten minutes to the decks
Was more than human flesh could stand.

Friday was a bitter day
For any man to see
In the chilly months of winter,
Exposed to frost and snow
An to make thing go much harder
About 12 o'clock that day
With a heavy slap of water
Our foresail it gave away.

We had another foresail
In our ship down below
We watched our chance
And got it up through water, wind and snow
We bent, reefed and hoist it up
With water to our knees
But we will never forget
That Friday until our dying days.

No doubt the sea was raging
But we pulled through all right
Our tiny little lifeboat
No doubt she tossed about
We got some slaps of water
Just while we lay hull to
But when we hoist the foresail
She showed us who was who.

We watched her for a few minutes
In the companion way
Our skipper said, "God bless her.
See how she heads to sea."
You would think to them rolling down
They would cause her downfall
But our tiny little fishing boat
She climbs on top of all.

When we had all cleared away
And we were down below
With the marrow frozen in our bones
And baked with frost and snow
We viewed our situation
But over it did not fret
We knew we were not in a hotel,
Smoking a cigarette.

We never thought of friend at home
To make our courage fail
But offered up a prayer to God
To stop that dismal gale
We were not unbelievers
But wasn't skilled with faith
We knew that the Almighty
Would alter our sad state.

Now when you are out in a storm of wind
Satan is always near
To put you through all hardships
To make you curse and swear
And put you in all misery
Hoping your soul to get
But God said, "Be gone Satan,
You are not master yet."

When you are in danger
Upon the stormy sea
With nothing to protect you
But a string tied to the stay
But if you do believe in it,
You will see what it will do
For that cord of your foster father
Will surely bring you through.

Come all ye first proud landsmen
That's in your houses warm
Get all you want brought in to you
By the men who brave the storm
And then they'll of time scold them
If they owe them a few signs
But you find in stormy weather,
They're not fit to wipe their shoes.

It was on the following Sunday
We had another veer
With the wind off from the north northwest
Likewise brought us good cheer
Our skipper he gave orders
And told us what to do
We danced the stack of barley
When Lawn Islands came in view.

Come all ye Newfoundlanders
And listen onto me
Don't look for style or beauty
To take you out to sea
Just buy one like the *Garfield*
God bless her night and day
She brought those five young sailors
Safe home to Little Bay.

Appendix F

Shipwrecks in the Port aux Basques Area Since 1900

Although the list is incomplete, for many ships and crews were lost without knowledge of landsmen and other wrecks were never written down or otherwise documented, the following vessels met their fate between Port aux Basques and Rose Blanche. The year 1900 was chosen arbitrarily since most larger vessels after that date would have been Newfoundland owned.

Montpelier	4 May 1900	near Gull Island, Channel
Heroine	22 November 1911	near Channel
Lloydsen	10 March 1913	Channel
Ascania	13 June 1918	off Petites
Albert Moulton	2 January 1924	sandbar near Channel
Magno	27 August 1924	between Port aux Basques and Sydney, N.S.
Eva Gertrude	30 May 1925	Western Baldwin Shoals
Annie Jean	25 August 1927	Sailed out of Isle aux Morts and disappeared
Vienna	25 August 1927	Sailed out of Isle aux Morts and disappeared
Latona	8 June 1930	3 miles east of Isle aux Morts
Monica Hartery	24 December 1933	Rose Blanche Point
Julia A. Anderson	27 April 1936	Wreckage found at Rose Blanche
Caribou	14 October 1942	App. 40 miles out of Port aux Basques
Robert Frampton	5 December 1945	off Port aux Basques
Rameaux	August 13 1947	Green Island Shoal, Cape Ray
Mary H. Hirtle	28 December 1950	Codroy Island
Lloyd Hounsell	30 November 1951	Rhode Island Reef
Olga M. Netta	11 July 1953	southwest of Cape Ray
Jock Scott	29 April 1962	southeast of Isle aux Morts
Leaside	10 March 1966	off Isle aux Morts
Loretta & Marion	27 July 1966	Burnt Island
Zilch	5 December 1966	off Isle aux Morts
Stalbas	4 July 1974	White Sunker Rocks, Isle aux Morts

Appendix G

By the 1940s many South Coast fishermen worked on schooners out of Lunenburg, Nova Scotia. Wages were higher, food and working conditions were better. Some of those who fished on Nova Scotian-owned *Sherman Zwicker*, (above, on a visit to Grand Bank harbour, 1994) were: Captain Frank Thornhill, born in Anderson's Cove; Hubert Harris, Hermitage; Clayton Johnson, Freeman Johnson, Abram Johnson, Aaron Johnson, Tom Harris, Fred Harris, Jacques Fontain; Ira Barter, Ramea; Richard Brushett, Burin; John Douglas, Grand Bank; Belah Brown, Marystown; Merrill Bullen, Vincent Baker, Chesley Rose, John Pierce, William J. Baker, John Wells, Tom Simms, Norman Day, Alex Grant, Charles Snook, Harbour Breton; John Sheppard, Tom Cox, Wreck Cove; Alex Drake, Freeman G. Savoury, John Martin Dominix, Belleoram; John Wells, Philip Hynes, Sandy Hynes, St. Jacques; Wilson Labour, English Harbour East; Len Anderson, Norman Francis, John Harris, Lou Anderson, George Rose, Clayton Wells, Eli Short, Lloyd Douglas, Henry Poole, Jack Goods, Eric Simms and Sam McDonald, Hermitage; Sam Snook, Red Cove; Isaac Prior, 2nd Engineer, Jersey Harbour; Tom Roff, Mortier.

INDEX OF VESSELS, SEAMEN AND TOWNS

Vessels

Seamen

Towns

Glossary

These may be local words for their meaning could not be found in the Kerchove's *International Maritime Dictionary* (1961).

August gale — tail end of a hurricane or tropical wind storm which usually swept southern latitudes in late summer. By the time hurricane force winds reached the maritimes, the force had dissipated to a gale. Usually they inflicted devastation to the Newfoundland schooner fleet in August or September.

bare poles — with no sail or canvas on the masts or poles. When wind conditions were high, a schooner was driven by the force of wind on her superstructure, masts and rigging.

battings — boards to fasten the canvas covering the hatch covers

blown away — in high winds sails were blown or torn off the booms

butts — large barrels used to hold drinking and cooking water, water butt; also, blubber butt which stored cod liver on fishing voyages.

coasting trade; coaster — a vessel equipped and manned to carry cargo and goods on short voyages along the coast. Banking schooners in the off-season voyaged to the mainland bringing coal and food. As the salt-fish industry declined, bankers were altered to adapt to carry supplies.

cross-handed — short handed; one person trying to do the work of two. An experienced dory man having a green or seasick dorymate would be working crosshanded.

Dirty Thirties — With the advent of world depression after World War I, the 1930s, for Newfoundlanders, became a time to go reluctantly on relief or "on the dole." Government handouts, lack of employment and hard cash, rations and reduced food have etched the years 1930-38 firmly in the minds of Newfoundlanders who survived the era.

dory stick — large tree suitable for cutting and sawing into wide planks for dories or schooners.

down north — as used by the fishermen of the South Coast, it was Newfoundland's north east coast, roughly Notre Dame Bay, Bonavista Bay, Trinity Bay and the Straight Shore. When an inadequate or aged vessel was sold to this area, she became obscure in local knowledge. If asked a south coast seaman might say, "I don't really know what happened to that vessel. I think she was sold down north."

draft bars — a flat board with two handles on opposite sides used to carry loads. Two men would carry a draft of dry fish, two quintals, from the shed to the boat on a draft bar. According to one fishermen it was a wheelbarrow with no wheel and no barrow (tub).

dubber — person, using an adze or plane, who cuts and smooths the planks to fit when building a boat.

foreign going — vessel engaged in long ocean voyages from the South Coast to Europe, West Indies or Brazil. Banking schooners in the off season carried dried fish to Portugal and Spain and the men were paid by the month on foreign going voyages.

goose sail — small sail used on a banking dory

herring baiting — frozen baiting; first fishing voyage usually in March-April. Herring, obtained during the winter, would be frozen from January to March, and kept in ice in the spring. Schoonermen also referred to this as the frozen baiting whereas later baitings of capelin or squid in the fall would be iced down.

kedgie — deck boy or cook's helper on a banking schooner. With a crew of twenty to twenty-five hungry men, the cook would have the kedgie peel potatoes, wash and dry dishes, clean up. When the dories came alongside to offload fish, the cook and captain could not be free to help, the kedgie caught the painters or dory lines to secure the dory by the schooner.

Ladies' Day — August 15, the Day of Assumption. In many Placentia Bay towns it was the custom to hold a celebration — a town social equivalent to a "Garden Party."

lying to; lie to — When seas and wind were such a schooner could not continue her course, it only puts up enough sail to steady it and keep the sea on the weather bow. When sailing or fishing was stopped in heavy weather and the vessel lay to, in the slow, heavy motion the vessel was jogging.

pounds — large box-like enclosure about twelve by twelve where fishermen stood to wash and clean the salt from heavily salted cod. Pounds could be inmmersed in a foot or two of water near the shore or hung over the side of the schooner.

rampike — logs of lighter spruce or fir attached to heavier sticks of birch or witchhazel to keep them afloat on their journey downriver.

Sankey — Old or traditional Salvation Army song usually with familiar words and heavy beat; named for songwriter Ira Sankey who composed many church hymns. Some old favourites, although these may not have been written by Sankey, were: "We Have an Anchor," "Let the Lower Lights be Burning," "Pull for the Shore."

second hand — On South Coast banking schooners, the mate was second hand and next in charge to the captain or skipper.

speed boat — a fast, low vessel with powerful engines and often with no functional masts; these were generally American or Canadian ex-rum running vessels built for speed and later sold to the South Coast when prohibition ended. There they were used as coasting vessels e.g. Administratrix; Reo II; Gertrude Jean.

stick — timber suitable for use as a mast or spar.

three master — tern schooner or three masted vessel.

trawl tub — wooden container, half barrels, where the trawl lines were coiled.

waterhorse — salted fish piled to allow the water to drain out of it in preparation for spreading to dry on a beach or flake.

western boat — fishing vessel smaller than a schooner used, for the most part, in Placentia Bay especially in the Cape Shore fishery.

Western Ocean — North West Atlantic Ocean.

widow's walk — a belvedere or standing area with a rail around it on the roof of a large home. Accessible from the inside, wives and relatives stood there to look for incoming vessels.